We Will Be Heard

We Will Be Heard

Women's Struggles for Political Power in the United States

Jo Freeman

ROWMAN & LITTLEFIELD PUBLISHERS, INC.
Lanham • Boulder • New York • Toronto • Plymouth, UK

ROWMAN & LITTLEFIELD PUBLISHERS, INC.

Published in the United States of America
by Rowman & Littlefield Publishers, Inc.
A wholly owned subsidary of The Rowman & Littlefield Publishing Group, Inc.
4501 Forbes Boulevard, Suite 200, Lanham, Maryland 20706
www.rowmanlittlefield.com

Estover Road, Plymouth PL6 7PY, United Kingdom

British Library Cataloguing in Publication Information Available

Library of Congress Cataloging-in-Publication Data

Freeman, Jo.
  We will be heard : women's struggles for political power in the United States /
Jo Freeman.
    p. cm.
  Includes bibliographical references and index.
  ISBN-13: 978-0-7425-5607-2 (cloth : alk. paper)
  ISBN-10: 0-7425-5607-7 (cloth : alk. paper)
  ISBN-13: 978-0-7425-5608-9 (pbk. : alk. paper)
  ISBN-10: 0-7425-5608-5 (pbk. : alk. paper)
  1. Women—United States—Politics and government. 2. Power (Social sciences)—
United States—History. 3. Feminism—United States. 4. Political participation—United
States—History. 5. Women in politics—United States—History. 6. United States—
Politics and government. I. Title.
  HQ1236.5.U6F746 2008
  324.082'0973—dc22
                                    2007038762
Printed in the United States of America

∞™ The paper used in this publication meets the minimum requirements of
American National Standard for Information Sciences—Permanence of Paper
for Printed Library Materials, ANSI/NISO Z39.48-1992.

To
Ted Lowi
Aaron Wildavsky
and Ed Artinian

Three men who encouraged me to write about women.

When you enter the party . . . you will find yourself in a political penumbra where most of the men are. . . . If you stay long enough . . . you will discover a little denser thing . . . the numbra of the . . . party, the people . . . planning the platform and picking out the candidates doing the real work that you and the men sanction at the polls. You won't be so welcome, but there is the place to go.

—Carrie Chapman Catt,
speech at NAWSA's Victory Convention,
held in Chicago in February 1920

Contents

~

Preface and Acknowledgments

Only in the last twenty years has women and politics been accepted as a legitimate field of scholarly inquiry, yet women have been involved in mainstream electoral politics in the United States for over 120 years. This book looks at some of their struggles to participate in U.S. politics from the first attempt to *organize* women as a crucial component of a major political party in 1892 to the swearing in of a woman as Speaker of the U.S. House of Representatives on January 4, 2007—the highest elected position attained by a woman to date. It describes some of women's many efforts to practice electoral politics even before most women could vote, some of the barriers they had to confront and break even after they could vote equally with men, and a few of the policies they have pursued—and debated—since achieving equal suffrage throughout the country.

There are many ways to write a book. This one is a series of case studies: some of people, some of institutions, some of actions. Case studies allow the reader to see what happened in depth, in the same way that a photograph allows one to study a scene and see details that would be missed in the flow of a movie. Together they present a panorama of women's political history from the late nineteenth through the early twenty-first centuries.

The prologue explores when and how women came to be seen as a legitimate field of study in political science. What is striking is how far behind scholarship trailed reality. Women's participation in politics was documented in their own publications and in the popular press during decades that political scientists were oblivious to their existence as political actors. It took the emergence of organized women loudly making demands on our political institutions for scholars to take notice.

The epilogue—written after the book was finished because the elections of November 7, 2006, changed history—looks at women's slow movement into Congress and into influential positions within Congress. Using the life of Nancy Pelosi as a tree on which to place important events, this chapter identifies key changes and circumstances that made her election as Speaker possible.

In between I have organized the selections into different sections, and within each section into a rough chronological order (complicated by the fact that some chapters cover many decades and some only a few months). Part I documents four efforts to practice politics, nationally and locally, and what the consequences were. Part II looks at some of the women who broke barriers and some of the barriers that were broken. Part III explores efforts to get issues of particular interest to women on to the national agenda, and the conflict between women's organizations that made that harder to do.

These pieces were written over twenty years. Six have previously appeared in print, albeit in fairly obscure places. A couple were written in expectation of being published, but for various reasons, never were. Two were cannibalized from a book I started in the 1980s but never finished. One or two started as invited lectures. The rest were written either for my web page or specifically for this book, though some of the latter pieces were based on earlier work. Because each stands alone, the reader can mix them up. It's not necessary to know what's in the early chapters in order to understand the later ones. This independence means that there is a little bit of overlap, but I have edited and revised the original words to minimize this. For the two pieces that were originally written before the story fully ended, I've added a postscript at the end to summarize what happened next.

Because they were written at different times and not all explicitly for this book, the chapters use different citation forms. I've provided suggested readings for those pieces that did not originally include sources. I also changed language to fill in blanks created by the passage of time. Readers may find some of the terms I use to be archaic, so let me provide my usual explanation that I try to use the language of the era in which I am writing. If I call a woman a chairman, it's because that was the title commonly used at that time (and in some places still is the title commonly used). Ditto for the use of "Mrs.," especially when I couldn't find a woman's personal name.

Rather than list here all the people I have to thank, I've included their names in the sources to the relevant chapters. The fact that these were written over several years means that I often consulted quite different persons for the different topics. Here I would particularly like to thank Amy Hackett, Elizabeth M. Cox, and Phillippa Strum for their ongoing assistance over many years. Amy's fine editorial eye has caught the glitches in all of these pieces at some point. Elizabeth Cox has shared her own research into our mutual interest in women and politics. Phillippa Strum continues to open doors.

I'd also like to thank Matthew Wasniewski for assistance in getting digitized images from the Prints and Photographs Division of the Library of Congress, and Olga Kirsanova and Susan Klebick for help in digitizing some of the other images.

Here I will thank the libraries and institutions whose resources and personnel facilitated my research. At the top of the list is Brooklyn College Library, where I have done research for many years. The Research Libraries of the New York Public Library is a close second. Added to these are the libraries and librarians of New York University, Brooklyn Public Library, Special Collections and Oral History Archives of Columbia University, Howard University, George Washington University, the Brookings Institution, the Woodrow Wilson International Center for Scholars, and the Library of Congress.

In the 1980s I spent a lot of time reading original documents and burning my eyes on microfilm readers. In the twenty-first century I spent equivalent time on the Internet, sometimes reading documents digitized by the same libraries whose microfilm I used to read. The willingness of many libraries to digitize unique materials means I could read a lot of things residing at places that I don't have time to visit. One of these days we'll all be able to do most of our research from our own desks. Now, we can at least do some of it.

Figure 1. Clockwise from top: Sophonisba Preston Breckinridge, date unknown (image no. LC-USZ62-44900 from the George Grantham Bain Collection at the Library of Congress); Louise Young in the 1940s (photo provided by M. Crawford Young); Jeane Kirkpatrick on April 7, 2006 (photograph by Jo Freeman); Martin Gruberg in the 1960s (photo provided by Martin Gruberg).

~

The Search for Political Woman*

Long ago social scientists created a hypothetical construct which they called "political man." While those who used this term probably thought of it as a generic reference rather than sex specific, it wasn't. If asked, they probably would have said there was no such creature as "political woman." Although women's arrival as a factor in politics, in the 1880s and 1890s, coincided with the emergence of the social science disciplines, social scientists simply didn't see them. To them, political woman was neither distinct from political man, nor part of political man. She simply didn't exist.

When sociologist Seymour Martin Lipset published his book on *Political Man* in 1960, he said in the foreward that a principal topic was "the factors which affect men's participation in politics, particularly their behavior as voters" (1960, x). Women are not mentioned at all and sex differences only on one page, where he observes without further comment that women in Germany in the 1920s and 1930s were more likely to vote for the conservative or religious parties than were men. That same year the Democratic National Committee issued a short pamphlet on the "History of Democratic Women" (prepared by the Democratic Congressional Wives Forum); both the *New York Times Magazine* and the *Saturday Evening Post* published articles on the woman voter (Hastings 1960; Shalett 1960); Perle Mesta, who

---

*Presented at a panel on "Culture and Knowledge: How Social Scientists Discovered Women" at the Conference on Jesuit Humanism: Faith, Justice, and Empiricism in the Liberal Arts, in celebration of the 150th anniversary of the founding of Santa Clara University in California, on May 5, 2001.

had been a major contributor to *both* parties and minister to Luxembourg under Truman, published *My Story*; Maude Wood Park published her lengthy inside story of how women won the Nineteenth Amendment, and John Talmadge published a book-length biography of the first woman appointed to the U.S. Senate. Rebecca Latimer Felton had been a major factor in Georgia politics for several decades even though she was only senator for a day. While this isn't much for one year, especially a presidential election year, it does illustrate that at least some people knew women were working in politics and had been for some time, but they weren't social scientists.

I'd like to think that political scientists, especially those that studied voting behavior, were a little more aware of "political woman" than political sociologists such as Lipset. But, as documented by Flammang (1997) and Nelson (1989), they weren't. Although a gender gap of 5–6 percent had appeared in the elections of 1952 and 1956, leading Republican women to crow that "Women Elected Ike" (Priest 1953; Shelton 1955; Republican National Committee 1962), political scientists barely noticed.

The mainstream press saw women that were invisible to social scientists. *Newsweek* covered "Women in National Politics" in 1955. In 1956 the *New York Times* sent reporters into several states to find out why women favored Eisenhower. In 1958 *U.S. News and World Report* published a cover story on "What women do in politics," and in 1960 it asked "Will women decide the election?" In the 1950s, political campaigns were labor intensive, and women provided 80 to 90 percent of that labor. But political scientists had nothing to say about women in politics.

In 1968, when I started graduate school in political science at the University of Chicago, I didn't expect to find a course on women and politics. The women's liberation movement had barely started and was not yet public. The National Organization for Women (NOW) was founded in 1966. The small groups of what I later called the younger branch of the movement were just appearing. I had helped start one of them in Chicago in 1967 and was one of thirty women from five states to go to our first national gathering in August 1968 (Freeman 1975). I knew we were doing something new. But I also knew we were doing something old because we were not the first women to protest our lowly status. I entered grad school hoping to find out something about my predecessors. While I didn't expect to find that political science had much to say about women, I did expect to find *something*. I found virtually *nothing*.

That same year, freelance writer Peggy Lamson published a book of biographies of ten political women, aptly titled *Few Are Chosen*, and political scientist Martin Gruberg published the first book-length study of

Women in American Politics. Born in 1935 and raised in the Bronx, Gruberg stumbled into this topic from a background in public law. On completing his dissertation at Columbia University in 1963, he started teaching in Oshkosh, Wisconsin. Needing a book to get tenure, he looked around for a hole crying to be filled to serve as a subject. Gruberg saw women as a minority group in politics that had been largely ignored. Encouraged by his academic advisors and by two women he met at a March 1964 conference on getting women into politics (women who would help found NOW in 1966) held in Madison, Wisconsin, he collected data eclectically. At the 1964 national nominating conventions he interviewed whomever he could find willing to talk about women in politics. Although he had no outside financing, Gruberg traveled to New York City and to party headquarters in Washington, DC, to do more interviews and visited the Schlesinger Library in Boston. He picked up some basic pamphlets from the national committees and found a few articles in the popular press, but little scholarship. He couldn't synthesize the scholarly literature because there wasn't any to synthesize. What he found out about political woman came from anecdotes, newspaper clippings, booklets, and a few statistics. Persuading a publisher to tackle a new topic was also difficult. "Women" had a niche in the popular press, but scholars did not take it seriously.

I went to both party conventions as well—to picket and vigil for civil rights. I was about to begin my senior year at Berkeley, and had been working for Democratic Party candidates since 1952. To give you some idea of how remote "women in politics" was from public consciousness, the only thing Maine Senator Margaret Chase Smith's campaign for president meant to me was that she put out a unique oval pin with a rose on it. I was totally oblivious to the fact that she was the first woman to actively campaign for a major party nomination for president, and so was everyone else I encountered at those conventions.

At the 1968 Democratic convention (conveniently held in Chicago) I was a budding feminist and no longer oblivious, but I neither met nor saw anyone I recognized as a political woman. Berkeley political scientist Aaron Wildavsky came to Chicago to study delegate decision making, in expectation of a contested convention. As one of several students he hired to do interviews, and the only one with convention press credentials, I talked to a lot of people that week. No one—not political scientists, students, delegates, the press, or protestors—had one word to say about women; nor did I see any programs, posters, or panels on women's rights or women in politics.

In fact, women *were* making noise that year, but they were drowned out by all the other protests. Sen. Eugene McCarthy (D-MN) had challenged

President Johnson in the Democratic primaries. While his focus was the war in Viet Nam, as the chief Senate sponsor of the Equal Rights Amendment (ERA), he made statements for it as part of his campaign. In fact, *all* of the candidates running in both major party primaries in 1968 (except Robert Kennedy) supported the ERA, though the others said little. Representatives from NOW and from the National Woman's Party (NWP) testified in favor of an ERA plank before the Platform Committees of both parties, but the final documents said somewhere between little and nothing about women, let alone the ERA.

Some signs of change were appearing. In my home state of California, the Democratic Party added a very strong plank on women's rights to its 1968 state party platform. Women headed the Republican state party in three states. What would come to be known as the gender gap was shifting. While men and women voted equally for Nixon for president that year, men were 4 percent more likely to vote for George Wallace (16 percent to 12 percent) while women were more likely to vote for Hubert Humphrey (45 percent to 41 percent). Very little notice was taken of any of these facts. The revolution was coming, but no one knew it.

I began my own search for political woman in order to write a term paper for a course on public policy at the university taught by Theodore Lowi, who was also my academic advisor. While he encouraged me to pursue the topic, the only help he could give me was a copy of Gruberg's book after I told him about it. Entering grad students were encouraged to do library research rather than field research, but I found nothing there. In the Law Library I found some law review articles on women and the law, which Leo Kanowitz aptly called "The Unfinished Revolution." Apart from Kanowitz, most of these articles were written in the 1920s and 1930s. There were a few recent pieces, enough to cobble into a suitable term paper, but "women and the law" was not about "political woman."

The articles in Gruberg's bibliography specifically on political women were in popular magazines like the *Ladies' Home Journal* and *Woman's Home Companion*, and most had been written many years earlier. Decades later I would learn that women's magazines and the women's pages in newspapers were where information on women in politics was to be found. But these publications did not grace the shelves of the University of Chicago library; if I had found and cited them in a term paper, my work would have been dismissed as trivial.

I met my first political woman in the archives of the university, where she had been buried for many years. Inspired by an undergraduate sit-in during the Winter 1969 quarter to protest the firing of sociologist Marlene Dixon, I wanted to know just how many women had held faculty positions in that department. My quest led me to a small room where the course catalogs were stored. I spent a week reading and taking notes from every catalog put out since the university was founded in 1892. Finding too few women in sociology to count, I expanded my search to six departments. It was in these catalogs that I discovered Sophonisba Preston Breckinridge. After tracing her career, I returned to the library, where I discovered that entries for her books occupied three quarters of an inch in the card catalog. I also found an ancient historian, Bessie Pierce, who knew her before her death in 1948. Pierce was the only person I found on the campus in 1969 who had ever heard of Sophonisba Preston Breckinridge, even though she had been a prominent and distinguished professor at the university for many decades.

The more I learned about Breckinridge the more she became my model of a political woman, the one whose path I would have followed if fate had been so kind. What appealed to me was how she combined scholarship with activism in pursuit of public policy to better the lives of everyone, but especially women. Born in 1866 into a distinguished Kentucky political family, she was the first woman to be admitted to the Kentucky Bar and practice law. In the mid-1890s she moved to Chicago where she entered the university and received a joint PhD in the departments of political science and economics in 1901. She promptly enrolled in the Law School, getting her JD in 1904. Armed with three doctorates, she became an instructor at the university, in the Department of Household Administration. This was the "women's studies" department of its day; here Breckinridge taught courses on the legal and economic position of women.

Today her career would be characterized as one in social work education. She helped pioneer that profession, arranging for the university to adopt what became the School of Social Service Administration in 1920. But underneath those academic robes she was a political woman—working in the Progressive Movement through such organizations as the Women's Trade Union League to write laws she felt would benefit women, serving as vice president of the National American Woman Suffrage Association and campaigning for the Progressive Party in the election of 1912. As a social scientist, she did extensive field research, making observations and taking detailed notes on how people lived and worked. She did not gather these facts for their own sake, but so that government could better tend to the needs of people. To Breckinridge, knowledge needed to be useful, and action needed to be informed.

When the Depression began, President Herbert Hoover named a Research Committee on Social Trends to provide scientific information on the problems now confronting the country. Breckinridge was commissioned to write a monograph on women, financed by the Rockefeller Foundation. Published in 1933 as *Women in the Twentieth Century: A Study of Their Political, Social and Economic Activities*, roughly one-third of its 364 pages are on "Women and Government." Surveying women as voters, lobbyists, party workers and office holders, it was the first comprehensive study of women in politics. She concluded that women had made great strides in organizing voluntary associations, and through them could affect some kinds of public policy, but the formal institutions of government and the parties had barely cracked open the door to women (Breckinridge 1933, 288).

The 1969 UC sit-in created much interest in the status of women. I gave four lectures on my archival findings at rallies, seminars, and colloquia that quarter. I also wrote a pamphlet using data from the *Handbook on Women Workers* which was widely distributed, and published an article in *The Nation* on "The New Feminists." As a result quite a few students asked me to teach a course on women in the Spring quarter. Of course, the course was noncredit and I was not paid; just putting it together was a challenge. To get a room on campus I needed a faculty sponsor. All the left-leaning men and every woman faculty member I asked turned me down. Finally, Don Scott, a very junior history professor in the undergraduate college, agreed to "front" the course. He made copies of the syllabus and some of the readings for us and gave independent study credit to any student who needed it, even though he had to read term papers to do this. UC didn't give him tenure, and probably didn't even give him credit for this extra work. The "Sophonisba Preston Breckinridge Memorial Course on the Legal and Economic Position of Women—(formerly H.A. 21)" included material on public policy issues of relevance to women, such as Title VII and the ERA, but women's political work was notable by its absence.

Politics was left out of my course because Gruberg's book only existed in hardcover, was not in the library, and I couldn't find anything else for my "students" to read. What I needed was a current version of the ninety-page paper on "The Political Role of Women in the United States" written by Louise Young in 1952 for UNESCO (United Nations Economic, Social and Cultural Organization). At the request of the UN's Commission on the Status of Women, UNESCO asked the International Political Science Association to conduct a survey of member nations on women in political life. IPSA asked the League of Women Voters to prepare the U.S. report, and it asked Louise Young to do so, pro bono. An active League member, Young had published a small book on *Understanding Politics: A Practical Guide for Women* in 1950. She reported later that "American political scientists were either indifferent or regarded the survey as of no importance and none offered to help" (oral history 1982, 116).

Seventeen countries submitted reports—four of them written by women. Several of these were presented at a conference held at The Hague on September 8–12, 1952. Louise Young borrowed money from her father to attend the conference and present the U.S. report. Surveys from four countries became the basis of a short book written by Maurice Duverger on *The Political Role of Women*. Norway, West Germany, France, and Yugoslavia were chosen because they had the best data. Young's report became a pamphlet distributed overseas by the US Information Agency. However, I did not know about this pamphlet in 1969, and despite some serious searching, I've never seen a copy.

Louise Young was one of the few scholars looking at political women who bridged the gap between Breckinridge and Gruberg, but she did her work largely as a labor of love. Born in Ohio in 1903, she came of age with the suffrage movement in a family that followed politics closely. She always remembered the excitement of the 1912 election. Following her husband to the University of Pennsylvania in 1925, she did graduate work in English. Her 1939 PhD did not bring paid employment. In the 1930s and 1940s married women were not expected to work, especially while raising their children. They were hired for professional jobs, even teaching, only when men or single women were not available. It was the League of Women Voters, which she joined as a suburban Philadelphia housewife in the 1940s, that became the base for her scholarly as well as public activity for the rest of her life.

After the family moved to Washington, DC, in 1946 Young combined raising three children, scholarly research, and volunteer work. Her research was facilitated by a cubicle in the Library of Congress from which she catalogued and archived the League's papers for the Library, edited a special volume of the *Annals of the American Academy of Political and Social Science* on "women's opportunities and responsibilities" (May 1947), and collected information on the history of women in politics. She did all this, she later said, in the "interstices" of her life (oral history 1982, 89). In 1953 the president of American University, who was the husband of a childhood friend, asked her to teach part time to help alleviate the shortage of PhDs on the faculty. She became a full-time faculty member in 1955 and taught until 1971.

In 1967 Young was invited to prepare a major history of the League of Women Voters to commemorate its fiftieth anniversary in 1970. This project took more time than she expected, and by the time it was finished in 1973, both the publisher and the League had lost interest. It was put on the back burner for another decade, until finally published in 1989 as *In the Public*

Interest: The League of Women Voters, 1920–1970. Young learned from her study of League history what Breckinridge had concluded in 1933—that women influenced public policy through voluntary associations rather than by working to elect sympathetic individuals to office. While women were politically active everywhere as individuals, only when they organized as women did anyone listen to their concerns.

The anniversary Young missed—1970—was the takeoff point of the new feminist movement. That was the year all the major media "discovered" women's liberation and did major news stories about it. When NOW held its march down New York City's Fifth Avenue on August 26 to commemorate the fiftieth anniversary of the Nineteenth Amendment, the world witnessed an uprising of American women (Freeman 1975, ch. 5).

Even political science, which had successfully ignored women for so long, had to pay attention. Although women were less than 10 percent of the profession (how much less depends on what is measured), in 1969 an official Committee on the Status of Women was appointed and an unofficial women's caucus organized to press for equal opportunity for women in the discipline. While neither of these groups had the study of political woman on its agenda, panels on women soon proliferated at the annual meetings of both national and regional associations. Jane Jaquette gathered many of these papers into an anthology on *Women in Politics,* published in hardcover in 1974. Marianne Githens and Jewel L. Prestage brought out another paperback collection in 1977. Its title—*A Portrait of Marginality*—summarized its message: five of its twenty-four chapters were specifically on black women in politics.

The causal connection was very clear. The new feminist movement attracted press attention, media coverage created scholarly interest across disciplines in what women were doing, convention organizers looked for panels that would bring audiences, and scholars responded by writing papers. In effect, demand created supply. It wasn't the curiosity of scholars or the availability of research data that prompted the search for political woman; it was trendiness. Soon journals were looking for special editions and publishers were looking for books on this hot new topic. In 1967, Martin Gruberg found little interest by publishers in his book. By 1972, publishers were writing *me,* a mere graduate student (albeit well-published), asking if I had a book in hand. In that period of emerging interest in women and resulting high demand, I found it easier to write for publication than to write term papers.

Many others rode this wave, to judge by the sudden profusion of articles on women, feminism, and related topics to appear first in the popular press and then in scholarly journals. Louise Young was asked by the *Journal of Pol-*

itics to contribute an article on women to commemorate the 1976 Bicentennial. She had on hand enough pages for a book on two hundred years of women's involvement in American politics, which she compressed into nine thousand words. The full manuscript was never published, but articles and books by others elaborating on what Young said in 1976 have been appearing ever since.

Institutions as well as individuals joined the search for political woman. In 1971 the Eagleton Institute of Politics at Rutgers University, established in 1956 with a small endowment from suffragist Florence Peshine Eagleton, secured $50,000 from the Ford Foundation to create a Center for the American Woman and Politics (CAWP). It opened in July with Ruth Mandel, another English PhD, and Ida Schmertz, an ABD in Russian studies, as codirectors. Since Eagleton's primary focus is on state politics, CAWP's first major project was a conference of women as one of several meetings of "up-and-coming" state legislators. Of the 344 women then holding this office, the League of Women Voters (LWV), the National Federation of Business and Professional Women's Clubs (BPW), and the American Association of University Women (AAUW) nominated two each from twenty-five states, who were perceived as influential. The Carnegie Corporation of New York provided $15,000 to bring them to a Pennsylvania retreat for three days in May 1972.

Mandel and Schmertz thought this was a marvelous opportunity to learn who these women were and what it was like to be a political woman. After Basic Books expressed interest in publishing something broader than a conference report, they invited Jeane Kirkpatrick to design a study and obtained $71,000 from the Carnegie Corporation to fund it. The women who came to the conference filled out a long questionnaire and submitted to individual interviews of two to three hours. This information and transcripts from the discussions were turned over to Kirkpatrick for assessment and analysis. The result was her 1974 book *Political Woman*. Her "most important finding . . . [was] that political woman exists." But she recognized that "for women to achieve de facto political equality, . . . both a cultural and a social revolution is required" (1974, 217, 244).

Kirkpatrick was the ideal person for this job. One of only a handful of women to hold the rank of full professor in a PhD-granting department of political science, she was well connected in the discipline, well respected, and personally interested in the position of women, especially as political actors. Born Jeane Duane Jordan in 1926 in Oklahoma, she too came from a family with strong political interests. Her childhood in Oklahoma, Illinois, and Missouri led her to New York, where she completed her BA at Barnard in 1948 and her MA at Columbia in 1950. After working for a few years, she married Dr. Evron M. Kirkpatrick, the new executive director of the American Political Science Association. Like Louise Young, she devoted the next few years to raising their three sons while continuing with her research and writing in Washington, DC. In 1962 she began teaching at Trinity College. After she finished her PhD at Columbia in 1968 she moved to Georgetown University and was promoted to full professor in 1973. As a political scientist, her training was in political theory and comparative government, but when she met Harold Lasswell she became very interested in behaviorism. She thought women were a distinct group, and was puzzled as to why they did not have a distinct political behavior. The CAWP study provided a welcome opportunity to answer some of her questions.

Her own search for political woman began well before CAWP tapped her to author its study of state legislators. In August of 1970 Warren Miller, director of the Center for Political Studies at the University of Michigan, brought together a group to design a study of delegates to the 1972 national nominating conventions. Kirkpatrick was invited in because they wanted to compare men and women delegates. Traditionally, women were only 12 to 15 percent of the delegates to the Democratic Party convention, and 15 to 18 percent of Republican delegates. However, in response to its tumultuous 1968 convention, the Democrats were revising their delegate selection rules. Guidelines were proposed that required minorities, youth, and women to be represented in each state's delegation "in reasonable relationship to their presence in the population of the state." Women's presence at the 1972 convention seemed likely to increase significantly. Although the Republicans were not considering a similar requirement, spillover from the Democratic efforts and new consciousness by women was having an effect. The investigators felt that women would be numerous enough to examine as a class, and not as "idiosyncratic individuals." Furthermore, women delegates could be matched with an equivalent sample of men.

The Russell Sage Foundation gave $125,000 to the University of Michigan for a study on "Women in Politics." A questionnaire was sent to all delegates attending both conventions, and personal interviews were done with a carefully chosen sample. With $124,804 in additional funding from the Twentieth Century Fund, Kirkpatrick wrote a six-hundred-page book on *The New Presidential Elite* that was published in 1976. The book shifted focus when she found party differences more important than sex differences. However, unlike prior studies of delegates, roughly one-fourth of her book emphasized "Women in the Presidential Elite." She concluded that "women's low participation in power today derives from relatively low political ambition *and* from male prejudice," but that the women delegates (and a lot of men) believed "that there would be a major change in women's political roles in the next ten years" (1976, 488–49).

I went to the 1972 Democratic convention as an alternate with the Chicago Challenge Delegation that unseated Mayor Daley's handpicked delegates. I had run for delegate committed to Shirley Chisholm—the first woman to actively campaign for the Democratic nomination—in order to get her name on the ballot in Illinois' First District. Coming in ninth among the twenty-four who ran in that district enabled me to claim a spot among those who finally got those seats. The eight who won in the primary were all Daley delegates and all male, running uncommitted. I was a beneficiary of the "affirmative action" policies in force that year, which created such a storm they were altered for 1976. Unlike 1968, women were a real presence at both conventions, both numerically and politically. It was a good year to study political woman.

As an alternate I didn't get Kirkpatrick's questionnaire or see any interviewers, and was completely unaware of her study. None of the people in my delegation mentioned it (and may have received the questionnaire after returning home) and none of my faculty at the University of Chicago knew of it either. There was so much going on at that convention that it was easy for a political science study to be hidden from those who didn't know to look for it. I did go to a lot of caucuses and would have welcomed someone to talk to about my observations. But Ted Lowi had left for Cornell and none of the Chicago faculty had any interest in American political parties, let alone political women. In December I went to Berkeley where I had a long talk with Aaron Wildavksy, who helped me to better understand what I had seen and experienced. I mention this to show how hard it was for those who had common research interests in women to find each other, and how easy it was to be isolated. Even Young and Kirkpatrick never met. Although women political scientists were few, and those interested in political women were fewer, we did not yet know each other, though we did know *of* each other. Until the women's movement got off the ground, communications networks among women scholars or scholars of women did not exist.

Kirkpatrick's work helped legitimate the study of women as a field within political science. But acceptance was delayed until the 1980s—at the earliest. Some resistance was due to inertia. Men were 90 percent of all political scientists, and more at the higher levels where decisions about hiring and tenure were made. Some came from a perception about who did politics and why. As Jaquette said in her preface, "Politics has traditionally viewed itself as a male field, and, with the possible exception of economics, it is the social science discipline which has responded with the least enthusiasm to the impact of the modern feminist movement" (1974, v).

If one looks at the speed with which the study of women became accepted in the different disciplines, the most important factor appears to be the number and the percent of women already in each discipline in the late 1960s, when the feminist movement emerged, women became a hot topic in the popular press, and complaints were filed with the Department of Health, Education and Welfare demanding that government contracts be rescinded until sex discrimination was eliminated. Acceptance was most rapid in those fields which already had a critical mass of women—somewhere between 20 and 30 percent—even though the women were at the lowest levels and in the least prestigious schools. Women begot more women. And more women fostered the study of women. Greater numbers of scholars studying women made the creation of specialty journals economically feasible and conferences on "women in . . ." realistic. Many other scholarly phenomena—regular local meetings, research support, courses, the sharing of knowledge and interests—also require minimum numbers to exist and a critical mass to flourish. After economics, political science had the lowest percentage of women of the social sciences at that time, and, except for economics, was the last to consider the study of women a legitimate field of inquiry.

Contributing to the resistance was the "affirmative action scare" which pervaded academia in the 1970s. While the idea that those who had traditionally been excluded from the academic disciplines should now be particularly sought after was originally intended to benefit scholars from racial minorities, it was the possible impact of the much greater numbers of women that really scared the men. Sheer numbers made women a much greater threat than minorities, though both were seen as invaders with an alien agenda. Declining budgets for hiring new faculty exacerbated turf battles as insiders circled their wagons against outsiders. Women scholars who wrote about women were automatically viewed with suspicion. Even Kirkpatrick, who was as much in the political science establishment as a woman could be, ran into raised eyebrows when she told colleagues she was writing about women.

The backlash caused many casualties among pioneer scholars, especially those who did not have tenure. While Gruberg got tenure in 1968, I don't know of any woman whose primary research was on women in politics who got tenure in a department of political science before the mid-1980s. Those who did publish on women were told to leave it off of their resumes when coming up for review. Others joined shaky women's studies programs just making their appearance on the academic scene, or held joint appointments. Many downgraded their aspirations to junior colleges, or full-time adjunct-ing, or did something else.

Even established political scientists did not foresee that the trendy topic of the early 1970s would become a scarlet letter by the mid- to late 1970s. In 1972 both Ted Lowi and Aaron Wildavsky encouraged me to write my dissertation on the new feminist movement; neither expressed concern that this might adversely affect my job prospects. In 1975 I published two books on women. One quickly became the leading introductory women's studies textbook. The other—the published version of my 1973 dissertation—won a $1,000 prize as the Best Scholarly Work on Women in Politics, given that year by the American Political Science Association to commemorate International Women's Year. My last academic job offer was in 1974. I received two one-year fellowships in Washington, DC, but the gates to academe were locked and I could not find a key. Before I gave up and went to law school in 1979, I probably applied for every job in American government advertised in the APSA personnel newsletter. The feedback I received, second or third hand, was that "we don't need anyone to teach women and politics." Of course I never taught such a course; I taught basic American government. But I wrote about women and politics.

Word soon got out that "women" was no longer "in." When I guest lectured at universities and gave papers at political science meetings, graduate students told me that their advisors told them not to write their dissertations on political women, and particularly not on feminism; it was too risky. Writing about political women paused for about a decade before picking up again. I too stopped researching and writing about women in politics, except for going to the quadrennial party conventions as a journalist for feminist publications. Not until 2000 did I publish another major book on women and politics. *A Room at a Time: How Women Entered Party Politics* also won a political science prize for scholarship (no prize money for this one). Like Louise Young I wrote on my own, as a labor of love, in the interstices of my life, with a little help from my friends.

Writing this book convinced me that academic researchers were not *merely* ignorant of the presence of political women, but *willfully* ignorant. Although "political woman" as a hypothetical construct did not exist until the 1970s, political women as active participants in the political process and influencers of public policy had been quite common for at least a century. Party women, as a specific type of politically active woman, emerged in numbers worthy of note in the 1880s, and were extensively described and commented on in 1890s newspapers. Women were a major component of the Progressive

Movement in the early twentieth century, and not just in organizations devoted to women's issues. Women expanded the definition of politics and contributed enormously to the creation of interest groups as major players in the political process. Women particularly utilized this avenue to influence public policy because the parties made it clear that they wanted women's labor, but not their ideas. Nonetheless, many women organized their own party clubs and spent their time electing "good men" to public office, sometimes making a crucial difference in who won.

I discovered that the common wisdom that "feminism failed" after suffrage, because women did not vote as a bloc to reform the political system, was a myth. Suffragists never claimed that women would vote as a bloc. That assertion was made by those who opposed giving women the vote. Nonetheless, there was a "gender gap" in the 1920s, with more women voting for the Republican Party, which the Democratic Party closed in the 1930s. It reappeared in the 1950s. Nor were women unorganized. The "Women's Lobby on Capitol Hill" was called by the American Medical Association the "most highly organized and powerful lobby ever seen in Washington" (Breckinridge 1933, 259–60). The major political parties were so afraid that women would organize to exercise influence as women that in the years immediately following the Nineteenth Amendment they campaigned against "sex solidarity." Political leaders denounced women's political organizations as un-American unless organized within an existing political party, and demanded that political women choose between their party and their sex. The parties worked hard to co-opt women in order to control them, and largely succeeded. Party women were not complacent about this but their complaints were ignored. (Freeman 2000, 123–27)

While it *may be* true that history is written by the victors, and it *is* true that women were not the victors in the postsuffrage struggle for political power, it is *also* true that scholars were blind to the battle. Political women commented on it; journalists wrote about it; but most scholars missed it almost entirely. When Roy Peel wrote his book on *The Political Clubs of New York City* covering the years 1927 to 1933 he saw women's clubs only as auxiliaries to the 1,200 regular male clubs. During those years there were hundreds of separate women's party clubs in New York City whose meetings and work were reported on in the newspapers. New York party women published three magazines for several thousand readers, but Peel appears not to have known they existed.

There were several presidential elections in which women's participation as orators, campaign workers, and/or voters received major attention in the newspapers: specifically 1896, 1912, 1916, 1928, 1952, and 1956.

The New York Times Index for 1936 has two pages of entries on women in the presidential campaign. Yet books written about these elections seldom give women more than a sentence or two. In the 1920s both major parties gave women equal representation on their national committees; in the 1940s they were given equal representation on the national convention committees. When equal representation for delegates to the national conventions was being debated in the 1970s, no one seemed aware that this was not a radical new idea. Indeed, the concept that men and women should have equal representation on party committees started in Colorado in the 1890s, and was particularly popular in the 1920s and 1930s when many states first required it.

My study of women's political history disclosed that Breckinridge was asked to write her pathbreaking volume in a similar context to that which existed when Kirkpatrick was asked to write hers. Consciousness about women in politics was high because 1928 was the "year of the woman voter." Throughout the 1920s the mass of women had been relatively apathetic about politics, enthused by only a few local candidates and none of the national ones. But Hoover was so popular that he became known as "the woman's candidate." (McCormick 1928, 22; Smith 1929, 126; Barnard 1928, 555). Some of his popularity derived from his role as food administrator during the Great War, and some from the importance of Prohibition in the election of 1928. Hoover was "dry," Smith was "wet," and it was commonly assumed that women wanted Prohibition to be enforced. Women registered to vote in record numbers, and the Republican Party's Women's Division was "besieged by unprecedented numbers of women who wanted to participate in the campaign" (Morrison 1978, 84). Hoover was endorsed by the National Woman's Party, the only major party presidential candidate to be endorsed by a specifically feminist organization prior to 1984.

Knowing history shapes our sense of the possible. Leaving women out of political science and political history let students falsely believe that political woman did not exist, that politics was something properly reserved to men, and that women who tried to participate were "idiosyncratic individuals" rather than engaged and effective political actors who faced a lot of resistance.

Sometime in the 1980s political woman took her place in political science, recognized as a topic of inquiry, even one that warranted an entire course. Perhaps acceptance finally came through sheer persistence, augmented by the willingness of political scientists to reexamine the suppositions of the discipline. But I suspect it was because a highly publicized gender gap appeared in the polls done for the election of 1980. The fact that a lot of women were voting differently than men demanded an explanation.

Once there was a market for knowing why women voted the way they did, political scientists rushed to fill the void. Women politicians were also moving into public office in numbers too big to ignore. Their presence in state legislatures had taken a great leap upward in the 1970s, and their presence in Congress jumped in the 1990s. These provided incentives to study political woman. Once again demand created supply.

Sources

In addition to the sources cited below, information for this chapter came from personal conversations with Jeane Kirkpatrick, correspondence with Martin Gruberg, and material supplied by Louise Young's son, Crawford. I also interviewed Ruth Mandel, director of the Eagleton Institute; Teresa Levitin, Warren Miller's former research assistant; and was sent information from the Carnegie Foundation's annual reports by Debra Brookhart, archives specialist at Indiana University, Indianapolis, where the foundation archives are stored.

Barnard, Eunice Fuller. 1928. Madame arrives in politics. *North American Review* 226 (November): 551–56.

Breckinridge, Sophonisba Preston. 1933. *Women in the twentieth century: A study of their political, social and economic activities*. New York: McGraw-Hill. Reprinted by Arno Press, New York, 1972.

Democratic Congressional Wives Forum (DCWF). 1960. *History of Democratic women*. 43-page pamphlet prepared under the auspices of the Democratic National Committee.

Duverger, Maurice. 1955. *The political role of women*. New York: UNESCO.

Flammang, Janet A. 1997. *Women's political voice: How women are transforming the practice and study of politics*. Philadelphia, Pa.: Temple University Press.

Freeman, Jo. 1969. The new feminists. *Nation* 208, no. 8 (February 24): 241.

———. 1971. Women on the social science faculties since 1892 at the University of Chicago. In *Discrimination against women*, Hearings before the Special Subcommittee on Education of the House Committee on Education and Labor, on Section 805 of H.R. 16098, 994–1003, June–July 1970. Washington, D.C.: U.S. Government Printing Office.

———. 1975. *The politics of women's liberation: A case study of an emerging social movement and its relation to the policy process*. New York: Longman Inc.

———. 2000. *A room at a time: How women entered party politics*. Lanham, Md.: Rowman & Littlefield.

Githens, Marianne, and Jewel Prestage, eds. 1977. *A portrait of marginality: The political behavior of American women*. New York: McKay.

Gruberg, Martin. 1968. *Women in American politics: An assessment and sourcebook*. Oshkosh, Wisc.: Academia Press.

Hastings, Philip K. 1960. Hows and howevers of the woman voter. *New York Times Magazine*, June 12, VI:14, 80–81.

Jaquette, Jane S., ed. 1974. *Women in politics*. New York: Wiley.

Kanowitz, Leo. 1969. *Women and the law: The unfinished revolution*. Albuquerque: University of New Mexico Press.

Kirkpatrick, Jeane. 1974. *Political woman*. New York: Basic Books.

———. 1976. *The new presidential elite*. New York: Russell Sage Foundation.

Lasch, Christopher. 1971. Sophonisba Preston Breckinridge. In *Notable American women, 1607–1950: A biographical dictionary*, ed. Edward James, Janet Wilson James, and Paul S. Boyer, I: 233–36. Cambridge, Mass.: Belknap Press of Harvard University Press.

Lamson, Peggy. 1968. *Few are chosen: American women in political life today*. Boston: Houghton Mifflin.

Lipset, Seymour Martin. 1960. *Political man: The social bases of politics*. New York: Doubleday.

McCormick, Anne O'Hare. 1928. Enter women, the new boss of politics. *New York Times Magazine*, October 21, 3, 23.

Mesta, Perle, with Robert Cahn. 1960. *Perle: My story*. New York: McGraw Hill.

Moritz, Charles, ed. 1981. *Current Biography Yearbook*. Kirkpatrick, Jeane (Duane) J(ordan), 255–59. New York: HW Wilson Co.

Morrison, Glenda E. 1978. Women's participation in the 1928 presidential campaign. PhD diss., University of Kansas.

Nelson, Barbara. 1989. Women and knowledge in political science: Texts, histories and epistomologies. *Women and Politics* 9, no. 2 (Summer): 1–25.

Newsweek. 1955. Women in national politics. May 9, 30–32.

Park, Maud Wood. 1960. *Front door lobby*. Boston: Beacon Press.

Peel, Roy V. 1935. *The political clubs of New York City*. New York: Putnam's Sons.

Priest, Ivy Baker. 1953. The ladies elected Ike. *American Mercury* 75, no. 350 (February): 23–28.

Republican National Committee, Women's Division. 1962. *Win with womanpower*. 16-page pamphlet.

Schuck, Victoria. 1970. Some comparative statistics on women in political science and other social sciences. *P.S.* 3 (Summer): 357–61.

Shalett, Sidney. 1960. Is there a "women's vote"? *Saturday Evening Post* 233 (September 17): 31, 78–80.

Shanley, Mary L., and Victoria Schuck. 1974. In search of political woman. *Social Science Quarterly* 55 (December): 632–44.

Shelton, Isabelle. 1955. Spotlight pinpoints the woman voter, though '56 campaign is still off stage. Women's World column, *Sunday Star* (Washington, D.C.), May 15, D-1.

Smith, Helena Huntington. 1929. Weighing the women's vote. *Outlook and Independent* 151 (January 23): 126–28.

Talmadge, John E. 1960. *Rebecca Latimer Felton: Nine stormy decades*. Athens: University of Georgia Press.

U.S. *News and World Report*. 1958. What women do in politics. December 12, cover + 72–9.

———. 1960. Will women decide the election? October 3, 61–65.

Young, Louise M. 1950. *Understanding politics: A practical guide for women*. New York: Pellegrini & Cudahy.

———. 1976. Women's place in American politics: The historical perspective. *Journal of Politics* 38, no. 3 (August): 300–20.

———. 1982. Oral history interview with Jeanette B. Cheek, September 27, Schlesinger Library.

———. 1989. *In the public interest: The League of Women Voters, 1920–1970*. Westport, Conn.: Greenwood Press.

PART I

PRACTICING POLITICS

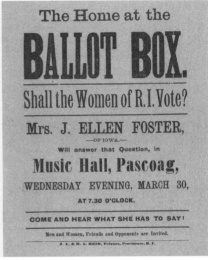

Figure 2.   Left: J. Ellen Foster in 1908 (image no. LC-USZ62-102556 from the Library of Congress). Right: Flyer for lecture, exact year unknown, but most likely 1898 (provided by Linda Rivet, Reference Librarian at the Jesse M. Smith Memorial Library in Harrisville, RI).

~

CHAPTER ONE

The Iowa Origins of
Organized Republican Women

At the Republican convention of 1892, Iowa lawyer J. Ellen Foster stood before the delegates assembled in Minneapolis to introduce the Woman's National Republican Association. "We are here to help you," she told them. "And we have come to stay" (Foster 1904, 251).

With this presentation Foster was proclaimed by the Republican National Committee as their organizer of Republican women. Before she died in 1910 Foster campaigned throughout the country for Republican candidates and helped local women organize Republican women's clubs in many states, even though women could only vote in a few of them.

Born Judith Ellen Horton in 1840 in Lowell, Massachusetts, she came to Iowa in 1869 as the wife of lawyer Elijah Foster. She read for the law while raising her children. After admission to the bar in 1872 she practiced with her husband, becoming the first woman to appear before the Supreme Court of Iowa.

Foster's real calling, however, was as an orator and political organizer. The "Woman's Crusade" against the saloon that began in Ohio in 1874 aroused her reform instincts. She spread its message in Iowa, helping found the Woman's Christian Temperance Union later that year. As head of the WCTU's legislative department, she wrote state laws and constitutional amendments limiting the sale and manufacture of alcohol and campaigned for their passage.

Her fame attracted much attention. Opponents of temperance burned her home in Clinton, Iowa. James S. Clarkson, editor and part-owner of the Des

Moines *Iowa State Register*, and member of the Republican National Committee from Iowa, recruited her considerable oratorical talents for the Republican party.

Throughout the 1880s, the Republican Party lost elections due to the acrimonious cultural conflict created by prohibition, especially in the Midwest. Either those favoring prohibition ran their own candidates, taking enough votes away from Republicans for the Democrats to win, or they took over local party committees to run prohibitionists as Republicans, alienating enough normal Republican voters for the Democrats to win (Kleppner 1970, 138; Jensen 1971, ch. 4).

In 1884 the Republican Party blamed the Prohibition Party for the loss of the White House to Grover Cleveland, the first Democrat to be elected president since 1856. Its candidate, aided by active campaigning by the WCTU, won just enough votes in crucial states for Cleveland to win in the electoral college.

Foster had campaigned for Republican James G. Blaine, and for the next few years campaigned within the WCTU for it to get out of electoral politics. When Foster could not persuade the WCTU to become and stay non-partisan, she seceded and formed her own organization, the Non-Partisan WCTU, in 1889.

Encouraged by the Republican National Committee, Foster had already made plans for an organization of women's Republican clubs. In 1887 she had visited England, where she was quite impressed by the work of the Women's Liberal Federation for the Liberal Party and the Primrose Dames for the Conservative Party (*Woman's Journal* 1888, 276). Clarkson had organized the National League of Republican Clubs in 1887, and Republican women regularly organized campaign clubs for major elections in about half the states. The time seemed ripe for Republican women to have their own national organization.

The WNRA didn't get off the ground until 1892, and never quite made it as a federation of women's Republican clubs. It operated as the women's committee of the RNC during campaigns and as an advisory body in between. However, Foster traveled widely to speak for the Republican party and encourage the organization of local women's Republican clubs. These helped Republican candidates during campaigns and educated women about politics between them.

Foster actively discouraged Republican women from merging reform and partisanship. She felt that women could participate in reform work, including the movement for woman suffrage, as individuals, but that as Republicans they should support the party's candidates, whomever they might be.

Throughout the 1890s women moved into politics, organizing hundreds of political clubs to campaign for their party's candidates, and sometimes for other women. Kansas elected fifteen women mayors. In 1894 women ran for public office in thirteen states. In the 1896 presidential campaign Republican women had their own headquarters in New York City. By the century's end, sixteen women had been elected to the legislatures of three states, and several as state superintendents of public instruction.

Not until 1912 would the national Democratic Party make a serious effort to organize women, even in the six states where they could vote for president. By then, the legacy of Iowan J. Ellen Foster was that Republican women in many more states were experienced campaign workers.

References

Adams, Elmer Cleveland, and Warren Dunham Foster. 1913. J. Ellen Foster. In *Heroines of modern progress*, 245–79. New York: Sturgis & Walton Co.

Foster, J. Ellen. 1904. Work of Republican women. Address before the 1892 Republican National Convention, June 6, 1892. In Francis Curtis, *The Republican Party: A history of its fifty years experience and a record of its measures and leaders, 1854–1904*, 2 vols, II: 251–53. New York: G. P. Putnam's Sons.

Gustafson, Melanie Susan. 1999. Partisan and nonpartisan: The political career of Judith Ellen Foster, 1881–1910. In *We have come to stay: American women and political parties 1880–1960*, ed. Melanie S. Gustafson, Kristie Miller, and Elisabeth I. Perry, 1–12. Albuquerque: University of New Mexico Press.

Jensen, Richard. 1971. *The winning of the Midwest*. Chicago: University of Chicago Press.

Kleppner, Paul. 1970. *The cross of culture: A social analysis of Midwestern politics, 1850–1900*. New York.

Mott, David C. 1933. Judith Ellen Foster. *Annals of Iowa: A Historical Quarterly* 19, no. 2 (October): 126–38.

New York Times. 1891. Mrs. Ole Bull's opinions: She sharply criticises "non-partisan" Mrs. Foster. March 8, 3:3.

Willard, Frances, and Mary A. Livermore. 1897. J. Ellen Foster. In *Women of the century: A comprehensive encyclopedia of the lives and achievements of American women during the nineteenth century*, 296–97. New York: Mast, Crowell & Kirkpatrick. Reprinted as *American women*. Detroit: Gale, 1973.

Woman's Journal. 1888. Woman's National Republican League. September 1, 276.

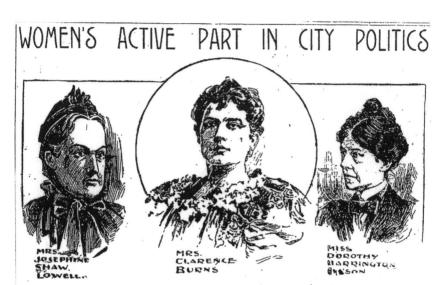

WOMEN'S ACTIVE PART IN CITY POLITICS

MRS. JOSEPHINE SHAW LOWELL

MRS. CLARENCE BURNS

MISS DOROTHY HARRINGTON BYNSON

Each Expects to Help Elect the Mayor of Her Choice.

Three Distinct Organizations Already Hard at Work—Municipal League Women Enter the Campaign for Seth Low, While Their Equally Enthusiastic Sisters Will Work for the Democratic and Republican Nominee Respectively.

NYJ 9·27·1897:43

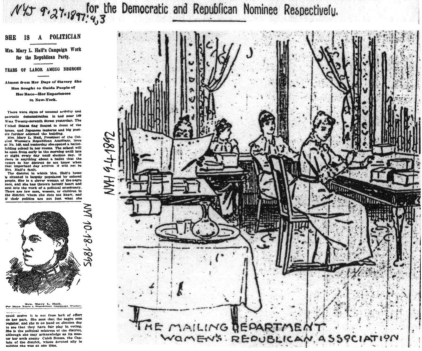

SHE IS A POLITICIAN

Mrs. Mary L. Hall's Campaign Work for the Republican Party.

YEARS OF LABOR AMONG NEGROES

Almost from Her Days of Slavery She Has Sought to Guide People of Her Race—Her Experiences in New-York.

There were signs of unusual activity and patriotic demonstration in and near 149 West Twenty-seventh Street yesterday. The United States flag floated in front of the house, and Japanese lanterns and big posters further adorned the building.

Mrs. Mary L. Hall, President of the Colored Women's Republican Auxiliary, lives at No. 149, and yesterday she opened a ballot-folding school in her rooms. The school will be open from early in the morning until late at night every day until election day. If there is anything about a ballot that the voters in her district do not know when that important day arrives it will not be Mrs. Hall's fault.

The district in which Mrs. Hall's home is situated is largely populated by colored people. She is a clever woman of the negro race, and she has thrown herself heart and soul into the work of a political missionary. There are few men, women, or children in the district whom she does not know, and if their politics are not just what she

NYT 10-18-1895

Mrs. Mary L. Hall,
For Many Years a Republican Campaign Worker.

could desire it is not from lack of effort on her part. She sees that the negro men register, and she is on hand on election day to see that they have fair play in voting. She is the political mistress of the district, although she may acknowledge as its master her arch enemy Caleb Simms, the Captain of the district, whose devoted ally in politics she was at one time.

THE MAILING DEPARTMENT
WOMEN'S REPUBLICAN ASSOCIATION

Figure 3. Clockwise from top: Collage of drawings and clips from the *New York Journal*, September 27, 1897; the *New York Herald*, September 4, 1892; the *New York Times*, October 18, 1895.

CHAPTER TWO

~

"One Man, One Vote; One Woman, One Throat": Women in New York City Politics, 1890–1910*

In the approaching municipal campaign in New York, women politicians are to play an important part. About 1,000 of them, representing the Women's Republican organizations of New York, are already sharpening their scalping knives and preparing to work havoc in the ranks of the Tammanyites.

—*New York Herald*, September 19, 1897, V:1:1

While it is commonly assumed that women went into politics after getting the right to vote, in New York City at least it was the other way around. Indeed, one could argue that it was regular experience with political women that eventually convinced men that women were capable of and entitled to exercise the franchise, a prerogative of nineteenth-century men. This didn't happen quickly; the women who worked in political campaigns did not demand suffrage as their reward. They deliberately avoided the issue of suffrage in order not to antagonize men. Instead the suffrage movement and the movement of women into politics proceeded on parallel tracks until at least 1912, with some organized women demanding the right to vote, and others acting to influence the men who could vote. Among the latter, there were also two tracks. On one were the "good government" reformers who rode the

*Published in *American Nineteenth Century History* 1, no. 3 (Autumn 2001): 101–23. In this chapter I use the words "Mrs." and "colored" because those were the proper terms for their time. I used a married woman's given name when I could find it, but that was not always possible.

train of nonpartisanship. On the other were party women, who were no less passionate in their partisanship than were party men.

By the time New York women won the right to vote in 1917, among them was a large cadre of trained political workers, some with a quarter century of experience. Although New York City was dominated by the Democratic Party, most of the women active in politics were Republicans, because the Republican Party began organizing women in the 1890s while the Democratic Party dallied.

Municipal Reform

Nineteenth-century New York City was run by Tammany Hall. Founded in 1789 as a fraternal and social organization, Tammany became synonymous with the Democratic Party Central Committee for New York County (Manhattan) because the leaders of both groups were the same. It maintained its power among voters through the liberal use of patronage and welfare, while taking bribes, providing "protection," and dipping into the public treasury. In the 1880s a growing class of business and professional men challenged Tammany's control. Theodore Roosevelt organized the City Reform Club of New York in 1882, though it barely scratched Tammany's hide for reasons he himself analyzed when he ran for mayor in 1886 (Roosevelt 1886). In 1890 some of the more prominent citizens of New York City organized a People's Municipal League to challenge Tammany Hall and convinced some independent men in both parties to run a slate of opposition candidates. They wanted to take politics out of municipal government and run it on a businesslike basis, without corruption or patronage. They were aided in this by a Ladies Committee, which raised funds and sent out letters soliciting men's votes for the league candidates (*New York Times*, Oct. 22, 1890, 5:2; Oct. 27, 1890, 4:2; *New York Herald*, Oct. 27, 1890, 3:4). They lost.

The Democratic Party celebrated its success in the 1892 elections by shifting control of important jobs and contracts to party bosses throughout the state. This power grab, combined with a major recession in 1893, prompted public outrage at dishonesty and revived the urban reform movement. Reformers demanded once again that municipal government be sundered from partisanship. Nonpartisanship was not only tactical—Democratic votes were needed to win—but ideological. Only a nonpartisan municipal administration, reformers argued, would offer "cleanliness, peace, and order rather than special favors and franchises" (McCormick 1981, 49).

Tammany Hall was only one of several urban Democratic machines in New York State. Hugh McLaughlin ran Brooklyn, the big city across the East

River. In the 1893 Brooklyn election, reformers joined with dissident Democrats and Republicans to elect Charles A. Schieren, the Republican candidate for mayor (McCormick 1981, 43–44). This effort was aided by the Brooklyn Woman's Health Protective Association (BWHPA). Organized in 1890 to keep the streets clean and the health laws enforced (*Brooklyn Eagle Almanac* 1891, 138), the women found the Democratic administration to be more of a hindrance than a help. As the fall campaign took off, the BWHPA "added its voice to the general cry of denunciation against the corrupt municipal administration of the ring" (*New York Times*, Oct. 7, 1893, 8:3). It called a mass meeting of Brooklyn women for October 19, where the BWHPA's founder and president, Mrs. James Scrimgeour, said that "it was time women's influence was felt in municipal affairs." She went on to note that the Republicans had nominated good men and "it was the duty of the women to urge the Republicans along" (*New York Times*, Oct. 20, 1893, 9:3). After endorsing Schieren, the BWHPA distributed eight thousand copies of an "Appeal to Voters" and asked women to "arouse indifferent citizens to a sense of their duty as voters" (*Brooklyn Eagle*, June 8, 1894, 12:5).

Schieren's election was the first sign of a major electoral shift favoring the Republican Party, nationally and statewide. This and other Republican victories in the state split the Democratic Party into quarreling factions. Across the river, reformers formed a Committee of Seventy, "drawn from the city's commercial, financial, and legal elite," to wrest city government from Tammany Hall (McCormick 1981, 47). One of these was the Rev. Charles H. Parkhurst of the Madison Square Presbyterian Church, who preached regularly against police protection of crime and Tammany protection of police. Impressed with women's work in the Brooklyn election, and the amount of talk generated by the agitation for woman suffrage at the New York State constitutional convention the previous summer, he repeatedly and publicly asked the "wives, mothers, sisters, and daughters of our city . . . to take a hand in the regeneration. There is no politics in the matter," he went on to say. "It is a question of right against wrong, of righteousness against trickery, and our women ought to feel proud to be able to help the movement onward." Parkhurst was an outspoken antisuffragist, but saw no inconsistency between this position and his call to women to help cleanse the city and curb corruption. The role of women, he felt, was to shape public sentiment (*New York Times*, Oct. 5, 1894, 8:1; Marshall 1997, 84; Edwards 1997, 117).

Parkhurst first asked Mayor Schieren, who also opposed woman suffrage, how helpful the women had been, and then published both letters in the *New York Times* (Sept. 25, 1894, 9:7; Sept. 26, 1894, 2:7). Schieren confirmed that the BWHPA took the lead among the several women's organizations that "were very active during the campaign, and enlisted their husbands to active duty and in various ways aided the reform movement by holding public meetings, and asking women of the city to influence their husbands to work for reform." Furthermore, "the women were also very careful not to bring up the suffrage question in the reform movement of last year, which would have met with antagonism and hurt the movement." Indeed, at the BWHPA's first mass meeting, several women speakers had reassured their audience that they were opposed to woman suffrage, but said it was patriotic for women to use their influence to remove from government "people who care more for spoils than for the honor of serving the city" (*Brooklyn Eagle*, Oct. 20, 1893, 2:1).

In October, Parkhurst made several speeches throughout New York City on "The Condition of Our City and Woman's Relation to It." He urged women to hold parlor conferences and mass meetings, to talk to women and talk to men (*New York Times*, Oct. 5, 1894, 8:1; Oct. 13, 1894, 9:4; Oct. 20, 1894, 9:5; Oct. 25, 1894, 9:3). He also looked for a woman to organize and lead women in the aid of his crusade, eventually settling on Josephine Shaw Lowell, a wealthy and respected charity worker (Lowell 1898, 465). Lowell, herself a suffrage supporter, called a meeting of women on October 12 to work for the reform candidate, William L. Strong. Invited were "women interested in philanthropy and reform and society women of different religious sects and various political opinions," including those for and against suffrage. In deference to her sponsor, Lowell represented the Woman's Municipal Purity Auxiliary as nonpartisan, non-political, and definitely not interested in suffrage (*New York Times*, Oct. 7, 1894, 4:6; Oct. 11, 1894, 9:7; Oct. 13, 1894, 9:4).

The new organization soon changed its name to the Woman's Municipal League (WML) and organized seventeen public meetings (*New York Times*, Nov. 4, 1894, 18:1). At one of these Mrs. Alfred Bishop Mason spoke on "The Woman's Part in American Politics." She said:

> An old English saying is: "One man, one vote; one woman, one throat." That means that one man can cast only one vote, while one woman can make many right votes by talking when it will do the most good.
>
> What we must do is to inaugurate a system of meetings which will not be all talk, but which will instruct the ignorant people of the slums what right and purity of politics are. (*New York Times*, Oct. 31, 1894, 5:1)

Although it was in existence for only a short time before the November election, the WML was much lauded for rousing voters otherwise indifferent to municipal reform. Not only was William Strong elected mayor in

1894, but the Republican Party captured a majority of the seats on the board of aldermen. A few days after the election, Mrs. Charles Parkhurst announced that the WML would continue. "It is to be a thoroughly feminine work," she told the *New York Times*, "and will not be conducted in any way along the lines of a man's club. The fundamental idea is educational—to educate women in regard to all lines of municipal affairs. We have found that their knowledge of such things is very limited" (*New York Times*, Nov. 4, 1894, 18:1; Nov. 9, 1894, 9:3,4).

Republican Women

Several of the anti-Tammany meetings were held under the auspices of the Woman's National Republican Association (WNRA) founded by J. Ellen Foster (*New York Times*, Oct. 25, 1894, 9:3; Oct. 27, 1894, 5:3). Foster was an Iowa lawyer who was active in both the Republican Party and the temperance movement. In July of 1888, after the Republican Convention, she met with the Republican National Committee and agreed to organize women for the party (*New York Tribune*, July 12, 1888, 2:6). She and her husband moved to Washington, DC, where he was given a patronage job by the Benjamin Harrison administration, and she embarked on a twenty-year career as a traveling organizer, lecturer, and campaigner for the Republican party (*New York Times*, March 8, 1891, 3:3). Foster remained president of the WNRA until her death in 1910, when it was taken over by her protégé, Helen Varick Boswell. The WNRA did not have members. It operated as the women's committee of the RNC during campaigns, and as an advisory body in between.

For the election of 1892, the RNC set aside several rooms for women's work on the top floor of the Hotel Savoy with Foster in charge (*New York Herald*, Sept. 4, 1892, 11:2,3). While she gave speeches, urging men to vote for Republican candidates and women to get men to vote, Boswell supervised the women workers (*Brooklyn Eagle*, Oct. 4, 1892, 8:5). Boswell had been raised in Baltimore in a Democratic household where discussion of "woman's rights" was taboo; her association with Foster made her a true believer in Republicanism (Boswell, *National Republican [NR]*, Nov. 23, 1918, 7). By the 1894 Congressional campaigns, Boswell had complete charge of women's work. She hired women speakers for "the political mass meetings at which women are becoming so interested," and focused her efforts on "the wage earning women, the girls in the factories, shops and large stores, holding meetings among them during the noon hour, to enlist their interest as rapidly as possible" (*New York Herald*, Oct. 11, 1894, 12:2).

Boswell attended several of the WML's meetings, and after Strong won the election, she asked the Republican Party leader if she could form a club for Republican women. On December 13 the "first auxiliary of the Woman's Republican Association was organized . . . in the West Side Republican Club rooms," choosing as its president Mrs. Clarence Burns, a well-known charity worker (*New York Tribune*, Dec. 14, 1894, 5:5,6; Boswell, *NR*, Nov. 23, 1918, 8). Soon called the West End Woman's Republican Association (WEA), within six years it would be "the most widely known political club in the State" (*New York Tribune*, Sept. 8, 1900, 7:1).

Although the best known, the WEA was not the first permanent women's Republican club in New York City. In 1892 Foster had helped Mary Hall and "thirty-one colored women of the Eleventh Assembly District" found a Colored Woman's Republican Association (*New York Herald*, Sept. 27, 1892, 6:5). Hall had come from Georgia, where she had escorted colored men to the polls to vote Republican. In the early 1880s she became the political apprentice to the colored boss of her district until she found he was jealous of her ability to turn out votes. With Boswell's encouragement, she put together her own organization of women, and proceeded to become a "power" in her district (*New York Times*, Oct. 18, 1895, 8:1; Boswell, *NR*, March 8, 1919, 8:6).

Throughout 1895 Boswell organized clubs in New York City, including a Business Women's Republican Club, one for working women, and a variety of "neighborhood influence clubs" of twelve to twenty women. In 1895 there were several women's Republican clubs in New York City. These were permanent clubs, not just temporary campaign organizations. At regular meetings club members gave papers on current events and discussed such issues as health, schools, and Sunday closing of saloons. Often they were addressed by distinguished guests. Sometimes socials or outings were held. During campaigns, club members provided a core of experienced workers ready to work for Republican candidates, and their meetings discussed election mechanics. Club women were instructed how to get men to vote and held classes for men on how to mark a ballot. One meeting discussed whether it was OK for women to give soup and coffee to Democrats as well as to Republicans waiting in the cold to vote (*New York Herald*, May 28, 1895, 11:1; July 2, 1895, 7:2; Nov. 6, 1895, 5:6; *New York Times*, May 23, 1895, 8:3; May 28, 1895, 9:4; Oct. 5, 1895, 2:7; July 12, 1896, 8:1; Aug. 22, 1896, 2:3).

In June of 1895 Boswell was selected to be the only woman among 149 New York delegates to go to the national convention of the League of Republican Clubs, where she was thrilled to meet party women from western states where women could vote. She also went to the state convention in September, and reported back that the men now wanted to meet with women rather than separately. There were seventeen Republican women's clubs in upstate New York (*New York Herald*, May 28, 1895, 11:1; June 15, 1895, 7:1; Sept. 11, 1895, 11:1.). In 1896 she went to the Republican Convention as an observer, where "the women were treated as distinguished guests although they had no part in the proceedings" (*New York Herald*, June 27, 1896, 10:1). By 1897 she was the "recognized head of the Women's Republican movement in New York" and "the only woman in the direct employ of the Republican County Committee" (*New York Herald*, Sept. 19, 1897, V:12:1).

Women's eagerness to join Republican women's clubs came from many sources. By the 1890s there were large numbers of middle-class women, especially in the cities, with time on their hands. Many were educated, and, if married, were not expected to engage in gainful employment. But neither were they "willing to become simply social butterflies" (Lockwood 1893, 385). Reform was within woman's sphere and forming and joining women's clubs was quite the thing to do. The municipal reform movement invited women in and simultaneously gave them a rationale for political work. Indeed they were told by leading men, many of whom opposed the radicalism of woman suffrage, that working to clean up the city by electing good men was their duty (*New York Times*, Oct. 25, 1894, 9:3; *New York Tribune*, Oct. 31, 1894, 7:1).

Nor was partisanship a problem. Strong party loyalties were the norm in the late nineteenth century. Boswell felt that "women have ever been partisan" because "[a]ll healthy, intelligent persons are partisan by nature" (Boswell, *NR*, Dec. 7, 1918, 8). Kate Bostwick, who described herself as a "rabid Republican," explained in 1896 that the prospect of taming the Tammany tiger prompted many women to become active Republicans: "The fever of reform was coursing through the veins of these women, and they formed the first regular Republican club . . . of college women and others of ability and executive knowledge" (Bostwick 1896). This was echoed by Mrs. Jane Pierce, a schoolteacher from New England. "I had never taken more than a general interest in politics," she told the *New York Herald*, "until the pressure came for fighting Tammany" (Oct. 10, 1895, VI:9:1). Four years later Mrs. Clarence Burns, first president of the West End WRA, wrote, "The best thing Tammany ever did was to drive women into politics. I was born a republican, but if it had not been for Tammany I probably never would have taken a prominent part in politics, nor would any other of the conservative women of this city" (*New York Herald*, Oct. 7, 1900, 7:2).

Once involved in political work women stayed because they found it to be pleasing, demanding both social and organizational skills. In 1896 Bostwick started her own club in Brooklyn, the Woman's Republican Union League. Among its founders were Mrs. James Scrimgeour, who was still the president of the BWHPA (*Brooklyn Eagle*, Sept. 17, 1896, 7:6). Quite a few were the wives of Republican politicians (*Brooklyn Eagle*, Sept. 23, 1896, 7:7; *New York Herald*, Sept. 19, 1897, V:12; *New York Tribune*, June 21, 1899, 7:3.). It is not surprising that political wives and daughters would want to campaign in organizations analogous to those of their husbands and fathers, even when the latter were not public or party officials. These women in turn would bring in their friends. Indeed the party clubs had more staying power than women's nonpartisan organizations because recurring campaigns created a permanent need for women political workers. After winning in 1894, the reform committees and the WML lapsed, while women's Republican clubs expanded for the 1896 presidential campaign (Lowell 1898; Monoson 1990, 106).

The Election of 1897

Republican women's loyalties were sorely tested in 1897, when voters would elect the first mayor of Greater New York City to govern the five boroughs. Consolidation was the pet project of state Republican leader Thomas C. Platt. After the Republican electoral sweep in 1896 gave his party full control of the state government, the legislature mandated it. The new state constitution required that municipal elections be held in odd-numbered years (McCormick 1981, 54–55, 90–94). Mayor Strong declined to run, and reformers, regular Republicans, and dissident Democrats could not agree on a candidate. The reformers organized into the Citizens' Union (CU) and drafted Seth Low, former mayor of Brooklyn and current president of Columbia University, to be their candidate. Low was a Republican, but independent of Boss Platt's machine. Although Platt had helped reformers to elect Strong, he received few benefits from doing so, and concluded that he could probably get more patronage from Tammany than from Low. The Republican convention nominated his good friend Benjamin F. Tracy, a "stalwart among stalwarts" (McCormick 1981, 123–24; Kurland 1971, ch. 5).

Republican women were painfully conflicted. An axiom of reform was that municipal politics should be separated from state and national politics. Parties and partisanship were fine in their place, but cities should be run like a large business, guided by the principles of efficiency and competency, not party loyalty (Kurland 1971, 85). As part of New York City's social and economic elite, Republican women were cut from the same cloth as reformers. Reform men, like Low, were much more likely to vote Republican than Democratic. In 1894, it did not matter if one was partisan or nonpartisan; there was a common candidate for whom to work. In 1897, the clash between party loyalty and reform sentiments was profoundly disturbing to many. The WEA discussed and debated what to do at several meetings.

Boswell exhorted them to party loyalty, bringing in speakers to talk on "The Interdependence of National and Municipal Politics." Some members claimed that Low was not really a Republican, and therefore not deserving of the support of Republican women. They attacked Low for not always voting Republican, for not favoring tariff protection, and even for his disapproval of suffrage and higher education for women. Several prominent women, such as Mrs. James G. Wentz, said they did not see what tariff protection had to do with Greater New York City. Unless everyone united behind Low, she said, Tammany would win and the city would lose. Finally J. Ellen Foster was brought in to convince the women that city, state, and national politics "cannot be divorced"; adherence to principle required party loyalty at every level. She urged the WEA to support Tracy because he was the *Republican* candidate. It did (*New York Tribune*, Oct. 2, 1897, 5:5; Oct. 16, 1897, 9:7; Oct. 30, 1897, 5:1).

Party loyalty did not triumph everywhere. In Low's hometown of Brooklyn the Woman's Republican Union League endorsed Low over the objections of its founder and president, Kate Bostwick, as did some of the Brooklyn Republican men's clubs (*Brooklyn Eagle*, Oct. 27, 1897, 7:3; *New York Times*, June 21, 1899, 3:6). The women split so badly that club officers were in court two years later fighting over the remains (*New York Tribune*, Sept. 28, 1898, 5:3; June 21, 1899, 7:3). But the Low campaign united antagonists as well as dividing allies. At one large Low meeting the presidents of the suffrage association and the antisuffrage society sat side by side on the stage. When asked what they were doing there, the antis replied, "Oh, but this is for Mr. Low" (*New York Tribune*, Nov. 15, 1897, 5:5).

Political enthusiasm among women was even higher in 1897 than in 1894. Reform women raised money, distributed circulars, and held meetings. One piece titled "The Women of Manhattan to the Voters of Manhattan" stated that "the women of every city have a stake as great in its just and enlightened government as the men" followed by five reasons why the women supported Low (*New York Times*, Oct. 26, 1897, 2:2). Even in meetings not specifically aimed at women they were 35 percent of those attending (*New York Times*, Oct. 27, 1897, 2:3). In Brooklyn, the BWHPA brought three thousand women to a large hall to hear him speak. Reported the *New York Times*:

> The scene that was presented in the hall where they met was unique—and yet it was very like the politics of men, with the shouts and the applause, and all

the other things that carry the latter from their equilibrium in time of political excitement, for these members of the feebler sex, young and old, cheered at the mention of Low's name, stamped their feet, waved their handkerchiefs in the air. (*New York Times*, Oct. 23, 1897, 2:5)

Seth Low told the Brooklyn women, to great applause:

In my last campaign (in 1883) one woman said that she had gained twenty-two votes for me, and I told her that was twenty-one more than she would have gotten if she had been a man. Mrs. Scrimgeour (BWHPA President) has said that each woman represents twenty votes, but I think, from looking at this audience, that each of you represents forty votes, at least. (*New York Times*, Oct. 23, 1897, 2:5)

Women's "forty votes" weren't sufficient to overcome the crowded field of candidates. Lack of unity was fatal to Low's campaign. He came in second and Tracy ran third. Tammany Hall retook city hall.

Activity in the Interim

The Citizens' Union attributed its loss to their lack of continuity. After considerable debate over whether to disband or remain as a nonpartisan political party, it chose the latter, though not without much dismay and dissension. Some reformers felt that a permanent political organization would inevitably become more concerned with its own welfare than that of the city and slowly become corrupt. They argued that the *principle* of nonpartisanship would be preempted with permanent organization. This position lost to those who felt that until reformers "met the social needs of the masses" the masses would not support reform (Kurland 1971, 108–11). The WML had reconstituted itself for the 1897 campaign. In March of 1898 it adopted a formal constitution which declared its objective to be "to secure active support for such movements and candidates as may give promise of the best government for the city without regard to party lines" (Lowell 1898). For the next four years it worked to expand its membership among younger women, though its meetings were rarely reported in the press (Monoson 1990, 109). It organized independently of the Citizens' Union but never strayed far from its parent, publicly affirming its support for whomever the Citizens' Union endorsed.

Both the Woman's Municipal League and the women's Republican clubs avoided the issue of suffrage, which was widely debated in the 1890s. The WML was constrained by its close association with suffrage opponents, who were prominent among the male leaders in the anti-Tammany movement (e.g., Parkhurst, Elihu Root, Everett P. Wheeler; see Marshall 1997, 66, 76), and served on the WML board (e.g., Mrs. Parkhurst). Even when suffrage agitation lapsed, the WML carefully kept its distance. In 1904 its *Bulletin* said that "Most of us are content to work, nay, prefer to work, without the suffrage" (*Women's Municipal League Bulletin [WMLB]*, July 1904, 2). In 1911, as public discussion of suffrage was reviving, its *Yearbook* reassured its 1,800 members that "it has no part whatever, either for or against, in the suffrage movement" (*WML Yearbook*, Nov. 1911, 3).

Republican women were constrained by their priorities. To emphasize that party loyalty eclipsed issues, Article VI of *The Constitution and Bylaws of the West End Auxiliary* declared: "Let it always be clearly understood that this organization is for the study of simple republicanism, that it is contrary to its design to attempt any diversion of the organization's work or influence to such reform movements as temperance, woman suffrage &c, with which many republican women are individually associated." Even though the Republican Party occasionally let woman suffragists use their meeting hall for suffrage meetings (*New York Tribune*, April 28, 1894, 7:4), Boswell told a meeting of Republican men that "I am not crying out for a vote just now. I can generally influence three or four votes, at least, and I think it is better to have these votes cast as I wish them than to cast a solitary vote myself" (*New York Times*, Oct. 18, 1895, 6:2). In 1903, newer members of the WEA wanted to take a position on suffrage. After a heated debate, a majority voted to bar it (*New York Tribune*, Dec. 18, 1903, 7:3). Mrs. Wentz, who later became active in the Woman Suffrage Party, estimated that 5 percent of the members of the early Republican women's clubs actively opposed woman suffrage (*New York Mail*, June 10, 1918).

Nor were the suffrage women interested in party work. Susan B. Anthony and Elizabeth Cady Stanton, both of whom lived in New York, had become increasingly alienated from the major political parties since 1884 when they had urged "earnest and conscientious support of the Republican National ticket" (*New York Tribune*, Aug. 1, 1884, 2). In 1897 Anthony criticized New York women for working in the municipal elections without first getting a party commitment to woman suffrage. By 1900 she was counseling women to stay out of political parties and work only to enfranchise themselves (Harper 1898, 928; Anthony 1900). In 1894 Stanton wrote approvingly to Lowell of women's work for municipal reform, even though none of the men running for mayor supported woman suffrage (*New York Times*, Oct. 11, 1894, 9:7). In 1900 she wrote that "it is not of the slightest consequence to me whether McKinley or Bryan is elected . . . [because it] will not make the least difference in the present position of women"

(Stanton 1900). This attitude by the leaders was reflected in the resistance of active suffragists to joining in party work. Boswell tried to recruit those from Republican families into her women's Republican Clubs in the 1890s, and was quite surprised when they told her, "No, the Republican party has never done anything for us, so we shall not do anything for the Republican party" (Boswell, *NR*, March 1, 1919, 7).

Undistracted by "other" issues, Republican women perfected their campaign techniques, adding door-to-door canvassing to literature distribution and meetings. In the 1896 presidential campaign Republican women opened their own headquarters at 1473 Broadway in August. They prepared campaign literature in German, Bohemian, and English, and divided up the tenement districts, which were Tammany strongholds. Within a week, 1,500 women had literature and instructions on how to canvass (*New York Tribune*, Aug. 22, 1896, 2:2; Aug. 29, 1896, 4:5). Mrs. Clarence Burns, director of the canvassing, wrote of their experience: "During the first McKinley and Bryan campaign we distributed two hundred thousand booklets, and interviewed as many women, endeavoring to instruct them in the awful effects of the 16 to 1 policy should Bryan be elected" (*New York Herald*, Oct. 7, 1900, 7:2). Boswell later recounted their mixed reception: "Our women were often met with derision and with threats of boiling water poured over them, and a few potatoes were thrown by the irate Irish ladies, but no one was ever hurt" (Boswell, *NR*, Dec. 7, 1918, 8).

In 1898 the WNRA headquarters was in Washington, DC. New York City Republican women worked to elect Colonel Roosevelt as their governor (*New York Times*, Sept. 30, 1898, 3:6; *New York Tribune*, Oct. 5, 1898, 5:1). Roosevelt had been the New York City police commissioner under the Strong administration. His attacks on police graft propelled him into the governorship, while his vigorous enforcement of the Sunday closing law (of saloons) alienated the German vote, contributing to the reform movement's loss of the mayoralty in 1897 (Kurland 1971, 86, 105, 114).

The election of 1900 was widely called a "petticoat" campaign because unprecedented numbers of women came to meetings, gave speeches, and otherwise worked for candidates, even in states where they could not vote. McKinley headquarters was in Chicago, but the "Women's Republican Headquarters" opened its doors at 139 Fifth Avenue in New York, even though there was no official women's bureau as there had been in the 1896 campaign. From here women were deployed to intensively canvass the tenement districts of Manhattan, particularly Tammany Hall strongholds where Republican men were not welcome. Boswell explained to one reporter that "[t]his tenement house work necessitates tact and energy on the part of the participants." The men readily conceded that women were better at it. Boswell described their approach:

> No house or room is invaded without the invitation of the inmates, but the universal experience of the visiting women has been that the dwellers in tenements are glad to see them and hear what they have to say in reference to the opportunities which the Republican party affords the laboring man in the way of work, high wages and sound money. (*New York Tribune*, Oct. 21, 1900, II:6)

Several newspapers wrote lengthy stories on women in the election of 1900. In its regular column on women's work the *Evening Post* wrote that:

> Early in this campaign the State committee apportioned the lower part of the city among the members of the West End Women's Republican Club, . . . Their districts once assigned, with plenty of "literature" on hand, they pursue their own methods. . . .
>
> Visits are made to the Russian and Polish Jewish quarters, to Little Italy, Little Syria, and other foreign settlements. The number of men old enough to vote and the number of the unnaturalized are learned. The women of the Republican Club get this information from their foreign sisters rather than from the men themselves who are less approachable. But sometimes a wife does not know her husband's politics, and protests that he would beat her should she ask. The visitor inquires whether he would beat herself if she put the question, and usually receiving a negative answer, returns at meal-time. If she can gain his confidence, he will listen to her respectfully, and even seek enlightenment upon questions of the day, which it would lower his dignity in his own eyes to ask from another man. Literature is left, and knotty points explained in subsequent interviews. A daily report is sent to State headquarters, whence agents are dispatched to the addresses of unnaturalized men to urge them to take out their papers, and to facilitate the metamorphosis of the alien into the citizen by explaining the legal formalities that seem too formidable to the ignorant. His naturalization accomplished, it is easy enough to persuade the regenerated foreigner to register and vote—and "to vote right" from his sponsor's view point.
>
> Meanwhile the feminine campaigner is making herself agreeable to the woman of the tenement . . . [and] explains the doctrines of her party. Mrs. Cornelia S. Robinson, president of the West End Club, says that the women of the poorer classes are much quicker than the men to grasp the importance of the monetary question, accustomed as they are to handling all the money earned by the family. In the case of a sick baby a doctor may be sent, if the mother agrees, or at any rate an ordinary prescription is ordered from some neighboring pharmacy. If want is apparent, it is met with temporary relief, and then called to the attention of the authorities. A women with half-a-dozen small

children in need of food or clothing, will use all her influence for the first person who alleviates her sufferings, and can usually be counted upon to control her husband's vote.

The three hundred members in the Women's Republican Club . . . [also] labor among clerks and factory hands of their own sex; handicapped, however by the attitude of employers, who fear that the girls might use their organization, even if ostensibly political, to make a united demand for better pay. . . .

In general, the women do all the tedious preliminary work in the wide area referred to, and the men follow up their efforts after the way has been opened. (*Evening Post* [New York], Oct. 18, 1900, 8:1)

By the 1900 campaign, New York Republican women had become a force to be reckoned with. The *Tribune* reported that "the Republican women of New York City have been most effective helpers to the Republican party, whose leaders have been glad to utilize the women's services" (*New York Tribune*, Sept. 8, 1900, 7:1).

The Campaigns of 1901 and 1903

During the four years that Robert A. Van Wyck was mayor of Greater New York City, he ran "a brilliantly ineffectual, superbly corrupt, and downright malevolent administration," as the puppet of Tammany boss Richard Croker (Kurland 1971, 114). Tammany coffers were filled from payoffs to police for protecting brothels and gambling dens, augmented by shakedowns of municipal employees. Judgeships were sold and city franchises auctioned to the highest bidder. Public schools were starved; thousands of students were denied entrance due to lack of seats. By 1901 reformers and Republicans once again saw the virtues of fusion. They jointly agreed to run Seth Low for mayor, and, in hopes of pulling votes away from Tammany, ran independent Democrats for the other citywide offices (McCormick 1981, 134; Kurland 1971, 136).

The Woman's Municipal League held meetings as it had before. Ten days before the election it released what became the central piece of campaign literature. A sixteen-page pamphlet, *Facts for Fathers and Mothers*, described how the police protected vice, especially the luring of young girls into prostitution. The WML raised twenty thousand dollars (including one hundred dollars from the antisuffrage society) to print hundreds of thousands of copies, but relied on many others for distribution (Villard 1902, 79). The relationship between the WML and the women's Republican clubs was captured by a headline: "Municipal League Working Hard to Secure Campaign

Fund—Two Hundred Thousand Leaflets Distributed by Republican Women" (*New York Tribune*, Oct. 25, 1901, 7:1).

Republican women were much better organized than the WML. In April of 1901, they organized a state association. It took official responsibility for women's work for the party in the municipal campaign, under Boswell's general direction. After conferring with the Republican leader of New York County (Manhattan), the women opened two headquarters "in the heart of the districts that have been considered hopelessly Democratic" and commenced canvassing. Mrs. Burns, "who understands the districts in New York better than any other woman in the organization," laid out the routes. When the Kings County (Brooklyn) Republican leader asked for help, the presidents of the two Brooklyn clubs, Kate Bostwick and Mrs. C. W. (Emma) Fisk, were assigned to take charge of the Brooklyn work; they opened their own headquarters in Brooklyn (*New York Tribune*, April 24, 1901, 5:1; Oct. 9, 1901, 7:2; Oct. 17, 1901, 5:3; *Brooklyn Eagle*, Oct. 18, 1901, 1:4).

Tammany boss Croker craftily tried to beat the reformers at their own game by running Edward M. Shepard, an independent Democrat from Brooklyn, who had denounced Tammany and ardently supported Low in 1897 (Kurland 1971, 137). While Low won, he did so with a bare 52 percent of the vote, running behind the independent Democrats on the ticket. "Low took the mayoralty by over thirty-one thousand votes, and his election was made possible because Democrats by the tens of thousands, especially on the Jewish Lower East Side, abandoned Tammany for fusion" (Kurland 1971, 139). This was precisely the area in which the Women's Republican Clubs had been canvassing in every election since 1896. Only the year before, Boswell had explained that they were canvassing in an "almost solid Tammany district" in hopes that "they will sow a seed which will result in the reduction of the usual Tammany majority" (*New York Tribune*, Oct. 24, 1900, 3:1). Seth Low was the beneficiary of that work.

Seth Low only served for two years because the Republican state legislature had cut the mayor's term of office in half in 1900 in hopes of limiting Tammany's control. When Low ran for reelection in 1903 the fusion coalition dissolved along party lines. After losing in 1901, Croker retired to his baronial estate in England, leaving Tammany Hall in the hands of a triumvirate. By 1903 Charles Frances Murphy, an owner of several saloons, "was in absolute command" and proceeded to woo the independent Democrats away from the reform coalition by convincing them that the national party needed a Democratic mayor in New York City (Kurland 1971, 185). The fusion Democrats elected in 1901 ran for reelection on the same ticket as the Tammany nominee for mayor, Congressman George B. McClellan Jr., the son of the Civil War general. While the Republicans nominated Low, they were unhappy at his failure to reward their 1901 support with patronage and unenthusiastic in campaigning (Kurland 1971, 192).

Republican women did not sit on their hands. The *Herald* reported that women were more active than ever, largely through three organizations: the Woman's Municipal League, the Woman's Republican Club, and the West End Woman's Republican Association. "They represent 1,500 New York women, many of them women of wealth and social prominence." The WML raised one thousand dollars a day for Low's campaign, organized several mass meetings with men and women speakers, and published "campaign literature in Italian and Hebrew newspapers." Its eight hundred members spent their time writing letters to friends asking for money and other support, and mailing circulars. The Republican women's clubs also sent "out campaign literature to the wives of men who we know are Tammany men and who live in the tenement districts," and organized their own meetings (*New York Herald*, Oct. 25, 1903, II:4:1).

However, the work of the women did not make up for the lethargy of the men. The Democrats won with 55 percent of the vote.

Aftermath

After losing the 1903 mayor's race, the municipal reform movement declined. It would be another ten years before reformers could agree on a candidate for mayor, let alone elect him. The nonpartisan organizations that it spawned continued, but concentrated on nonelectoral solutions of urban problems. The BWHPA campaigned against spitting on the sidewalks and monitored the enforcement of street sanitation and pure milk and food laws until it dissolved in 1927. However, Mrs. Scrimgeour, its president until she died in 1903, actively worked for several Republican candidates. The Citizens' Union became a municipal watchdog, exposing the underside of city politics when Tammany became too gross.

Josephine Shaw Lowell died in 1905 (*New York Tribune*, Oct. 14, 1905, 5:1) but the WML continued until it merged with the Citizens' Union in 1923. Between 1902 and 1911 the WML published a monthly *Bulletin* on its activities, branches, and committees, except during the summer. It concentrated on neighborhood problems, such as better parks and cleaner streets, and promoting protective legislation, such as bills to regulate employment offices. Its only venture back into the world of elections was in 1905, when it backed William Travers Jerome's race for reelection as district attorney. That year it raised and spent nine thousand dollars on 350,000 copies of

"Why New York Women Stand Back of Jerome," which it distributed at meetings and published in German and English newspapers (*New York Tribune*, Nov. 7, 1905, 5:1; Arthur, *WMLB*, Jan. 1906, 6–9). In 1906 it obtained a building at 19 W. 26th Street, which it hoped would become a "real women's building" (*New York Tribune*, April 13, 1906, 5:1).

Women's interest in municipal reform revived in 1913, but when the "Women's Fusion League for Good Government" opened its headquarters on Fifth Avenue, it was women in the three political parties (Boswell for the Republicans, Mrs. J. Borden (Daisy) Harriman for non-Tammany Democrats, and Ann Rhodes for the Progressives), not the nonpartisan WML, that were behind it (Boswell, *NR*, April 5, 1919, 8; NY *Sun*, Aug. 19, 1921). However, women were not consulted on the choice of fusion candidates until 1921, the first mayoral election in which women could vote (New York *Sun*, Aug. 24, 1921).

Republican women's clubs continued but their activities were less frequently reported in the press. Mrs. Wentz, who had campaigned for Harrison in 1892 but spoken out for Low in 1897 when the WEA supported Tracy, formed her own Woman's Republican Club in 1900 to appeal specifically to society women (*New York Tribune*, Nov. 9, 1900, 8:2) and remained its president until 1931. The club dissolved in 1940. Although she actively supported woman suffrage in the New York referenda of 1915 and 1917, her other causes were quite conservative (*New York Times*, July 29, 1945, 39:3). Mrs. Burns returned to philanthropic work (New York *Sun*, March 2, 1900). Republican women worked for Republican candidates in state and national races, continuing to build their presence in the party. Helen Varick Boswell graduated from Washington (DC) College of Law in 1902, but made her permanent home in New York and dedicated her life to working for the Republican Party. In 1908 she and Foster were once again in charge of mobilizing Republican women for the presidential campaign. They gave speeches, organized meetings, and oversaw the mailing of one thousand circulars a day (New York *Sun*, Oct. 25, 1908, 6:1). When the party split over Theodore Roosevelt's candidacy for president in 1912, she directed women's work for Taft (*New York Times*, Sept. 1, 1912, 5:9:1; *NR*, March 1, 1919, 7). In December of 1917 she was appointed Republican vice-chairman of New York County with responsibility for organizing women. By March she had appointed women leaders in all assembly districts, and by April half the election districts had female captains (*New York Times*, March 24, 1918, 24:1; April 18, 1918, 12:8). The fates of other individual Republican women are harder to trace, but some are mentioned in newspaper stories on Republican activities decades later. When New York women gained suffrage in 1917, there was already an organizational framework for women who wanted to work for the Republican Party and quite a few women with years of political experience to induct them into the party. It took little adjustment to incorporate women into the formal party machinery.

The Democrats

The New York Democratic Party contributed little to the movement of women into politics, waiting until 1918 before taking women seriously as party workers. In 1897, as Republican and reform women were holding meetings and distributing literature, the *New York Evening Journal*, a Democratic newspaper owned by William Randolph Hearst, asked editorially "Where are the Democratic Women?" It called for "some Democratic Woman's Clubs" (Sept. 19, 1897, 50:2), and only a week later claimed one had been organized by Dorothy Harrington Mason, with headquarters at the Hotel Bartholdt (Sept. 27, 1897, 4:3). However, when the *New York Times* reported on a Woman's Tammany Club meeting held the following month, it said, "of the four hundred persons present, only about fifteen were women" (Oct. 28, 1897, 2:2).

While there are dozens of newspaper stories about the work of Republican women between 1892 and 1910, there are few on Tammany women. Most are interviews with Mrs. Julius Harburger, "wife of the Assemblyman and Tammany leader of the Xth District," who said she was president of the Women's Democratic Club of the East Side. In 1901, as women were organizing for Low, Mrs. Harburger only said that "active campaign work" had begun (*New York Tribune*, Oct. 9, 1901, 7:2). But when journalist Oswald Garrison Villard reported on the 1901 campaign to the 1902 national suffrage convention he observed that "no body of women worthy of notice has yet been got together to campaign for Tammany Hall" (Villard 1902, 78). In a 1903 interview Harburger claimed that "we had the largest mass meeting of women exclusively ever held" (*New York Herald Magazine*, Oct. 25, 1903, 8), but there is no newspaper report of such a meeting of Democratic women. A 1904 story was aptly headlined "Women Helping in the Campaign" as the five Democratic women interviewed were helping their fathers, sons, and husbands (*New York World*, Aug. 28, 1904, 7:1). One of these was Barbara Porges, who had a reputation as a "boss" on the lower East Side. But while she helped people in her district, all she asked in return was that they support her husband's reelection as alderman. She did not organize women into a political force, and when suffrage became an issue, urged men to vote against it because the women weren't ready for the vote (New York *Sun*, Oct. 21, 1931).

There were a few attempts by women to organize Democrats but not by the party itself. In 1880 several suffragists who were also Democrats tried to organize New York voters to support the Democratic presidential ticket (*Daily Picayune*, New Orleans, Nov. 2, 1880, 6:1). While local campaign clubs for women appeared during national elections, not until 1912 did the Democratic National Committee authorize an organization of women to support a presidential campaign. In 1892 Mary Frost Ormsby started a Democratic Influence Club for women in New York City, which was publicly disapproved of by presidential candidate Grover Cleveland (*New York Tribune*, July 10, 1892, 8:2), and disappeared in 1893 (*New York Herald*, Feb. 15, 1893, 10:6). In 1905 the *New York Tribune* announced that Mrs. J. S. Crosby would organize a Democratic Club because there were no women working for the Democratic Party. Eventually incorporating as the Woman's Democratic Club of New York, it held its first meeting in September (*New York Tribune*, Sept. 15, 1905, 5:1; *New York Times*, Feb. 9, 1912, 6:4).

Mrs. Crosby's political loyalties were independent of the Democratic machine. She and her husband had followed Henry George, a radical but non-Marxist social theorist who twice ran for mayor of New York City and once for secretary of New York State. George campaigned for the Citizens' Union candidate in 1894, but ran himself in 1897. His candidacies attracted labor votes and thus were threats to Tammany hegemony. George died right before the 1897 election but his legacy lived on. In 1901 Mrs. Crosby became president of the Henry George League of Women (*New York Times*, Jan. 14, 1901, 7:2). During the 1903 mayoral campaign, the City Federation of Women's Clubs almost endorsed Seth Low, and Mrs. Crosby decided it was time to organize Democratic women. When she finally did so two years later, she acknowledged that she had no plan of action, would not do house-to-house canvassing, and didn't expect to "purify Tammany Hall." The members of her club were from the same social elites as Republican women (*New York Tribune*, Aug. 15, 1905, 5:1).

Despite its lack of purpose or program, the club survived, and stayed loyal to the Democratic Party. It held its collective nose and endorsed Tammany candidates for public office (*New York Tribune*, Oct. 7, 1905, 5:4). It ridiculed "reformers and googoos" at its first dinner a few months later (*New York Times*, April 6, 1906, 6:3). It endorsed William Randolph Hearst in 1906 after he was nominated for governor by the state Democratic convention, but without enthusiasm. "It doesn't make any difference anyway, said Mrs.

Wood. 'The Party does not know that we are in existence, and doesn't care what we think one way or the other.'" (*New York Tribune*, Sept. 29, 1906, 10:2). In the 1908 presidential campaign Mrs. Crosby raised several hundred dollars to support her club's work for Bryan, who was a family friend as well as the Democratic Party standard bearer. But still her Democratic women did not canvass, speak, or mail. They gave literature to their friends and prodded their men to vote (New York *Sun*, Oct. 25, 1908, 6:2).

Mrs. Crosby was the permanent president of her club for many years but Tammany Hall remained in control of the New York City Democracy, and except for 1913–1917, the New York City government. After women got suffrage in 1917 Tammany women took over her Woman's Democratic Club, electing as its president the sister of Tammany boss John Curry (*New York Times*, April 13, 1918, 22:1). In 1920 Mrs. Crosby took the radical step of supporting the Republican ticket and was expelled (*New York Herald*, Oct. 22, 1920, Oct. 23, 1920). Nonetheless, when she died in 1924 she was eulogized as the "mother of New York Democrats" (*New York Times*, Jan. 31, 1924, 15:6). Over twenty years after the Republican Party welcomed women into the ranks of party workers, the New York City Democratic Party began to make a place for women, at least *loyal* party women. By the time Tammany brought women into the Democratic tent, it had long forgotten the woman who served as district leader and a member of the general committee in the 1890s. Until she died in 1901, everyone thought Murray Hall was a man (*New York Times*, Jan. 19, 1901, 3:4).

Conclusion

The movement of women into active participation in politics in New York City was largely independent of the movement for woman suffrage. The two movements rose to prominence about the same time, in the early to mid-1890s, but kept their distance until at least the second decade of the twentieth century. While there was some overlap in personnel, judging from names in the newspaper reports there was not much. Active suffragists did not campaign for specific candidates for public office, and women's political organizations, whatever the interests of individual members, avoided suffrage. These organizations found a place for both suffragists and antisuffragists, partisans and nonpartisans, in their campaign for better municipal government.

The women who occupied these places generally came through two routes: Some were invited in and others "glided" in. The *New York Times* editorialized its pleasure in the "substantial service" rendered by the women in the 1890 election, as "logical, proper, and justified" (Oct. 27, 1890, 4:2). The

Rev. Dr. Parkhurst invited women to join in the 1894 campaign to elect a good man as mayor of New York. As a respected clergyman with conservative views on women, his invitation legitimated political activity by women by labeling it as moral, not political. Other respectable men did the same. In 1901, women of the Civitas Club of Brooklyn heard a lecture on the "Civic Duty of Women" to get their male friends and relatives to vote for "decent, clean men" (*Brooklyn Eagle,* Nov. 29, 1901, 12:1).

While Republican men did not initiate women's participation in the local party, they did welcome them. In an 1897 article on "Leaders of the Women in Politics," the *Herald* reported:

> [Republican County Committee] Chairman Hatch is a thorough believer in the efficiency of women's work in politics, and speaks in flattering terms of the results achieved by them three years ago and also in the last Presidential campaign. [State Party Chairman] Thomas C. Platt coincides with his lieutenant. He cordially approves of the work done by the Women's Republican clubs and favors any plan tending to widen their opportunities and add to their influence. (*New York Herald,* Sept. 19, 1897, V:12)

In 1900 the *Herald* published another full-page spread on "The Woman in Politics" with comments by two party leaders. Platt affirmed that "I have always regarded with great favor the activity of the ladies whose names you submit in matters political. I think that their influence has been very wholesome, and it is my conviction that their work in the present campaign will be potential" (*New York Herald,* Oct. 7, 1900, V:2). In contrast, Tammany Hall boss Richard Croker's statement equated political activity with suffrage, and expressed his ambivalence:

> Personally I do not approve of women going to the polls, and I think there are very few men who would like to see their wives attending mass meetings and being jostled about by crowds surrounding the booths. In many cases I can see where women might be of valuable assistance in a political campaign.
>
> Of course, I believe that a woman should have a voice in the election of our representatives, and I think that the time will come when we may have to confer with them.
>
> I respect woman too much to ever wish to see her at the polls.

Although Murphy proved to be a more liberal and enlightened boss than Croker, there's no evidence that he was any warmer toward women's political work until women could vote. He made overtures to independent Democratic men, but ignored the one independent Women's Democratic Club. If

Tammany women organized or worked in campaigns, they were largely unnoticed by the press and contemporary observers. It is more likely that Murphy arranged for Mrs. Harburger to lead a "paper" club and give interviews to the press to maintain the image of the party as open to all, but did little to encourage women's participation.

Not all women waited for an invitation. Boswell said in 1918 that women had "glided" into politics through the study of political issues (*NR*, Dec. 7, 1918, 8). Others also made this observation. In 1893, attorney Belva Lockwood, who had run for president on the Equal Rights ticket in 1884 and 1888, wrote that "Women have come into politics in recent years, not only because there has been a demand for them there, but because they have been forced by a logic of events beyond their control." She saw education, not suffrage, as "paving the way" for women's movement into politics (Lockwood 1893, 386). Mrs. Joseph Mumford of Philadelphia told the BWHPA that women, much more than men, had the leisure to study municipal problems and propose solutions. "Education and enlightenment" had shown them their responsibility to "come into politics" (*Brooklyn Eagle*, April 18, 1894, 9:2). Journalist Ida Husted Harper wrote in 1912 that women had moved from church work to club work to civic improvement and into political work (*Los Angeles Examiner*, Sept. 15, 1912).

Villard, in 1902, also observed the gradual acceptance of women's participation in politics even without the ballot.

> Twenty-five years ago such a thing as a woman's headquarters, distributing pamphlets, raising money, getting up meetings, supplying speakers, and furnishing one of the most effective arguments of the entire campaign, would have aroused a storm of indignation and scorn . . . ; and indeed in 1894 there were not a few protests. . . . In 1897 the women workers for the Citizens' Union were heartily welcomed . . . , but they were still regarded as curiosities. In the campaign of 1901 public sentiment had been so far educated that [I] was unable to find a trace of a protest against women's taking part in the battle against Tammany. (Villard 1902, 79)

Some have argued that because nineteenth-century political parties were essentially male social clubs, nonpartisan politics was the only way women could work in campaigns (Monoson 1990). While 1890s municipal reformers believed nonpartisanship was the best way to select a city government, there is no evidence that they believed that partisanship was acceptable for men and not for women. Nor is there any evidence that party men believed this, at least not Republican party men. While Republican women did emphasize that they were there for service, and did not expect pecuniary rewards, there is no evidence that being a party loyalist made them feel unwomanly. In the 1890s party loyalties were intensely felt, often defining people's identities and determining their close associates. Women felt these passions as much as men. The multiple campaigns and numerous political organizations in New York City in the 1890s and 1900s presented them with many choices. Women worked in all of these, partisan and nonpartisan. Their organizations were separate from men's, but not their principles. Nor was partisanship viewed as a radical departure from woman's proper role. Some of the women who worked in the Republican Party of the era were progressives; many were conservatives, and became more so over time. None were radicals. To judge by women's party activities and the statements to the press of party men and women, woman suffrage was radical; women in politics, including party politics, was not.

References

Anthony, Susan. 1900. Political women. *Daily Times* (Leavenworth, Kansas), September 11, on Reel #6 of "The Papers of Susan B. Anthony: 1820–1906," microfilm collection (Library of Congress Manuscript Division), and in Harper 1898, III:1214–15.

Arthur, Helen. 1906. The work of the Woman's Municipal League in the last campaign. *Women's Municipal League Bulletin* 4, no. 6 (January): 6–9.

Bostwick, Kate M. 1896. Women's political clubs. *Monthly Illustrator* 13: 304–8.

Boswell, Helen V. 1918–1919. A Republican woman in politics. A series of seventeen short articles in the *National Republican* (November 23, 1918–April 5, 1919).

Constitution and bylaws of the West End Auxiliary, Woman's Republican Association of the United States. Organized 1894; New York Public Library.

Edwards, Rebecca Brooks. 1997. *Angels in the machinery: Gender in American party politics from the Civil War to the Progressive Era*. New York: Oxford.

Harper, Ida Husted. 1898. *Life and work of Susan B. Anthony*, 3 vols. Indianapolis: Hollenbeck Press. Reprint: Salem, New Hampshire: Ayer Company, Publishers, 1983.

Kurland, Gerald. 1971. *Seth Low: The reformer in an urban and industrial age*. New York: Twayne.

Lockwood, Belva A. 1893. Women in politics. *American Journal of Politics* 2 (April): 385–87.

Lowell, Josephine Shaw. 1898. The Woman's Municipal League of New York City. *Municipal Affairs* 2, no. 3 (September): 465–66.

Marshall, Susan E. 1997. *Splintered sisterhood: Gender and class in the campaign against woman suffrage*. Madison, Wisc.: University of Wisconsin Press.

McCormick, Richard L. 1981. *From realignment to reform: Political change in New York State, 1893–1910*. Ithaca, N.Y.: Cornell University Press.

Monoson, S. Sara. 1990. The lady and the tiger: Women's electoral activism in New York City before suffrage. *Journal of Women's History* 2, no. 2 (Fall): 100–135.

Roosevelt, Theodore. 1886. Machine politics in New York City. *Century Magazine* 33 (November): 74–82.

Stanton, Elizabeth Cady. 1900. Mrs. Stanton doesn't care for either party in the woman in politics. *New York Herald*, October 7, V:7:2.

Villard, Oswald Garrison. 1902. Women in New York municipal campaign. *Woman's Journal*, March 8, 78–79.

CHAPTER THREE

~

The Rise of Political Woman
in the Election of 1912*

With a suddenness and force that have left observers gasping, women have injected themselves into the national campaign this year in a manner never before dreamed of in American politics.

—*New York Herald*, Aug. 11, 1912

Never before in the history of the United States have women taken a deeper interest in a presidential campaign than this year.

—*New Orleans Picayune*, Aug. 19, 1912

Unprecedented in this country is the prominent part which women are taking in the presidential campaign this year.

—*Calumet Michigan News*, Aug. 21, 1912

Woman's Day in national politics seems to many an editorial observer to be now dawning.

—*N.Y. Literary Digest*, Aug. 31, 1912

---

*I'd like to thank Amy Hackett and Kristie Miller for their useful suggestions to this chapter. This chapter uses "Mrs." and "Miss" because that is how women referred to themselves in 1912. "Afro-American" was also commonly used at that time.

Figure 4.   Clockwise from top left: Daisy Harriman watches the crowd as seventy-five-year-old Mrs. Abbie Vibbert of Springfield, MA, addresses a Democratic rally in Union Square, New York City on August 20, 1912 (image no. LC-DIG-ggbain-12784 from the George Grantham Bain Collection at the Library of Congress); "The Serenade" from the *St. Louis* (MO) *Post Dispatch*, August 20, 1912 (Daisy Harriman scrapbook at the Woman's National Democratic Club in Washington, DC); Helen Varick Boswell, date unknown (image no. LC-DIG-ggbain-07731 from the George Grantham Bain Collection at the Library of Congress); Frances A. Kellor, date unknown (image no. LC-DIG-ggbain-07807 from the George Grantham Bain Collection at the Library of Congress).

The election of 1912 marked the takeoff point for two progressive movements—that for woman suffrage and that of women into politics. Both movements had roots deep in the nineteenth century, both got a boost from the Populist Movement in the 1890s, and both saw a decline in public interest in the early 1900s. During these decades they had moved on parallel tracks, each movement working to bring women into public life, but only occasionally borrowing from or working with each other. The election of 1912 put both on the national agenda. It expanded their ranks and increased public awareness of women's political work. And, while suffragists still proclaimed their nonpartisanship and party women kept their official distance from suffrage, the election of 1912 saw the beginning of mutual support. The best-known party women—the ones quoted in the newspapers—admitted that they favored woman suffrage even while they said it wasn't an issue in the campaign. In previous elections such women had refused to state their own attitude toward suffrage out of fear of alienating men. Before the 1912 election, only a few women were active both for suffrage and in political campaigns; afterwards, women working in politics saw the need for both.

What was different about 1912? Although individual women had been active in political campaigns for many decades, by 1912 there was a critical mass of women eager and willing to work for the presidential candidates of all political parties. They were energized by the issues raised by the Progressive Movement and saw the outcome of the 1912 election as crucial to the country's future. In 1912 there were 1.3 million women of voting age in the six states where women had equal suffrage with men. When women were given the vote in Washington in 1910 and in California in 1911, the electoral college vote which women could affect more than doubled. The four states which had fully enfranchised women in the nineteenth century— Wyoming (1869), Utah (1870/1896), Colorado (1893), Idaho (1896)—had smaller populations.[†] For the first time all presidential candidates treated women as important to victory.

The presidential campaign of 1912 promised to be a highly competitive race. Deep divisions within both the Democratic and Republican parties portended close contests for each party's nomination, even for Republican incumbent William Howard Taft. An uncertain outcome gave all factions an incentive to look for new sources of support. Progressivism split the Republican Party. The new Progressive Party had the most to gain from spreading its net widely and made the biggest leap by endorsing woman suffrage in

---

[†]The electoral college votes were: California, 13; Colorado, 7; Idaho, 4; Utah, 4; Washington, 7; Wyoming, 3. Total: 38 out of 531.

its platform. The suffrage movement had been slowly pushing votes for women onto the political agenda for years, but it was acceptance by the Progressive Party that gave it legitimacy as a national issue. For the first time a major party candidate, Theodore Roosevelt, spoke in favor of woman suffrage as he campaigned.

Because of this split, 1912 was one of those rare elections in which there were *three* major candidates. As a former president, TR brought status and legitimacy to the Progressive Party that was created for his candidacy. As a reformer, he opened the door to new ideas. This combination made it possible for woman suffrage to move from being a state issue into the national debate. In turn, the sheer numbers of women working in the various campaigns demonstrated their value as a political resource and undermined the many objections to their voting as well as working for candidates.

The presidential campaigns had their headquarters in New York City, the political capitol of the country. It was common to have a second headquarters in Chicago to help with the Western campaign, and occasionally a third some place else. These headquarters housed different committees, which raised money; produced and distributed campaign literature, badges, and posters directed at different groups of voters; sent out surrogate speakers; and spoke to reporters. Presidential candidates relied on their friends to campaign for them in their own states. Some presidential candidates traveled to address mass audiences; others stayed at home and let their supporters visit them. In 1912, TR was a one-man locomotive until he was shot by a madman on October 14. Taft went on vacation, then returned to the White House, making a few speeches along the way. Wilson continued to govern New Jersey, making short trips to give carefully crafted speeches until he called a moratorium when TR was incapacitated by his wound.

All eyes were on California, where women would cast their third vote in a year in the November 5 general election. California was a progressive Republican state. Democratic candidates for president had won only four times since it joined the Union in 1850. Reformers and suffragists had worked together to achieve equal suffrage along with several other progressive measures in a statewide referendum held on October 10, 1911. The Women's Progressive League quickly organized a voter registration drive which helped over seventy thousand women register to vote in time for the December 5 municipal elections in Los Angeles; sixty-five thousand women actually voted—only a few thousand less than the number of men. California women were well organized and politically conscious; many quickly turned their attention to the presidential election. By the time California held its primary on May 14, women had organized for all the leading candidates. A greater proportion of eligible women registered and voted than men (letter to *New York Times*, May 17, 1912, 2:4). California women didn't wait for the national committees and the national candidates to tell them what to do.

This chapter will describe what women did in that election and the consequences for enlarging women's public role. Since women who supported candidates for president worked through political parties, each of the major parties will be treated separately. California women will receive special emphasis because of their importance to this election.

The Republican Party

The Republican Party had controlled the federal government since 1896 but it was not a united party. When an increasingly conservative president William Howard Taft tried to purge progressives during the 1910 primaries they coalesced against him. That year the Democrats captured the House for the first time since 1892. Several prominent progressive Republicans asked former president Theodore Roosevelt to challenge President Taft's renomination, and in February he announced that he would do so. By the time the Republican convention opened in Chicago on June 18, Roosevelt had won more of the popular votes in the fourteen states which held a primary, but Taft had more delegates. The turbulent convention was rife with controversy and heated by rhetoric, but was still controlled by the Taft forces, which won the nomination on the first ballot and wrote the party platform. Angry at the Taft steamroller, Roosevelt delegates bolted the convention to found a new Progressive Party. They included the only two women who were delegates, Florence C. Porter and Isabella W. Blaney, both from California.

Running the presidential campaign was the responsibility of the national committee. The Republican National Committee (RNC) lost no time in setting up headquarters in the Times Square Building in New York City. The Republican party had recognized the importance of women since 1888, when it asked J. Ellen Foster to form the Woman's National Republican Association. Although she mounted a major appeal to women during the campaigns of the 1890s, her efforts in the elections of 1904 and 1908 were subdued. Foster died in 1910, and her place as head of the WNRA was taken by her protégée, Helen Varick Boswell. Thus it was only natural for the party to turn to Boswell to be director of women's work in 1912. In Chicago, the director of the western headquarters named Mrs. J. D. Whitmore as head of his women's bureau (*Topeka Daily Capitol*, Sept. 10, 1912, 1). Taft women had already organized in California under the leadership of Mrs. Abbie E. Krebs and were putting out their own literature (*San Francisco Call*, May 1, 1912, 5:1).

Boswell was given two rooms on the ninth floor of the campaign head-quarters. She wanted her office to be in the Astor Hotel, where women often went for teas and lectures, but the campaign wanted it nearby so she "gracefully yielded . . . to the superior political wisdom of the men" (*New York Tribune*, Oct. 14, 1912 [5]; quote in the New York *Sun*, Oct. 18, 1912, 6). For a few weeks Boswell worked there with a small staff, including her assistant, Miss Elizabeth Toombs; a press agent, Miss Mary C. Francis; an organizational secretary, Miss Mary Woods; and two stenographers. When her office staff grew to thirty-five, an elaborate suite on the fourteenth floor was offered by a woman of means who was sailing for Europe. The Women's Department quickly moved upstairs (*New York Tribune*, Sept. 4, 1912 [32]). These rooms were so elegant that the men used them for special conferences, pushing the women out of sight when important visitors were present.

An experienced party worker with a network of Republican women to draw upon, Boswell immediately announced that "committees of women are being organized in the counties of all the States where women have the ballot" which will "work in harmony with the respective County Chairmen" (*New York Times*, Aug. 20, 1912, 18:2). Mary Woods was put in charge of organization. She contacted every Republican county chairman in the country, asking him to recommend women leaders. She also had "thousands of names of women given up by the women leaders." More names were culled from letters written by Taft supporters to the campaign offices. All of these were filed on index cards. Each woman county leader was asked to send a report weekly, and each state leader daily. Speakers were constantly recruited, cleared with the campaign's speaker's bureau, and sent out to address meetings. Researchers prepared packets of information, and even entire speeches with "the facts, the fancies and the eloquence that we hope is going to make converts," so that strict Republican doctrine would be adhered to. The Woman's Department also recommended items to the publicity bureau, which telegraphed material around the country every day. The women spoke to visiting reporters "each day between three and four o'clock." By the end of the campaign "there was a strong organization of women in almost every state, seconding the efforts of the men" (*National Republican [NR]*, March 8, 1919, 8:5,6; March 1, 1919, 7:3).

In 1912 Afro-American women were still loyal to the party of Lincoln. While some joined the Progressive cause, most were turned off by Roosevelt's refusal to seat black-and-tan delegations from the Southern states at the party convention, in preference to "lily white" ones. TR welcomed integrated delegations from Northern states, but most Afro-Americans stayed away from his campaign, even when they agreed with his platform. Some supported Wilson, but TR's "Southern strategy" and Wilson's Southern sentiments gave scant reason to desert Taft. Boswell wrote later that "we were fortunate in finding some excellent leaders for that race, both in speaking and organizational work" (*NR*, March 1, 1919, 7:3).

Mary Francis, an author of several books, wrote campaign literature while Boswell was one of the campaign's top speakers. Boswell became the first woman to address the New York State Republican convention, and that of Maryland, her home state. She also visited many other states, speaking and checking up on the Taft women's organization. She wrote later that "it became the fashion at every big dinner or large gathering to have women from the three parties" debate their choices. Most of the women who participated in these debates knew each other, having all been active in politics or women's clubs for many years; some were personal friends. Because of this, Boswell wrote, there was no acrimony among the speakers as they explained their positions. This did not always hold for their partisan followers; Boswell never forgot the time she was hissed.

The Progressive Party

The new Progressive Party held its first national convention in Chicago in early August. It aimed to be a major party—perhaps supplanting the Republican Party as the latter had the Whigs in the 1850s—and therefore created a party structure as well as a campaign organization. It selected a national committee and state committees, held state conventions, and ran candidates for state and local office. Western states in particular leaned to the Progressive Party. Women's Roosevelt Leagues had helped TR win the California Republican primary in May by two to one (*San Francisco Call*, March 17, 1912, 43:1; March 26, 1912, 2:6; March 29, 1912, 7:3).

As is true of all new parties, the Progressive Party sought to expand its reach by appealing to new constituencies which the old parties had neglected. TR had long been receptive to women's greater participation in public life, which he saw as an expansion of women's natural maternal role, not a derogation of it. In 1880 he had written his senior thesis at Harvard on the "Practicability of Equalizing Men and Women before the Law," toward which he was favorable if somewhat skeptical that it could be done. He voted for a woman suffrage bill while serving in the New York State Assembly (1881–1885) and urged the gradual expansion of suffrage for women in his speech to the legislature after election as governor in 1898 (HWS 1902, 4:1075). However, TR did not think that women voters would change electoral outcomes so he did nothing while president. Out of office he was more outspoken. In 1910, he told a meeting of Colorado women that "I am in favor of woman's suffrage." But, he added, "I think there are many more important questions to be settled. I am much more interested in the economic questions that affect the women than in those purely political" (*Rocky Mountain News*, Aug. 30, 1910, 10). A year later he wrote a suffrage opponent that "I am rather in favor of the suffrage, but very tepidly" (Morison 1954, 7:240).

TR changed his mind late in the spring of 1912. Right before the Republican convention, Judge "Ben" Lindsey of Denver, a progressive Democrat, persuaded him that a strong stand in favor of woman suffrage would benefit his campaign. Lindsey had been organizing Woodrow Wilson clubs until TR announced his candidacy in February. He subsequently became one of TR's closest advisors, mentioned as a possible running mate before the Progressive convention. Realizing "the advantage of enlisting the help of women who through their large organizations had become a strong factor in public life" (HWS 1922, 5:706), TR authorized Judge Lindsey to announce that there would be a woman suffrage plank in his platform (*New York Times*, June 13, 1912, 1:4; Washington, DC, *Evening Star*, June 13, 1912, 9:4). His conversion from passive to active supporter may have been prompted by the intention of Wisconsin Senator Robert M. LaFollette, one of his rivals for progressive support in the Republican primaries, to propose his own platform containing a strong suffrage plank (HWS 1922, 5:705).

Women were quite visible both at the Progressive Party convention and during the campaign. Reporting on the first day of the new party's convention, *New York Times* described it as "a convention managed by women and has-beens. . . . Everybody who is not an ex is a woman" (*New York Times*, Aug. 5, 1912, 1:1). When Jane Addams, the most prominent American woman of her time, seconded TR's nomination, the press loudly but wrongly proclaimed her to be the first woman to have such an honor. It also noted that women wrote, or helped write, important planks in the platform. Between twenty and forty women were official delegates, compared to two each at the Democratic and Republican conventions. Nineteen women from seven states signed a call "From the Women Delegates to the National Convention of The Progressive Party to the Women of the United States." Four women sat on the national committee and many others on state and local committees, though only one *headed* a county committee (Park County, Wyoming). One-fourth of the delegates to the New York state convention were women, where four women were chosen to be delegates to the national convention (*New York Times*, Aug. 4, 1912, 4:1). A third of those at ward meetings of the Progressive Party in Chicago were women (*Chicago Daily Tribune*, Sept. 3, 1912, 5:6).

TR greatly admired Addams and women like her. As was true of most progressives, he wanted to believe that women would add a finer, nobler element to the coarse world of party politics. On August 8 he telegraphed Addams to thank her for seconding his nomination at the Progressive Party convention and reiterate his commitment to women's full inclusion in the new party.

> In this great National Convention, starting the new party, women have thereby been shown to have their place to fill precisely as men have, and on an absolute equality. It is idle now to argue whether women can play their part in politics because in this convention we saw the accomplished fact, and moreover, the women who have actively participated in this work of launching the new party represent all that we are most proud to associate with American womanhood. (Morison 1954, 7:594–95)

Like Taft and Wilson, Roosevelt believed that woman's place was to care for home and family. Unlike them, he did not believe that this responsibility excluded participation in public life, or that suffrage unsexed or masculinized women. In a speech in Vermont later that month TR declared that "I have said not once but a score of times, that I put the domestic life above every other kind of life, and I honor the good wife and mother as I honor no other woman and no man. . . . Real issues affect women precisely as much as men. The women who bear children and attend to their own homes have precisely the same right to speak in politics that their husbands have who are the fathers of their children and who work to keep up their homes. . . . I do not believe that there is identity in functions between men and women, but I do believe that there should be equality of rights" (*New York Times*, Aug. 31, 1912, 2:4–6).

Within the Democratic and Republican parties women automatically organized themselves into separate sections and held separate meetings specifically for women. Because the Progressive Party had called for women to fully partake in the organization and management of the new party, women were urged to join regular party organizations and sit on state and local committees, in preference to forming auxiliaries or separate clubs. Some did. Most did not. In 1912 women were used to having their own organizations and their own meetings, where they specialized in appealing to women and did not have to defer to men. Women's Roosevelt Leagues and Clubs proliferated. A separate Women's National Finance Committee, headed by Mrs. Kellogg Fairbank in Chicago, focused on raising money. It "sold Bull Moose stamps in drugstores and started a People's Dollar Campaign," while staffing "Bull Moose stores in Chicago and New York [which] marketed TR badges, stuffed moose, bronze lapel pins, and red silk bandannas with the Colonel's face imprinted on them" (Dalton 2002, 399).

The Progressive Party attracted to it many women who had made their reputations and spent their careers working for reform. In addition to Jane Addams, these women included Lillian Wald, Frances Kellor, Alice Carpenter, Katherine Phillips Edson, Margaret Dreier Robbins, and her sister Mary Dreier. Most, though not all, of these women were Republicans. Only a few, such as Ruth Hanna McCormick of Illinois, had been active Republicans. Although these women supported woman suffrage, those women whose primary work had been in the suffrage movement were less active. Journalist and suffragist Ida Husted Harper wrote that while there were many women at the Progressive convention, there were only a few suffragists (*New York Times*, Aug. 10, 1912, 6:7).

When the new party set up its headquarters at the Manhattan Hotel, Alice Carpenter was initially put in charge of women. She soon left to go on the stump and Frances Kellor took over responsibility for organization. She wrote numerous letters looking for women ready to work for Roosevelt and the Progressive Party. She asked the national committeemen and the state and county chairmen to appoint women to their respective organizations whom she could aid to do "women's part of the work" of electing TR. She also wrote suffragists, extolling the opportunity the campaign presented as "an unparalleled training school for women who have not participated in political affairs." She urged them to "work for suffrage within party lines." To other women's clubs she asked the help of "every earnest and able woman in the work of promoting interest in suffrage and the protection of working women and children" (Jane Addams Papers, Reel 7:0023–30).

Under her direction, 250 female orators were deployed throughout the East Coast. Instructions to women speakers told them not to attack the other parties except on the issue of suffrage. The Progressive Party's first women's rally in New York City's Union Square featured two warhorses of reform: Mary Dreier and Mary Ellen Lease (Washington, DC, *Evening Star*, Aug. 24, 1912, 2:6). The former was president of the New York Women's Trade Union League. The latter had made a national name for herself as a Kansas agitator in the 1880s and a Populist speaker in the election of 1892. Progressives made the most of Jane Addams's support. In Los Angeles, a Woman's Rally Committee wrote campaign songs for a "Jane Addams Chorus" which debuted on August 26. The songs, and the chorus, soon spread throughout the country.

The Democratic Party

The Democratic Party had the most traditional attitude toward woman's place and was the least responsive to pleas for woman suffrage. While Democratic women had organized local campaign clubs during elections for decades, these were not encouraged or endorsed by the national party, and were sometimes actively discouraged. Only in states where women could vote were direct appeals made to women to support the party's candidates. The election of 1912 was the first time that the Democratic National Committee authorized and supported an appeal to women.

The opening move to organize Democratic women nationally was made by backers of Champ Clark, who had represented Missouri in Congress since the 1890s. When the Democrats gained a majority of House seats in 1910, he was elected Speaker. With a campaign based "mainly in Congress" (Goldman 1990, 224), Clark was the leading candidate for the Democratic nomination at the beginning of 1912. His sister, Mrs. Annie Pitzer of Colorado, would become one of the two women delegates to the Democratic National Convention in June. He had long supported William Jennings Bryan, who headed the party's ticket in 1896, 1900, and 1908. However, Bryan's radical populism alienated many voters, especially in the East, and he had always lost by substantial margins. Although many felt the Democratic Party had become more conservative and less receptive to "Bryanism" over time, division in the Republican party created a window of opportunity which others thought Bryan might use to advance his own candidacy one more time. This explained why Bryan had not declared his personal support for Clark even though he headed the Nebraska delegation to the national convention, which was pledged to Clark.

On February 28, 1912, the *Evening Star* in Washington, DC, announced that "Wives of Prominent Democrats to have Harmony Feast"—"Just Like the Men." The occasion would be a Dolly Madison Breakfast to be held on May 20 with Mrs. Clark presiding. The wives of prominent Democrats were invited to what was intended to be an annual event. Several hundred guests, mostly "wives, daughters and descendants of democratic statesmen," heard numerous orations and toasts. Two of these were given by the wives who sat on either side of Mrs. Clark: Mrs. William Jennings Bryan and Mrs. Judson Harmon, wife of the Ohio governor and dark horse presidential candidate. At the end it was announced that a meeting would be held in a few days to form a permanent organization of Democratic women (*Evening Star*, February 28, 1912, 7:5; quote in May 20, 1912, 1:8).

One of those attending the breakfast was Nellie Fassett (Mrs. John Sherwin) Crosby of New York City. She was not a political wife, but a political organizer and the personal friend of William Jennings Bryan. Mrs. Crosby had been organizing and presiding over women's political clubs since the 1890s. She had founded the Woman's Democratic Club of New York City in

1905—"the only organization of Democratic women [in New York] to out-live its birth year"—and was still its only president (*Philadelphia Telegraph*, Sept. 25, 1912 [48]). She had long wanted to head a national organization; the election of 1912 gave her the opportunity to do so. It's possible that Bryan or his wife had asked her to take control from Clark's wife and sup-porters, who did not have her organizational or political experience. It's also possible that her mentor was fellow New Yorker Norman Mack, chairman of the Democratic National Committee. Mack was the publisher and editor of the Buffalo *Daily Times* and a "regular" Democrat. In spite of the traditional alliance between New York and Southern Democrats, Mack was neutral in the presidential contest.

The organizing meeting of the Woman's National Democratic League (WNDL) was held on June 2 at Washington's Willard Hotel with fifty char-ter members. Mrs. Crosby was elected president. All of the officers and many members soon departed for the Democratic convention in Baltimore, where the WNDL "made its real debut" (Hopkins 1912). The fact that most of them were married to Members of Congress who were convention delegates made this easy. At the first meeting of the WNDL Executive Board, held on July 3, the day after the convention ended, the wives of the presidential and vice presidential nominees were promptly made the WNDL's honorary pres-ident and vice president. Its business completed, Mrs. Crosby returned to New York and incorporated the WNDL in New York state on June 27, 1912.

The women named in the newspapers as the new officers and directors of the WNDL did not include any of the women named as organizers of the Dolly Madison Breakfast, but at least five were wives and two were widows of Members of Congress. Among the latter was Phoebe Apperson Hearst, who was also the mother of prominent newspaper publisher William Randolph Hearst. He was a major Clark supporter, and quite antagonistic to the man who finally won the Democratic nomination on the forty-sixth ballot at the Baltimore convention—Woodrow Wilson (*New York Times*, June 1, 1912, 4:2; June 28, 1912, 7:12; Washinton, DC, *Evening Star*, June 2, 1912, 16:6).

These connections may explain why the Wilson campaign didn't want the WNDL to be Wilson's representative to women. Wilson was a political neophyte, having held no public office other than governor of New Jersey, and that only for a year and a half. Nor did he rise as a Democratic Party activist; indeed he often turned against the party bosses who helped elect him. Most likely he did not know, or did not trust, the men behind the WNDL. Instead, Wilson aide Archie Alexander decided that there needed to be a separate Woman's National Wilson and Marshall Association. His mother and her friend, society matron Florence J. Harriman, officially Mrs.

J. Borden Harriman, called "Daisy" by her many friends, drew it "up on paper" but couldn't find a prominent woman to head it. "All our birds had gone to perch on the suffrage plank" of the Progressive Party, Daisy wrote later (Harriman 1923, 111–12). In the end, Daisy agreed to be its head.

The new organization was announced in the press with the publication of a letter written on August 5, to Harriman from William F. McCombs, the new chairman of the Democratic National Committee (DNC). Thanking her for her July 31 letter asking the DNC's approval of a Woman's National Wilson and Marshall Organization (WNW&MO), McCombs assured her that "We welcome the support and aid of your organization." Within two days Harriman had issued a press release and settled herself to the task of mobilizing women to help elect Wilson. One of her first acts was to hire a professional clipping service to fill a scrapbook with newspaper stories about her activities.

Harriman claimed that her organization was nonpartisan—hence the lack of "Democrat" in its name—and that she was an "independent." She said that her "husband is a Republican, but he's going to vote for Wilson. . . . I believe in getting the best man for the place, whatever his party." Despite this disclaimer, the WNW&MO operated under the auspices of the DNC, which provided space in its campaign headquarters at 200 Fifth Avenue (*New York Times*, Aug. 7, 1912, 4:3).

The Wilson campaign didn't completely ignore the WNDL while it was arranging for its own women's group. Mrs. Wilson officially invited the WNDL officers to attend the traditional notification ceremony on August 7 at the Wilson summer cottage in Sea Girt, New Jersey (*Evening Star*, Aug. 4, 1912, 2:4; *New York Times*, Aug. 4, 1912, 5:3). There the WNDL executive board elected Mrs. Harriman to the League's board of directors.

The WNDL opened its headquarters at 1123 Broadway in New York City, two blocks away from DNC headquarters. The WNDL's corresponding secretary, Mrs. Steven B. Ayres, wife of a Bronx congressman, ran the office (*Iowa City Press*, Oct. 7, 1912 [54]). She immediately created a National Wilson-Marshall Women's League, through which little girls could recruit paying members to the WNDL (New York *Evening Sun*, Oct. 18, 1912 [86]).

Rather than explain why her group was not part of the official campaign, Mrs. Crosby bragged that "our work . . . is carried on without any expense to the men in the campaign work." She planned to raise money through teas and bridge parties, and use it to mail literature "full of good Democratic doctrines" (*Philadelphia Telegraph*, Sept. 25, 1912 [48]). The WNDL still had the support of Norman Mack, even though he was no longer DNC chairman. His wife was named vice president for New York, and his magazine, the *National*

Monthly, proclaimed itself "the official organ of the League." A column on the work of the WNDL appeared every month during the rest of 1912.

Unlike the WNW&MO, the WNDL was intended to be a permanent organization for Democratic women. Mrs. Crosby began appointing state vice presidents who are "carrying on the work of organizing permanent state and county organizations." Sometimes she appointed women known for their political work to head a state organization; other times she asked a prominent local politician to do so. By October there were eight state vice presidents, including Wyoming and Washington where women could vote for president (*National Monthly*, Oct. 1912, 123). Leading political women in a dozen other states announced the formation of statewide Democratic Leagues without the formality of official affiliation with the WNDL.

One of these was in Los Angeles, where the Los Angeles County Women's Democratic League set up headquarters on the third floor of the Alexandria Hotel. From there they organized mass meetings in halls and hotels and sent out speakers to address workers at factory gates, shops, and railroad yards. Women were asked to make their automobiles available on election day to bring voters to the polls (*Los Angeles Times*, Oct. 20, 1912 [98]).

Ten days after accepting the nomination, Woodrow Wilson welcomed women into "the field of politics." In a brief, impromptu speech to several hundred women who came to participate in "New Jersey Day" at Sea Girt, he said that "when the women come into politics they come in to show us all those little contacts between life and politics, on account of which I for myself rejoice that they have come to our assistance; they will be as indispensable as they are delightful" (quote in Washington, DC, *Evening Star*, Aug. 18, 1912, 1:1, *New York Times*, Aug. 18, 1912, 4:3). After listening to Wilson, women flocked to the booth of the WNW&M Club of New Jersey to hear Daisy speak and to sign up to help out in the campaign (*New York World*, Aug. 18, 1912 [9]).

Harriman set up her campaign office in Room 1058 of the Fifth Avenue Building. Aided by a group of society women, she gathered a mailing list of fifty thousand women from all over the country, especially those in women's clubs and professional positions. Harriman planned to send them a circular every week, discussing issues and explaining why women should use their indirect influence to get the men in their families to vote for Wilson, or vote for him themselves in the six states where they could do so (*New York Globe*, Aug. 12, 1912 [4], *Evening World*, Aug. 8, 1912 [18]). First the Wilson women prepared an eight-page document describing the work Governor Wilson had done for women, children, and working men in

New Jersey (*New York Times,* Aug. 9, 1912, 2:4). This was sent out two weeks later with a letter importuning women to join and make a small contribution (Trenton N.J., *Times,* Aug. 24, 1912 [6]).

Next the WNW&MO organized mass meetings for women throughout New York City. Harriman was often surprised to find that more men than women came to her meetings. At her first mass meeting on August 20 in Union Square, Harriman found herself addressing a crowd of 388 men and boys, but only 12 women. She asked the men to pass on her remarks to their wives, overlooking the fact that New York women were being appealed to solely so they could influence their husbands' votes. All went smoothly until Harriman and her band pulled out campaign buttons and started to toss them to the crowd. In the men's rush to grab the trinkets, the rally almost became a riot, and the police had to be called in (*New York Post,* Aug. 20, 1912 [12], New York *World, New York Herald,* Aug. 21, 1912 [14], *New York Globe,* Aug. 21, 1912 [16]). This got more press coverage than anything the women had to say.

Nonetheless, Harriman kept trying to reach housewives. She called for a housewives' meeting in Union Square on September 13, where she spoke to five hundred men and several dozen women (*New York Globe,* Sept. 13, 1912 [42]). A leaflet for a "Monster Mass-Meeting" in Brownsville declared that "THIS IS A WOMAN'S MEETING." "Women should come and be told the reason that they be in politics and for WILSON this year." Women did turn out, but not as many as men (*Brooklyn Eagle,* Sept. 10, 1912 [38]). This pattern prevailed even outside New York. Men outnumbered women in a luncheon at Chicago's Iroquois Club on September 17 called to organize a local Women's Wilson & Marshall Club. They applauded loudly when Harriman, the first woman to ever address the Iroquois Club, told her audience that "party alignments are rapidly disintegrating. . . . it is our opportunity, as loyal women, to turn [men] to the Democratic Party" (*Inter-Ocean,* Sept. 18, 1912 [39]). The WNDL apparently was more successful at appealing to housewives, which it claimed were 90 percent of its membership. It told them that "housewives know that the Republican Presidents and the Republican Congresses have proved bad housekeepers" (Ayres 1912, 146).

When Harrriman went to Chicago, she bypassed the men in the western Wilson headquarters and the local Democratic Party to seek the help of another society woman, Ruth Hanna McCormick. Unlike Daisy, Ruth was experienced in and knowledgeable of politics. She was a supporter of Roosevelt and a Republican by birth; her husband was running the Progressive Party's Chicago campaign office while also running for the Illinois legislature on its ticket. Ruth gave Daisy many names and lots of advice (Harriman 1923, 112). A month later Mrs. E. S. Borneman became Western director, after forming the Chicago Women's Wilson League (*Chicago American*, Oct. 19, 1912 [90]).

Daisy was soon sidelined by illness and spent the rest of the campaign directing her organization from her bed. This did not inhibit action because women in the states did not wait to be told what to do. All over the country they organized Women's Wilson and Marshall clubs, woman's Democratic Leagues, and just plain women's Democratic clubs. They set up meetings for local notables and local candidates to speak on behalf of the presidential candidates. Some women running for local office found audiences at these meetings larger than they could get on their own.

In Seattle, Washington, where women could vote, the local WNW&MO had a heated debate over whether to admit men to its big women's rally. According to the local newspapers, "It had been planned at first to exclude men entirely, but the fear was expressed that some of the men might refuse to let their wives go out in the evening, if they would have to stay at home. So the ban was lifted." Officially, "men would be tolerated" but not encouraged to attend, even in the audience. Presiding was Mrs. May Arkwright Hutton of Spokane, a mine owner known as "the richest woman in the West." As one of the two women delegates to the Democratic National Convention, "she came to fight for Clark; but she stays in the campaign to fight for Wilson." The featured speakers were Democratic candidates for the state legislature, superintendent of public instruction, and clerk of King County—all women (Seattle, Wash. *Intelligence* and *Times*, Oct. 10, 1912 [59], Dallas, Texas, *Herald*, Oct. 13, 1912 [70]).

California organized its Woman's Woodrow Wilson League soon after the Democratic convention (*San Francisco Call*, July 5, 1912, 5:3). Progressives in California were strong enough to put TR on the ballot as both the Republican and Progressive Party nominee, but he still attracted almost as much anger as adoration. One of the best-known women in that state was novelist Gertrude Atherton, who scathingly denounced Roosevelt in her effort to secure women's vote for Wilson. In her first campaign speech at San Francisco's Palace Hotel, she called him "a colossal bluffer, absolutely selfish" (*San Francisco Examiner*, Aug. 16, 1912). In the next two months she made thirty speeches for Wilson up and down the state, later confessing that she converted numerous Republican women but only three "Moosettes" (Letter to *New York Times*, Oct. 20, 1912, 14:7).

Not all Democratic women were welcome as speakers. The Ohio state committee rejected Dr. Mary Walker, famed Civil War surgeon, made even more famous for her insistence on wearing men's clothes. The state party chairman said he'd rather have a two-headed calf (Butler, Tenn., *Herald*, Oct. 11, 1912 [61]).

The Prohibition and Socialist Parties

The usual plethora of minor parties ran candidates in the 1912 election. Some had put woman suffrage in their platforms and women candidates on their slates for decades. The Prohibition Party had supported woman suffrage since its founding in 1872. Its 1912 platform said "We favor suffrage for women on the same terms as men." Although the party had declined considerably by 1912, women were integral; a woman defeated an incumbent man for election as secretary of its national committee (Washington, DC, *Evening Star*, July 13, 1912, 7:6).

The Socialist Party, with Eugene Debs as its perennial presidential standard-bearer, had also supported woman suffrage since its founding in 1901. Its 1912 platform declared that "We demand unrestricted and equal suffrage for men and women" and it ran women for office in several states, including governor of Washington (Bedford, Mass., *Standard*, Sept. 1, 1912 [31]). About 10 percent of the delegates to its 1912 convention were women; two women sat on its national committee and one on the executive committee.

The Issues

Regardless of what was in the party platforms, the actual issues of the campaign were chosen by the candidates and their campaign committees. They reflected a combination of the personal preferences of each candidate and what each committee thought would win the most votes. Some issues, such as the tariff and what to do about the trusts, were addressed by all three candidates, but on others they spoke past each other. The national Democratic and Republican parties had been fighting about the tariff for half a century. The Republican party favored protective tariffs, which the Democrats denounced as special privileges. While not quite committed to free trade, Democrats argued that tariffs should only be high enough to generate necessary revenue. Taft and Wilson took the traditional positions of their respective parties. Roosevelt disagreed with both on how to control the trusts, but on the tariff he was still a Republican. The parties also disagreed on how to achieve their goals. The Democrats were the party of states' rights and limited government. The Progressives favored strong national regulation, especially of corporations. Republicans were not opposed to national regulation, but thought it should be done lightly and not be destructive of business.

Wilson announced his themes in his speech accepting the nomination, at Sea Girt on August 7. From this, Democratic campaign managers chose two issues "by which they hope to make a bid for the feminine vote in the six woman suffrage states" (*Evening Star,* Aug. 12, 1912, 2:1). They were 1) the high cost of living, which could be cut back through reduction of the tariff; and 2) social legislation, in particular laws bettering the condition of women and children through protective labor laws. A postcard poll several weeks later, asking women what they considered the vital issues of the campaign, found that 40 percent identified the first issue and 30 percent the second as the most important (*Sacramento Sun,* Oct. 1, 1912 [48]).

At Sea Girt, Wilson had said that women should participate in politics because "nobody certainly is more directly in contact with the cost of living than the women are" (quote in Washington, DC, *Evening Star,* Aug. 18, 1912, 1:1). To demonstrate the importance of the tariff to women, Harriman's group calculated how it affected the cost of items women purchased for their homes and families. A letter sent out by the Wilson women claimed that the tariff cost each family $125 a year. It asked housewives how they managed to pay for commodities which had increased in price by 61 percent between 1896 and 1910, when wages had only gone up by 20 percent (*Los Angeles Examiner,* Aug. 21, 1912 [22]).

On September 9 the Democrats opened a Tariff "Chamber of Horrors" exhibit at 29 Union Square West in New York City to illustrate the effects of protection on prices. A booth aimed at housewives had a fully furnished three-room flat with tags on each item giving the cost at home and abroad. For example, a sewing machine cost $30 in New York and $24.83 in England; frying pans cost $.95 at home and $.64 abroad. Another "horror" was that the tariff reduced the amount of sugar that a dollar could buy from twenty-five to sixteen pounds (*Brooklyn Eagle,* Sept. 8, 1912; *New York Telegram,* Sept. 13, 1912 [37]). Deemed a rousing success, this exhibit was replicated elsewhere (*New York Globe,* Sept. 13, 1912 [41]). The WNW&MO and the WNDL shared responsibility for this exhibit on alternate Fridays.

The Republicans countered with a doll, known as the Protective Tariff Lady. The brainchild of Mary Francis, she was dressed as the wife of a man of modest means might wish to dress, with prices labeling all items of her attire. The purpose was to show that an American woman could dress well for between twenty-two and twenty-five dollars, even though every item she wore was made in America. Women did not need the lower-priced goods of Europe, made by men paid half what their husbands received for the same work. This doll was part of the Republicans' Dollar Wage Show, strategically placed near the Democratic exhibit (*New York Telegram,* "Tariff Doll is Terror to Foes," Oct. 19, 1912 [89]; *New York Times*, Oct. 11, 1912 1:2). While Republicans admitted that the cost of living was high, the official position—repeated frequently by Boswell in the tripartite debates—was that this was not caused by the protective tariff. The states took a somewhat different position on the tariff. California Taft women argued that "we have the best tariff schedule for California products in the history of the state" (*San Francisco Call*, May 5, 1912, 40:2).

Unlike with the tariff, the parties did not disagree on the desirability of protecting women, children, and workers. They competed on how much protection was desirable and who passed what laws first. Harriman's letter on all the "progressive and humanitarian" legislation enacted in New Jersey while Wilson was governor was quickly objected to by the chairman of the Republican State Committee, Edmund W. Wakelee. The credit, he insisted in a very lengthy letter to newspaper editors, belonged to the Republican-run legislature (Henderson, N.Y., *Gleaner*, Sept. 12, 1912 [35], Millville, N.J., *Republican*, Sept. 12, 1912 [43], *New York Tribune*, Sept. 14, 1912 [38]). Mary Woods, secretary for women's work for the RNC, wrote a letter to the *New York Times* claiming the "honor . . . [for] the clubwomen of New Jersey, who side by side have worked and at least succeeded in obtaining the passage of laws to ameliorate the conditions of women and children" (*New York Times*, Sept. 9, 1912, 8:5).

Progressive women claimed such "social legislation" as their mantra, highlighting the many planks in the Progressive Party platform for "the protection of home life against the hazards of sickness, irregular employment and old age through the adoption of a system of social insurance." They spoke about suffrage, but it was not the main topic on their agenda. Indeed Jane Addams would speak on suffrage only in those states where the men were to vote on it in a November referendum. Progressive women thought that trusts and tariffs were as important to women as to men, but did not emphasize these concerns in literature aimed at women. Literature aimed at women, mostly written by Frances Kellor, based its appeal on the need for "humanitarian measures" such as the prohibition of child labor, the "protection of the home," and "betterment of industrial conditions" and the role women played in achieving these.

There was another "women's issue," raised largely as part of the personal crusade of Dr. Harvey W. Wiley. He had been a chemist in the Federal Bureau of Pure Food, where he felt his efforts to curb food adulteration had been thwarted by both the Roosevelt and Taft administrations in deference to "special interests." He joined the Wilson campaign, and as a result the WNW&MO published a booklet documenting his charges called *The War of*

Wealth Against Health. In it Harriman appealed "to the patriotic women of America for their active participation . . . in behalf of these measures." She argued that "No function is so essentially the women's function as the protection of the food supply" (Omaha, Neb., *World Herald*, Oct. 9, 1912 [58]). Only Wilson campaigned on this issue; both TR's and Taft's campaigns ignored these charges (*New York Times*, Sept. 18, 1912, 3:4).

Although women were not an important constituency to the Democrats, Woodrow Wilson specifically addressed the women of the country in a widely reprinted article published in *Woman's Home Companion.* The "new meaning of government," he said, was that "those who exercise its authority must 'keep house' for the whole people." One example was pure food laws, properly administrated. Another was "conservation of our natural resources." He concluded by explaining why government had a "direct and manifest" interest "in high prices and an excessive cost of living." In effect, the governor was explaining that women should be interested in who governed because government was responsible for concerns within the realm of women.

It was harder for Republican women to find a theme because the Taft campaign wasn't doing much campaigning. Nonetheless Boswell declared that her purpose was to "show the women voters of the country why they must vote for President Taft in the interest of their homes, State and Union" (*New York Times*, Aug. 20, 1912, 18:2).

Woman Suffrage

Only the Progressive Party saw woman suffrage as an issue in the 1912 campaign. The Democratic and Republican parties continued to ignore it as they had in the past. The Socialist and Prohibition parties supported woman suffrage, but it was not a priority. The women in charge of women at the Democratic and Republican campaign headquarters personally favored woman suffrage, but, since their candidates did not, none thought it should be a campaign issue.

Wilson was personally opposed to suffrage but officially "on the fence." Harriman did not see it as her task to push him over (*New York Times*, Aug. 18, 1912, II:4:3). From the beginning she emphasized that "we don't want the idea of suffrage to enter the work of this committee at all" (*New York Tribune*, Aug. 7, 1912 [2]). While she did encourage women who wanted suffrage to join the campaign, she only wanted those "who are willing to leave the suffrage issue temporarily in abeyance" (*New York Herald*, Aug. 18, 1912, 2:1 [7]). In a letter to the *New York Times* she explained that while she endorsed suffrage, "there are . . . communities in this country where equal suffrage is not understood. . . . [where] there are women who can and will help women without regard to whether they vote or do not vote" (Sept. 7, 1912, 10:7).

The WNDL admitted that it attracted few suffragists to its ranks. Nonetheless, suffrage crept in. As Mrs. Crosby told the New York *Evening Sun,* "We are not working at suffrage over the campaign season, but we can't keep it out. None of us means to drag it in, but it crops up on every occasion. At our latest meeting Mrs. Stephen B. Ayres and Mrs. Eva MacDonald Valesh, neither of whom is an avowed suffragist, found themselves talking about suffrage" (Sept. 26, 1912 [35]).

Taft avoided suffrage, but since he did little campaigning, that was not hard to do. His public position had been stated earlier when he said he was willing to wait for "a substantial call from that sex before the suffrage is extended" (*HWS* 1922, 5:708). Boswell personally believed in suffrage as a right and a duty of all citizens, but followed the path laid out by her mentor, J. Ellen Foster, to keep politics and suffrage quite separate. In the Republican clubs that she organized as well as in the campaign, she welcomed both those who opposed and those who favored woman suffrage. Whether addressing men or women, Boswell always gave "straight political" speeches without mentioning woman suffrage or women's rights. She firmly believed that "the way to demonstrate one's fitness for the suffrage was to be intelligent on political matters, and be not only able but willing to do some party work" (*NR,* March 1, 1912, 7:1).

TR's own position on suffrage had moved considerably since he became a candidate. In February he had written an editorial in the *Outlook,* the progressive magazine where he was a contributing editor, proposing a special election at which only women would vote on the question of woman suffrage. "Where they do not want it the suffrage should not be forced upon them. . . . where the vote is so light, those not voting should be held to have voted no" (Roosevelt 1912, 262). This was also the plank he intended to propose to the Progressive convention. However, the members of the Resolutions Committee made sure that his plank did not get into the platform. The platform pledged the party "to the task of securing equal suffrage to men and women alike." In his keynote speech former senator Beveridge (R-IN) dwelt on it at length, declaring suffrage both a "matter of natural right" and a "matter of political wisdom." TR followed his August 8 telegram to Addams with a second one: "Did I put into telegram the flat-footed statement without qualification or equivocation that I was for woman suffrage, the Progressive Party is for woman suffrage, and that I believe within half a dozen years we shall have no one in the United States against it" (Morison 1954, 7:595).

TR explained his own conversion as a result of associating with women like Addams, Frances Kellor, and Florence Kelley,—all women who had devoted their lives to bettering the conditions of workers, the poor, and immigrants. In a speech given on August 30 he explained that "I grew to believe in woman suffrage not because of associating with women whose chief interest was in woman suffrage, but because of finding out that the women from whom I received most aid in endeavoring to grapple with the social and industrial problems of the day were themselves believers in woman suffrage." This, he added, was reinforced by what women did with the vote where they had it (*New York Times*, Aug. 31, 1912, 2:4–6).

TR articulated the position "that women should have the same right to vote as men have" as though it had been his from the beginning. He maintained that "I see no reason why voting should interfere with woman's home life any more than it interferes with the everyday work of the man which enables him to support the home" (*New York Times*, Aug. 31, 1912, 2:4–6). Several states were holding referenda on woman suffrage that fall. Campaigning in Oregon, TR urged it to "follow the example of other western states in giving women the right to vote" (Washington, DC, *Evening Star*, Sept. 12, 1912, 2:1). Even if he had embraced equal suffrage for political reasons at first, by late summer he was a believer.

This conversion was not accepted by suffrage leaders. The National American Woman Suffrage Association (NAWSA) was officially nonpartisan. The fact that one party and its candidates supported suffrage while the others ignored it put the organization in an awkward position. Many criticized Jane Addams, a NAWSA vice president, for violating the tradition of nonpartisanship. Although Addams generated much publicity for suffrage, no other national NAWSA officers and few state officers followed her lead into active partisanship. NAWSA's president, the Rev. Dr. Anna Howard Shaw, said "I have no use for Theodore Roosevelt." In a speech to the Detroit Equal Suffrage societies she denounced TR for supporting woman suffrage only when it was politically expedient to do so (*New York Times*, Sept. 6, 1912, 1:6). Harriet Stanton Blatch of the Woman's Political Union publicly criticized Roosevelt and the Progressive Party for not actively supporting the Ohio suffrage referendum on Sept. 3—the only proposed amendment to the state constitution that lost (*New York Times*, Sept. 4, 1912, 1:3; Sept. 5, 1912, 6:1; Sept. 6, 1912, 3:6). Ida Husted Harper published several letters to the editor attacking TR for "insincerity" and "political dishonesty" (*New York Times*, Aug. 10, 1912, 6:7; quotes in Aug. 22, 1912, 8:7).

While NAWSA officers stayed out of the partisan fray, not all suffragists stayed away from the candidates. Maud Malone made it a point to go to every speech given by a presidential candidate in New York City and yell out "What about woman suffrage?" from the audience. Malone heckled TR in March and Wilson in October. The male audience was hostile, demanding that she be thrown out, while both candidates insisted that she be allowed to stay. Malone persisted with her questions until physically carried from the scene. After heckling Wilson at the Brooklyn Academy of Music, she spent the night in jail (*Evening Star*, March 26, 1912, 10:2; Oct. 20, 1912, 2:7; Pueblo, Colo., *Chieftain*, Oct. 6, 1912 [54]; *New York Times*, March 26, 1912, 1:2; Oct. 20, 1912, II:4:4). The men she heckled did not ignore her question, but neither did they answer it. Roosevelt said he was in favor of woman suffrage if the women voted to have it—his standard position before the Progressive Party convention. Wilson insisted that suffrage was a state, not a national, matter and that he was "only here as a representative of the national party" (*New York Times*, June 13, 1912, 1:4; Washington, DC, *Evening Star*, Oct. 20, 1912, 2:7). Taft escaped being heckled by not speaking in New York, so he didn't need a reply.

Antisuffrage

While opposed to woman suffrage, the "antis" were not opposed to women helping in the presidential campaigns. Indeed Ida Tarbell, a well-known journalist who thought women didn't need to vote, was even offered the presidency of the WNW&MO. She demurred, saying she "could be more useful writing about the tariff" (*Kansas City Star*, Aug. 20, 1912 [23]). Quite a few female "antis" were caught up by the campaign. At a Woman's Day held at the Democratic "Chamber of Tariff Horrors" suffragists and antisuffragists sat side by side on the platform listening to speeches in support of Wilson (*New York Herald*, Sept. 14, 1912 [38]).

Nor did all progressives support suffrage. One reason the woman suffrage referendum lost so badly in Ohio was that the head of the Progressive Party was an ardent "anti," while the head of the Taft Republicans in that state was an outspoken suffragist.

Nonetheless, some women's groups found it hard to maintain their opposition to woman suffrage while actively participating in the campaign. The League for Civic Education of Women sponsored a debate between women supporting the three contenders. Its president, Mrs. John Jerome Rooney, explained that her League had abandoned active opposition to suffrage in favor of concentrating on civic education. Previously the League had sponsored lectures on eugenics, and discourses by physicians on the "probable effects of political excitement" to discourage support for woman suffrage. Helen Varick Boswell told the League that "having spent many years in political service, she could offer personal testimony that it in no wise affected the health" (New Brunswick, N.J., *News*, Oct. 19, 1912 [89]).

The Outcome

Wilson won with only 42 percent of the popular vote but 435 votes in the electoral college. Roosevelt came in second with 27 percent of the national vote, but only 88 electoral college votes. Taft, the incumbent, ran a very poor third with 23 percent of the popular vote. His plurality in Utah and Vermont gave him 8 votes in the electoral college. Socialist Eugene Debs made the best showing of his political career, getting 6 percent of the popular vote. The Prohibition Party got 1.4 percent. Nationally, fewer people voted for Wilson in 1912 than had voted for Bryan in 1896, 1900, or 1908, while the overall distribution of the Democratic vote remained the same. It appears that many Taft supporters, especially in states where he wasn't on the ballot, simply stayed home. This helped the Democrats increase their control in the House to over two-thirds and to capture a majority in the Senate for the first time in twenty years. In the six states where women could vote for president, Roosevelt won California and Washington; Taft took Utah; and Wilson won Colorado, Idaho, and Wyoming. There is no way of knowing *how* women voted, though most speculation was that women were more likely than men to favor Roosevelt. Estimates of *how many* women voted ranged from one-fifth to one-third of the total voters in those states (*New York Journal*, Nov. 6, 1912, 10:3). The registrar in Los Angeles reported that 80 percent of all registered women went to the polls. Roosevelt won California (where Taft was not on the ballot) by only 174 votes. It's quite possible that women gave him that margin of victory. The day after the election the *New York Times* reported that

> Women played even a more important part in California than was expected. . . . From all the large cities come reports of the great activity of women in bringing voters of their own sex to the polls and in doing effective work against such vicious measure as that which sought to reopen race tracks throughout the State.
>
> In Los Angeles many women who own autos used them to gather aged and infirm voters and carry them to the polls, as well as workers in shops and stores who had limited time. Many of the women workers in this city who were ardent Progressives appeared at the opening of the polls, at 6 o'clock, and remained throughout the day. (*New York Times*, Nov. 6, 1912, 13:4)

Everyone involved believed that the suffrage cause had been helped considerably by the campaigns of 1912. Referenda in Kansas, Oregon, and Arizona gave women equal suffrage—the most states to do so in a single year. Women came very close to winning in Michigan, though suffrage lost decisively in Wisconsin and Ohio. Jane Addams reported to NAWSA that "on the Progressive platform I had the best chance to talk woman suffrage that I ever had in my life. I talked it to vast audiences of men who would not have come to a suffrage meeting or to a social reform meeting, but they would come to a political meeting, and there they had it driven into them night after night and day after day" (*Woman's Journal*, Dec. 14, 1912, 400). National magazines described how woman suffrage worked in California and Washington. The issue was publicized in several journals which had heretofore ignored it; the *National Monthly* published several articles pro and con while the *Crisis* published a special symposium in September. The following year a record number of suffrage bills were introduced into state legislatures, setting the stage for more referenda asking men to give women the vote. In 1916 both the Republican and the Democratic platforms included support of woman suffrage by state, following rancorous debate and despite much opposition.

Although TR lost decisively, the Progressive Party made a better showing in 1912 than the Republican Party had in its first national campaign in 1856. It elected thirteen new Members of Congress and 260 state legislators. The latter were a sufficiently important bloc in the Illinois legislature for it to pass a law enfranchising women for all matters except those specifically mentioned in the Illinois constitution (which would have required a referendum); this included voting for president in 1916. To keep progressive ideas before the people, the party set up a Progressive Service Bureau headed by Frances Kellor.

However, the times were not auspicious and the party did not thrive. It lost in state and local elections in 1913 and 1914. In 1916 both the Republican Party and the Progressive Party held their conventions during the second week in June in Chicago. The former nominated Supreme Court Justice and former New York governor Charles Evans Hughes as its candidate. The latter nominated TR. When TR refused to accept the nomination so that Hughes could beat Wilson, the Progressive Party died. TR put in one last blow for suffrage by convincing Hughes to come out for a federal amendment even though the Republican Party platform only supported suffrage by state (*New York Times*, Aug. 2, 1916, 1:2).

Harriman's Woman's National Wilson and Marshall Organization folded after the election, though Democratic women continued to organize locally. The WNDL did survive until at least 1918, but as a Washington, DC, club rather than a national one. The Woman's National Republican Association, which was more of a shell than an organization, faded from view. In 1916 both the Democratic and Republican National Committees would organize women for the presidential campaigns from scratch, with new women at their head, but they would have a large number of state women's party organizations to work with. The one holdover from the election of 1912 was Frances Kellor, who organized Progressive Party women into the Women's Committee of the Hughes Alliance. In the election of 1916 its work received more press—not always favorable—than all the other women's campaign organizations combined.

Sources

The primary sources for this chapter are newspaper stories, which are referenced internally. Most of these were collected for Daisy Harriman by a professional clipping service and pasted into a scrapbook, which is now in the possession of the Woman's National Democratic Club in Washington, DC. The club graciously allowed me to spend time in its archives going through that scrapbook in the summers of 1999 and 2000 and the winter of 2002. I found other relevant stories from the indexes of the *New York Times*, the *Evening Star* (Washington, DC), the *New York Herald*, and the *San Francisco Call*, and read them on microfilm, mostly in Howard University and the New York Public Library. Clippings from the scrapbook are cited with a date and the page number from the scrapbook in square brackets. Stories that I read on microfilm are cited by page and column number from the newspaper. In addition I relied on the following secondary sources for background, but only cited them if quoted.

Addams, Jane. 1912a. Why I seconded Roosevelt's nomination. *Woman's Journal* (August 17): 257.

———. 1912b. My experience as a Progressive delegate. *McClure's Magazine* (November): 12–14.

Anthony, Susan B., and Ida Husted Harper, ed. 1902. "Eminent Advocates of Woman Suffrage." *The History of Woman Suffrage*, Vol. IV, 1883–1900, appendix. Indianapolis, Ind.: Hollenbeck Press.

Ayres, Mrs. Steven B. 1912. Woman's National Democratic League. *National Monthly* (November): 146, 151.

Boswell, Helen V. 1919. A Republican woman in politics. Parts XIII and XIV. *National Republican* 5, nos. 47 and 48 (March 1, 8).

———. 1936. Political episodes XII. *Woman Republican* 13, no. 5 (May): 9.

Dalton, Kathleen. 2002. *Theodore Roosevelt: A strenuous life*. New York: Knopf.

Freeman, Jo. 2000. *A room at a time: How women entered party politics*. Lanham, Md.: Rowman & Littlefield.

Goldman, Ralph. 1990. *The national party chairmen and committees: Factionalism at the top*. Armonk, N.Y.: M. E. Sharpe.

Guiterman, Arthur. 1912. Women of the campaign. *Woman's Home Companion* 39 (November): 22.

Gustafson, Melanie S. 2001. *Women and the Republican Party, 1854–1924*. Urbana: University of Illinois Press.

Harriman, Mrs. J. Borden. 1912a. "Enter politics" Mrs. J. Borden Harriman's message to American women. *New York Herald*, August 18, 2.

———. 1912b. Why women should aid Wilson. *National Monthly* (September), 97.

———. 1923. The Democrats come back. Chap. 6 in *From pinafores to politics*, 98–116. New York: Henry Holt and Company.

Harrison, Patricia Greenwood. 2000. *Connecting links: The British and American woman suffrage movements, 1900–1914*. Westport, Conn.: Greenwood Press.

History of Woman Suffrage (HWS), 6 vols. Unabridged republication of the original editions, 1969. New York: Arno Press. Vol. IV, 1883–1900, ed. by Susan B. Anthony and Ida Husted Harper, Indianapolis, Ind.: Hollenbeck Press, 1902, 1144 pp.; Vol. V, 1900–1920, ed. by Ida Husted Harper, NAWSA, 1922, 817 pp.

Hopkins, Grace Porter. 1912. Woman's National Democratic League. *National Monthly* (August), 78.

Miller, Kristie. 1999. Eager and anxious to work: Daisy Harriman and the presidential election of 1912. In *We have come to stay: American women and political parties 1880–1960*, ed. Melanie Gustafson, Kristie Miller, and Elisabeth I. Perry, 65–76. Albuquerque: University of New Mexico Press.

Morison, Elting E. 1954. *The letters of Theodore Roosevelt*. 8 vols. Cambridge, Mass.: Harvard University Press.

Mowry, George E. 1971. Election of 1912. In *History of American presidential elections 1789–1968*, gen. ed. Arthur M. Schlesinger, Jr., 3: 2135–66. New York: Chelsea House Publishers.

Roosevelt, Theodore. 1912. Women's rights and the duties of both men and women. *Outlook* 100 (February 3): 262–66.

Wilson, Woodrow. 1912. The new meaning of government. *Woman's Home Companion* 39 (November): 3–4.

Woman suffrage in national presidential conventions. Chap. 23 in *The history of woman suffrage*, vol. 6, *1900–1920*, ed. Ida Husted Harper. National American Woman Suffrage Association, 1922, 702–19.

Women as a factor in the political campaign. 1912. *New York Times*, September 1. Reprinted in *Women: Their changing roles*. New York: Arno Press, 1973, 83–86.

Women in politics. 1912. *Outlook* 102 (September 28): 162–64.

Women in the thick of political fight. 1912. *New York Tribune*, August 14.

Women leap suddenly into political favor, now courted by all parties. 1912. *New York Herald*, August 11, III:2:1.

Women's work in the campaign. 1912. *Literary Digest* 45 (August 31): 324–26.

Figure 5. Marianne Fowler addresses a rally after a labor march in Richmond on January 22, 1978, to persuade the Virginia legislature to ratify the Equal Rights Amendment. Photograph by Jo Freeman.

CHAPTER FOUR

∿

All the Way for the ERA:
Winning and Losing in Virginia*

The postelection cartoon on the editorial page of the *Alexandria* (Virginia) *Gazette* told it all: A determined young woman with a slingshot (in a dress) stood with one foot firmly planted on the back of a large fallen man. She was marked "Va. ERA" and he "House Leader James Thomson." This cartoon acknowledged a victory that political pros had said would be impossible to gain: A handful of women had defeated the majority leader of the House of Delegates, a twenty-two-year veteran of political fights, on the basis of a single issue: The Equal Rights Amendment. Furthermore, they had done it by persuading voters to elect one Republican and one Democrat out of three contestants in a two-seat district. Educating voters to split their ticket is extremely difficult in the best of circumstances, but doing so in order to defeat an incumbent Democrat in a district that hadn't elected a Republican in anyone's memory is a feat worthy of note in any electoral Hall of Fame.

This feat took planning. The groundwork was laid in 1975 when Alexandria resident Susan Marianchild Blair put an ad in a community newspaper asking all those interested in ratifying the ERA to come to her house for a meeting. One of those who came was Marianne Fowler, who had become active in the Democratic Party as part of the 1968 McCarthy for President campaign. A staunch supporter of the ERA, Fowler had a plan to remove Jim Thomson from office and was looking for supporters.

---

*This chapter was commissioned by Ms. magazine and was written in 1977, based on interviews with the principals involved. Submitted in February of 1978, it was neither rejected nor published.

Thomson was a focal point of feminist ire because he chaired the House Privileges and Elections Committee, which considered constitutional amendments. He had kept the ERA confined to committee so it would not come to the full House for a vote. The ERA was three states short of ratification. Virginia could be one of those states. Thomson was not keeping the lid on the ERA merely for political reasons. He said several times that he did "not believe in equality for women." He was also a die-hard segregationist. Since the district he represented was a Washington, DC, suburb, and more liberal than most areas in Virginia, ERA supporters felt he simply had to go.

Fowler's plan was elegant in its simplicity. She knew that Thomson had won his many reelections by very slim margins—winning him the ironic nickname of "landslide" Thomson—and that seven of the thirty-one precincts in his district were highly transient. Residents of these precincts were largely those who move in and out of the Washington scene. As a group they were quite liberal, and not tied into the Virginia political machine. Because they lacked long-term ties, a large proportion did not register to vote. But because they were also politically conscious and highly educated, they were open to register, and vote, for a good cause.

Her plan was to have phone calls made to every adult in those precincts, first to get them to register and then to get them to vote for the pro-ERA candidates in the upcoming Democratic primary. Running in that primary, in addition to Thomson, was a pro-ERA incumbent, and a pro-ERA challenger, Dick Hobson. The women meeting in Susan Blair's living room adopted Fowler's plan and organized the Alexandria Ad Hoc Citizens Committee. It recruited close to one hundred ERA supporters, and made thousands of phone calls before election day.

Although this group defeated Thomson in six of the seven targeted precincts, he retained his seat. It was the other incumbent who lost his office. Challenger Hobson had won with a vigorous campaign, but the other incumbent had done little and came in third. Consequently, the number of postelection pro-ERA Delegates from Alexandria still numbered only one. Nonetheless, what the women learned from this campaign and the incipient organization they created provided the foundation to topple Thomson in 1977.

In preparation for the next campaign the Ad Hoc Committee organized itself into VERA. VERA stood for Virginians for the ERA, and it also stood for truth. While VERA was only an Alexandria group, Fowler and members of the Virginia Ratification Council organized a statewide group which they called VERA-PAC (for Political Action Committee). It's purpose was to do in other districts what VERA planned to do in Alexandria: defeat foes of the ERA.

As the 1977 campaign approached, VERA ran into a problem: It couldn't find any candidates. None of the twenty-eight Alexandria Democrats—many of them women—it asked were willing to run against Thomson in the primary election. VERA wanted a candidate with some support in addition to that of the feminist movement because it knew that feminist voters alone would not defeat Thomson.

While VERA coordinators Blair and Mary Charles (Charlsey) Armstrong were pondering how to defeat Thomson without a candidate, Fowler was conferring with other women on the Democratic Party County Committee of which she was a member. One of these discussed the problem with the chair of the Republican County Committee. A short while later he called Blair and said he might have a candidate for them.

The potential candidate the chairman brought to Blair's house was Gary Meyers—a young, pro-ERA Republican lawyer. He was politically ambitious enough to have been active in his community, and politically astute enough to know that he couldn't win in heavily Democratic Alexandria with only the backing of the Republican Party. While the GOP chairman looked on grimly from the corner of the room, VERA leaders quizzed Meyers, and he them.

Once VERA was convinced that Meyers could and would run his own campaign (unlike the 1975 losing incumbent) and that he would promote the ERA once elected (unlike some other candidates who received pro-ERA support and changed their stand after the election), it began mobilizing ERA supporters to urge split-ticket voting on the basis of a single issue.

VERA had several assets for this campaign, including over one hundred names of contributors to the 1975 campaign. As president of Alexandria NOW (National Organization for Women), Susan Blair could readily draw upon that membership. Blurbs were placed in women's newsletters, pleas were made at NOW's national convention in April, and phone calls were made to any and all potential supporters. But the most important asset was commitment to the ERA. After the first month people came into the office just from word-of-mouth recruiting, some from as far away as Connecticut and Pennsylvania. One man from Indianapolis spent his week's vacation working to defeat Thomson.

The key to the strategy was locating every pro-ERA voter in Alexandria. This is a strategy that requires relatively little money, but lots of people and time. VERA spent less than seven thousand dollars for the entire campaign (most raised through a mailing to a Ms. subscribers list) but recruited close to two hundred people. Only about a quarter were feminists—many thought feminism was "awful"—but they were for the ERA.

There were forty-five thousand registered voters in Alexandria. Working from an official list of registered voters, pertinent information for every voter was put on a separate card. These cards were organized by streets, and a street directory was used to find every household phone number. A hundred and fifty people spent two months phoning every household to ask if they favored passage of the Equal Rights Amendment. Since the purpose of this survey was to locate *pro* voters, time was not spent debating the merits of the issue, or even explaining it to those who expressed unfamiliarity. Several weeks before the election, canvassers began visiting all of the "pros" at their home to bring them literature on the two candidates that VERA supported.

Promoting the ERA candidates had to be done subtly. VERA wanted to keep a low profile so it would not arouse the antis to a countercampaign. And it didn't want to embarrass Democrat Dick Hobson any more than necessary. Hobson knew that if he were seen supporting or even collaborating with a Republican, the Democratic Party would retaliate. Therefore, he publicly supported Thomson, and his campaign manager even persuaded VERA to put a disclaimer on the literature which linked the two pro-ERA candidates' names. But Hobson never asked that VERA take his name off of their literature or cease working for his reelection.

Since repetition is crucial to political persuasion, this literature was not only left under every door, but also mailed to the "pro" voters. Bulk mail is much cheaper than first-class postage, but a timely delivery is less likely. VERA organizers met with Post Office personnel to secure their cooperation, then carefully packaged and coded their mailing according to instructions. Not only was the first mailing delivered with dispatch, but the sample ballot mailed only a few days before the election arrived in time.

An election day "pulling" operation is key to any successful campaign. It does not matter how many voters have been persuaded to vote right if they don't go to the polls. In Virginia the list of those who have voted is not publicly posted; each voter's name is called out as it is checked on the registration list. This meant that a VERA poll watcher had to be at thirty of Alexandria's thirty-one precincts the entire day just to find out who did and did not vote. (They left Thomson's home precinct alone.) Toward the end of the day, the pullers found out from the watchers the names of those who had not yet voted. These names were taken to a phone bank, where volunteers phoned every pro-ERA registered voter who had not yet voted. VERA also provided baby-sitters and rides to the polls for those who needed them. Everyone was reminded that this was the day to vote for the ERA.

Vote for the ERA is what they did. Voter after voter interviewed by the local media said they were turning out to demonstrate their support for the

ERA. When the results were tallied, challenger Meyers, strongly identified with the ERA, led both incumbents, and "landslide" Thomson had lost—by a landslide.

By the rules of ordinary politics, this electoral confirmation of Virginia's support for the ERA should have served as a warning to the legislature that it was not listening properly to its constituents. But the rules of ordinary politics were not the ones the Democratic Party of Virginia was following. Instead the party responded with exactly the kind of retaliation that Dick Hobson had feared. But its anger wasn't directed against Hobson, or any other man. It was aimed at the women behind the campaign and the issue they had campaigned for.

Although Marianne Fowler had provided many of the ideas behind the VERA campaign, she studiously stayed out of it. She spent her time organizing statewide because she knew the party would not tolerate active support of a Republican. But she was the Democratic Party's most convenient scapegoat for losing their majority leader. Less than a month after the election the county committee voted by 42 to 4 to remove her. Her "trial" was more like a kangaroo court than a court of law. No explicit charges were made against her; she was merely told she could make a speech in her defense before the vote.

In her speech she pointed out that the party bylaws required county committee members to support both the candidates and the principles of the Democratic Party. The ERA is in the national platform. If Thomson's failure to support party principles forced her to choose between them and party candidates, why should she be penalized for giving the principles priority? "Why should I have to give up my feminism to be in the Democratic party?" she said.

The retributive attitude she encountered permeated the state party. On February 9, 1978, the Election Committee voted 12 to 8 against sending the ERA to the full House. Some pro-ERA representatives even threatened to vote against the ERA if it ever came to the floor in order to "get even" for the defeat of Jim Thomson. In Virginia, as in many other states, the "male club" was more sacred than the "rules of the game."

Postscript

Virginia never ratified the Equal Rights Amendment but Fowler was reelected to the Democratic county committee in 1978.

PART II

BREAKING BARRIERS

Figure 6.   Campaign buttons from the personal collection of Jo Freeman.

~

CHAPTER FIVE

The Women Who Ran for President*

Long before women could vote they ran for public office, including the high-est office—the presidency of the United States. They ran for the same rea-sons that men run who don't have a chance: because a presidential candidacy is a great platform from which to talk about issues and sometimes just to talk about yourself. Two women put themselves forward for the presidency in the nineteenth century. None did so in the twentieth before 1964. Between 1964 and 2004 over fifty women were on at least one ballot as candidates for pres-ident, both as minor party candidates and as candidates in primaries for the nomination of the Republican or Democratic parties. Only a few of these women were noticed by the national press. In 1987 and 1999 two women who had established their credentials as political professionals tested the wa-ters of the major parties, but decided they were too chilly because adequate funds were not available. Not until the twenty-first century was a woman's candidacy for president taken seriously.

Who were these women and why did they run?

The Nineteenth Century

In the nineteenth century political parties were private organizations. They decided who their candidates should be on every level from local to national

---

*This chapter was started in 2005 and completed in the winter of 2007 while I was a Senior Scholar at the Woodrow Wilson International Center for Scholars in Washington, DC.

and provided tickets which voters put into ballot boxes. A party ticket was just that, a ticket on which were printed the names of the party's candidates. There were no ballots as we now think of them. In the 1830s the national parties created national committees to run their presidential campaigns, but the actual campaigning and provision of tickets were still up to the local parties. If a particular party or candidate had local supporters they would provide tickets to local voters.

Two women ran for president under the label "Equal Rights Party" although there was no actual party with that name. Both women were suffragists and believers in equal rights for women, so the name had a symbolic meaning.

Victoria Claflin Woodhull is remembered as *The Woman Who Ran for President*, but whether she actually ran is debatable. She was a notorious woman. Born on September 23, 1838, in Homer, Ohio, she earned money as a clairvoyant healer, a stockbroker, and a newspaper publisher. She both charmed and frightened many men. On April 2, 1870, she announced that she would be a candidate for the presidency in a letter to the *New York Herald*. Soon thereafter she started *Woodhull & Claflin's Weekly* with her sister and through it invited all types of reformers to come to a convention in New York City in May of 1872. On May 10, 1872, after adopting a platform for the newly minted Equal Rights Party, several hundred people enthusiastically called on her to run as their candidate. She gladly accepted even though she was only thirty-three and thus could not legally be president. Frederick Douglass was chosen to be her running mate, but no one asked him and he never acknowledged the nomination. Soon thereafter she became embroiled in a series of scandals which left her with no time to campaign. On election day she was in jail, charged with sending obscene material through the U.S. mail. There is no record of any tickets with her name on them being put into a ballot box.

Woodhull may have been the first woman to be nominated for president but the first woman to actually campaign was Belva Ann Bennett Lockwood in 1884. Born in upper New York state on October 24, 1830, she had broken many barriers before insisting that she could receive votes even though she could not cast one. After earning her living by teaching school and managing property, she enrolled in a law program in Washington, DC. She passed her courses, but had to use political skill and her wits to get her diploma. Then she had to talk her way into admission to the bar and had to persuade Congress to pass a law in order to become the first woman admitted to practice before the U.S. Supreme Court in 1879. In addition to practicing law, she lobbied for woman suffrage and temperance, campaigned for candidates, and reported for newspapers. After failing to persuade the 1884 Republican convention to include a woman suffrage plank in its platform, she wrote Marietta Stow in California, editor of the *Woman's Herald of Industry*, that women should run for office, since no law prevented their serving if elected. Stow and attorney Clara Foltz subsequently telegraphed Lockwood that she had been nominated for president by the Equal Rights Party. Lockwood promptly accepted the nomination and later asked Stow to be her running mate.

Lockwood was one of many reform candidates running in 1884 and the platform she wrote contained numerous popular reform positions—many of which eventually came to pass. While hers paid particular attention to women's rights, promising woman suffrage and the removal of women's traditional legal disabilities, suffrage was only one of many issues covered in her campaign speeches. Since the tariff was the issue of the day, it occupied a prime spot in her talks, which thousands came to hear in a campaign of only a few weeks.

Running for president was harder than running for other offices because the voters could not vote directly for candidates. Each presidential aspirant had to have a slate of electors in each state committed to voting for that candidate in the electoral college. Voters voted for the electors. Lockwood's first campaign task was to find people to run as electors who were pledged to her candidacy. She later claimed that she had succeeded in nine states.

Her candidacy was opposed by some notable suffrage leaders, who thought that it brought ridicule upon their cause. They were right about the ridicule. Cartoonists made fun of her, and men organized "Belva Lockwood parades" in which they wore Mother Hubbard costumes as a way of mocking her. Some voters were not deterred. Lockwood claimed that she received 4,711 votes in seven states. Her success, and the attention it brought, convinced her to try again in 1888. This campaign was much more modest and there is no record of how successful it was.

The Twentieth Century

Not until 1964 did another woman get votes for president. Late in the nineteenth century states began passing laws regulating the election process. They replaced the party ticket with the Australian ballot, a long list of the candidates for each available office that was printed by the government. Political parties became quasi-public entities; how they were organized and how they selected their candidates was shaped by state law. All these rules, regulations, and qualifications made it much harder for candidates to be recognized and get votes than was true in the nineteenth century. Instead of printing tickets and giving them out to voters, candidates had to follow a legal procedure to get on the ballot. Ballot access became a hurdle in the twentieth century that did not exist in the nineteenth. Nonetheless, in the eleven presidential elections between 1964 and 2004, from ten to twenty small parties were on the ballot in at least one state every November.

Although several states held primary elections to pick a party's presidential candidates early in the twentieth century, during the middle of the century fewer and fewer did so. Usually state parties chose delegates to national conventions where the presidential ticket was chosen. Beginning in 1972, presidential primaries became popular again. However, the type of primary varies enormously depending on the rules of the national parties, the requirements of each state's law, and the choices of state parties. Different law usually applies to major and minor parties, and sometimes to the Democratic and Republican parties. Some primaries are easy to enter and some are not. Some states require petitions with numerous signatures; some only require a filing fee; and a few merely that a person be generally known to be a candidate for president.

This is also true of the general election. In some states ease of entry makes it possible for many parties to have candidates on the ballot for president and vice president; in other states only the major parties can qualify. In some years even incumbents running for reelection—for example President Taft in 1912 and President Truman in 1948—have not been on the November ballot in all states. For a minor party candidate to get on the ballot in every state is very difficult in any year, and has been achieved less than a dozen times.

Of course one can run for president without appearing on a ballot, or even getting votes (á la Woodhull). But since it takes a certain amount of determination to get a ballot listing, that seems like a reasonable threshold for counting as a candidate. It is the one that Congressional Quarterly Inc. uses for inclusion in its many reference books. Since I am using those books as my source of names, that is the criterion that I will use. Even with that limitation, questions over whom to include still remain. These will become evident as I review the women who got on the ballot. (See table 5.1.)

The Early Birds

When Margaret Chase Smith, the Republican senator from Maine, stood before a luncheon of the Women's National Press Club held at the Mayflower Hotel on January 27, 1964, and announced that she was running for president, she became the first woman to become a candidate for a major party nomination for the nation's highest office. Smith's announcement of her

Table 5.1.   Number of Women on a Ballot for President, 1964–2004

| | # Women in Primaries | | |
	Republican	Democrat	# Women in General Election
1964	1	1	—
1968	—	—	1
1972	—	2	1
1976	—	3	1
1980	—	—	3
1984	—	1	2
1988	2	1	2
1992	5	5	4
1996	8	3	5
2000	1	1	2
2004	1	9	—

Sources: America at the polls, 1960–2004, John F. Kennedy to George W. Bush: A handbook of American presidential election statistics, Vol. 2, Washington, D.C.: CQ Press, 2005. *Guide to U.S. elections*, 5th ed. Washington, D.C.: CQ Press, 2005.

Notes: Congressional Quarterly only lists those candidates for president who appear on at least one ballot. However, once this qualification is met, it counts write-in votes in all states. Because CQ only provides the number of votes, it is sometimes hard to tell how many state ballots carry a candidate's name. Therefore I have generally written that a candidate received X votes from Y states rather than was on the ballot in Y states. When I wrote that a candidate was on the ballot in Y states the information came from another source, such as a newspaper story, a book, or an interview. The District of Columbia counts as a state from 1964 onward because the U.S. Constitution was amended in 1961 to allow its residents to vote for president. I have found a couple of errors in CQ reference books and there may be more.

Between 1964 and 2004, eighteen women were on at least one state ballot as candidates for president in the general election; three were on a ballot in two years. I've counted the two women the SWP ran in 1972 as one, because Reed was a surrogate for Jenness. However, I also counted Gavrielle Holmes in 1988 even though she was a surrogate for Larry Holmes. Fourteen women were on at least one state ballot in a Republican primary election; two in two different years, and one in three different years. Twenty-two women were on at least one state ballot in a Democratic primary election; two in two different years, and one in three different years.

Four women are counted in two columns: Ellen McCormack ran in several Democratic primaries in 1976 and at the head of her own ticket in 1980. Lenora Fulani ran at the head of her own ticket in 1988 and 1992, and in the New Hampshire Democratic primary in 1992. Isabel Masters ran in two Republican primaries before running at the head of her own party in 1992 and in the Oklahoma Republican primary before heading her own ticket in 1996. Mary Jane Rachner was on the New Hampshire and North Dakota Republican primary ballots in 1988 and the Minnesota Democratic primary ballot in 1992.

candidacy was not spontaneous. For over a year she had received a steady flow of mail urging her to run. While flattered, she did not begin to take the possibility seriously until the quantity of her mail escalated after an AP story late in 1963 suggesting that she might run. It wasn't party leaders or women's groups that convinced her to do so; the former were flustered at the thought and the latter were silent. It was ordinary people.

Like Woodhull and Lockwood, one of her reasons for running was "to break the barrier against women being seriously considered for the presidency of the United States—to destroy any political bigotry against women on this score." She entered the March 10 New Hampshire Republican primary—then the first opportunity for voters to indicate their presidential preference—and got 2,120 votes, or 2.4 percent of the total vote in a field of seven candidates. She did better in the April 14 Illinois primary, getting 25 percent of the Republican vote due to the efforts of a dedicated band of Republican women. No one, including her, believed she would win the nomination. But no one believed most of the men running for president would either. Smith lasted to the bitter end of the contentious Republican convention held in San Francisco in July of 1964, where she was formally nominated for president and received twenty-seven delegate votes.

In 1968 Charlene Mitchell became the first woman to head a minor party ticket in the twentieth century, and also the first African American of any party to appear on a presidential ballot. She was officially nominated to head the first Communist Party ticket since 1940 by 179 delegates meeting at a hotel in New York City, after selection by party leaders behind closed doors. The thirty-eight-year-old woman and her twenty-three-year-old male running mate were chosen to appeal to youth, many of whom were protesting the war in Viet Nam. The Communist Party had run tickets every four years between 1924 and 1940, initially as the Workers' Party of America. In 1944 it supported Roosevelt and in 1948 it supported Progressive Party candidate Henry Wallace. Subsequently it laid low due to laws which made it virtually illegal.

When the Communist Party decided in 1968 that it was safe to run again it either did not know or did not care that it was breaking new ground for women. While the CP had long had "the woman question" on its agenda, its presence was passive while the party actively tried to appeal to African Americans and to youth. Mitchell was nominated as "the great granddaughter of a slave." Joining the CP in 1946, she had served on its national committee since 1957, while working as a bookkeeper in Los Angeles. She had recently joined the party's staff in New York City. Her nomination made the headlines of the *Worker,* a Communist newspaper since 1924. She and her running mate campaigned against the war in Viet Nam, in favor of the Soviet Union, and against "reactionary" labor unions. They received 1,075 votes from four states. That was the last time the Communist Party ran a woman at the head of its ticket, though another African American woman, Angela Davis, would occupy the second slot in 1980 and 1984.

Response to the New Feminist Movement

By 1972 the women's liberation movement was flourishing and consciousness of women's issues and women as a potential voting bloc was high. Three women ran for president that year. Linda Jenness was the candidate of the Socialist Workers Party (SWP). Congresswomen Patsy Mink (HI) and Shirley Chisholm (NY) ran in several Democratic Party primaries.

The SWP, officially founded in 1938, began as a faction within the Communist Party that supported Leon Trotsky. It has run presidential tickets since 1948. Unlike many socialist parties it frequently runs candidates for state and local office.

Only thirty-one, Linda Jenness did not meet the constitutional age requirement to hold the office of president, but the SWP was on the ballot in twenty-five states—six more than in 1968. She qualified for the Ohio ballot but was removed when she could not prove she was thirty-five. Jenness had grown up in a conservative family in Georgia, but sympathized with the civil rights movement. At Antioch College she became radicalized by the Cuban Missile Crisis and the Viet Nam War. After joining the SWP in 1966, she was often run as its candidate for different offices because she was such an excellent speaker. With the women's liberation movement highlighting women and feminism, she was a logical choice for the SWP to pick at its August 1971 convention.

In 1972, Jenness used the platform of her candidacy to speak out against the war and for women's liberation. Roughly $300,000 was raised by small donations and spent for the petition signatures necessary to get the SWP ticket on the ballot. Its literature was equally devoted to denouncing the presidential candidates of the Democrats (McGovern), the Republicans (Nixon), and the Communist Party (Gus Hall). Jenness was the last woman the SWP ran for president, though women have often occupied the second spot on its ticket since 1972. The SWP ran Evelyn Reed in place of Jenness in three states that would not permit Jenness to be on the ballot due to her age. Between the two of them, they received 66,677 votes in twenty-five states.

Patsy Takamoto Mink had been in public office most of her adult life, having served in the Hawaii legislature before being elected to the House of Representatives in 1964. Outspoken against the war in Viet Nam, she was asked by a group of progressives in Oregon to run in their state's May 23 Democratic primary to provide a platform to talk about the war. Most of them were founders of the Oregon branch of the National Women's Political Caucus so they consciously chose a woman as their candidate. Mink agreed to run if the group obtained the necessary four thousand petition signatures to put her on the ballot. Once this was done, she frequently stopped off in Oregon on her trips home to Hawaii to speak out against the war and in favor of her other concerns. Mink was busy as a congresswoman that spring. Among other duties, she shepherded Title IX of the 1972 Educational Amendments Act through the House. Written to prohibit sex discrimination in federally assisted education programs, it would have its biggest impact on women's participation in collegiate sports. In April, Mink traveled to Paris with New York congresswoman Bella Abzug to meet with Madam Nguyen Thi Binh, a negotiator for the North Viet Namese government. This generated a lot of criticism.

Mink's campaign was widely publicized in Oregon but virtually unknown elsewhere. In addition to her 5,082 votes in the Oregon primary she got 573 votes in Maryland and 913 votes in Wisconsin, even though she did not campaign in either state. In Maryland, the secretary of state is responsible for deciding whose names will appear on primary ballots, based on news media recognition that the person is a viable candidate. Wisconsin follows a similar procedure except that the decisions are made by a Presidential Preference Selection Committee for each political party recognized by the state. Mink did not have her name placed into nomination at the Democratic convention and did not get any delegate votes.

Shirley Chisholm's political roots were in Brooklyn, which she represented in the New York Assembly before becoming the first African American woman to be elected to Congress in 1968. After six months of "exploring" a candidacy she formally announced it on January 25, 1972. Although Chisholm made a point of saying that she was not the women's candidate, she had always been a strong supporter of women's rights. One of the four founders of the National Women's Political Caucus in 1971, she often said that during her twenty years in local politics "I had met far more discrimination because I am a woman than because I am black." Indeed Shirley Chisholm was so outspoken in favor of women's rights that she was often criticized for not paying enough attention to black issues. Of all the women who have run for president, she got the most votes. Over four hundred thousand people voted for her in fourteen Democratic primaries. On the first ballot at the Democratic convention, she got 151.95 delegate votes—largely from delegates who came committed to Hubert H. Humphrey (MN) but were released by him before the first ballot. No woman has done as well since.

Campaign Finance Acts Change the Rules

In the 1970s Congress passed several acts which regulate federal campaigns and provide public funding for presidential campaigns that meet certain criteria. All candidates for federal office who raise or spend over a certain amount of money have to register and file reports with the Federal Election Commission (FEC). Initially the threshold was one thousand dollars; now it is five thousand dollars. First affecting the 1976 presidential election, these requirements for political committees made it more difficult to run grassroots campaigns without running afoul of the law. Since most candidates running in the primaries and all candidates running on minor party tickets are perennially short on funds, all have been burdened by the new regulations and only a few (including three women) have benefitted from public funding.

Despite the uncertainty of how the new law would be applied, three women ran in at least one Democratic primary in 1976. Each one illustrated a different reason for running.

Gertrude W. Donahey ran only in Ohio, as a "favorite daughter." Before the primaries became the main means of choosing a major party candidate, state parties often ran one of their own as a "favorite son." These party stalwarts weren't serious candidates, but placeholders, to enable the party leaders to control the delegate votes of their states in negotiations with those candidates who were within striking distance of the nomination. Donahey had been elected Ohio's state treasurer in 1970—the first woman elected to a statewide office in that state. She may have been the only "favorite daughter" before this practice went out of style. Although she got 43,661 votes in Ohio's Democratic primary, she came in fifth out of six candidates with less than 4 percent of the vote.

Fifi Taft Rockefeller was a self-described "town character of Cincinnati." She liked running for office. In 1964 she entered Indiana's Democratic primary under the name of Fay T. Carpenter Swain (most likely her legal name), receiving 7,147 votes. In 1968 she tried to enter New Hampshire's, using the name Princess Running Waters Red Legs St. Swanee. In 1976 she ran in the Democratic primary of her home state of Kentucky as Fifi, getting 2,305 votes. She liked the publicity she got as a presidential candidate. When not running for office, she enjoyed attending trials.

Ellen McCormack was a single-issue, cause candidate. What motivated this housewife and mother of four from Long Island, New York, to twice run for president was her opposition to legalized abortion and her belief that the other candidates wouldn't talk about it if they could avoid it. Her campaign committee was composed of her friends on the Pro-Life Action Committee and her platform was a constitutional amendment to prohibit abortion. A registered Democrat, her 1976 campaign was her first run for public office. After visiting twenty-two states she received 238,000 votes in eighteen Democratic primaries. Although very few voters thought abortion was a priority issue that year, McCormack's campaign brought a lot of press. It also allowed her supporters podium time at the Democratic convention when they put her name into nomination. They used the opportunity to denounce the Democratic party for "becoming the Party of abortion." By raising $525,580 in donations of $250 or less per contributor from twenty states she qualified for $247,220.37 in federal matching funds for the primaries. She got twenty-two delegate votes from five states on the first ballot at the Democratic convention.

McCormack's success triggered a reaction from Congress, which had not intended cause candidates to receive federal matching funds. Congress added one more amendment to several already under consideration in the spring of 1976 to stop federal funds from going to any candidate for a presidential nomination who received less than 10 percent of the vote in two consecutive competitive primaries. For all practical purposes, that meant that funds raised in the year before the primaries began could be matched from federal coffers if otherwise qualified, but those raised after the first two primaries in which a losing candidate actively campaigned could not be. The Federal Election Commission interpreted "primary" to mean seeking the nomination of a party—even if it didn't have actual primary elections. Consequently, this new requirement was harder on candidates for major party nominations—which hold many primaries—than on those pursuing minor party nominations—which rarely have any. McCormack was the first and last woman seeking a major party nomination to receive federal matching funds.

In 1980 McCormack ran for president again, as the candidate of the Right-to-Life (RtL) Party. This party was founded in 1970 by the same group of mostly Catholic Long Island housewives behind the Pro-Life Action Committee. Becoming acquainted through a book club, they were radicalized by passage of New York's liberalized abortion law. RtL endorsed candidates in various races and also ran its own. In 1978 RtL ran Mary Tobin, another of its founders, for governor of New York and McCormack for lieutenant governor. When they received 2.6 percent of the vote, RtL qualified for a ballot line in New York. In 1980 Republican candidate Ronald Reagan lobbied for the RtL endorsement but didn't get it because of his support for pro-choice Republicans. RtL ran McCormack instead. She did not receive any federal matching funds for seeking her party's nomination. McCormack was on the ballot only in New York, New Jersey, and Kentucky (the latter two as an independent), but with write-ins received 32,327 votes in six states. The RtL Party continues to endorse candidates in New York which support its narrow anti-abortion stance.

The Left-Wing Parties
The movements of the 1960s—especially that against the war in Viet Nam—stimulated the formation of a lot of small parties; in 1968 nine ran their own candidates for president in twenty-five states. Some got enough votes to qualify for a semipermanent ballot line in different states, which

means they could run candidates without going through the more burdensome petition process for each election that was otherwise required. One of these was the California Peace and Freedom (P&F) Party. Founded on June 23, 1967, it has run hundreds of candidates in state and local elections in order to talk about its issues and maintain its ballot position, occasionally winning a few local offices.

As a left-wing party with a California ballot line, it has a valuable resource which it sometimes makes available to candidates from ideologically compatible parties. In 1971 it joined with similar parties in other states to form the national People's Party. This grouping ran tickets in 1972 and 1976 before being destroyed by the usual factional fights and attempted takeovers. Dr. Benjamin Spock, famous for his baby book before becoming an antiwar activist, had the top spot in 1972 and the second spot in 1976. Heading the People's Party ticket in 1976 was Margaret Wright, a black Los Angeles community activist. The Wright-Spock ticket got 49,024 votes from ten states, 85 percent from California. In some years P&F has run is own presidential ticket, but only in California. In 1980 Maureen Smith and Elizabeth Barron received 18,116 votes and in 1996 Marsha Feinland and Kate McClatchy received 25,332 votes. All four women are party leaders and regular candidates for various offices under its label.

Sonia Johnson was the official P&F Party candidate for president in 1984, as part of an arrangement with the Citizens Party, whose ticket she headed. Formed by disgruntled liberals in 1979, the Citizens Party was dedicated to returning government to the people, with a strong emphasis on environmental issues. Its 1980 candidate was founder Barry Commoner. Sonia Johnson had gained fame as a feminist. She founded Mormons for the Equal Rights Amendment in 1978, which led to her excommunication by the Mormon Church in 1979. In 1982 she staged a thirty-seven-day hunger strike in an unsuccessful effort to pressure the Illinois legislature to pass the ERA. On August 11, 1984, she was nominated as the second (and last) presidential candidate of the Citizens Party after former attorney general Ramsey Clark declined. Johnson ran as a feminist and a populist, demanding that minor party candidates be added to the televised debates. By raising $422,509 in contributions she qualified for $193,734.83 in federal matching funds for seeking the nomination. She was on the November ballot in twenty states and received 72,200 votes from twenty-six states, including write-ins. The Citizens Party soon died.

Not surprisingly, left-wing minor parties have been more likely than other parties to run a woman at the head of the ticket. Of the eighteen women to appear on a November ballot in the twentieth century, twelve headed the tickets of various socialist parties and two others were at least progressive. Of the explicitly socialist parties which have run presidential tickets, only the Socialist Labor Party has never run a woman for president. Founded in the 1870s, it fielded a presidential ticket every four years from 1892 through 1976. It did run a woman for vice president in 1972 and 1976.

Three other explicitly socialist parties have run women. The Socialist Party, founded in 1901, ran its first woman for governor (of Washington State) in 1912, and its first woman for president in 1988. Willa Kenoyer, a freelance writer from Michigan, received 3,882 votes from eleven states. Its second woman, Mary Cal Hollis, received 4,706 votes—mostly write-ins—from twelve states in 1996. Hollis was a self-described "stay-at-home mom" and former special education teacher who had once been a Democrat. These women illustrate the networks among left-wing parties. Kenoyer was formerly the national co-chair of the Citizens Party. Hollis sought the nomination of the Green Party, receiving 27 percent of the vote at its nominating convention (which Ralph Nader won).

The Workers World Party (WWP) has put the most women on at least one presidential ballot, though two of the four women were placeholders. They were the following: 1980, Deirdre Griswold and Larry Holmes; 1984, Gavrielle Holmes and Milton Vera in Ohio and Rhode Island (Larry Holmes with Gloria LaRiva in nine other states); 1992, Gloria LaRiva and Larry Holmes; 1996 and 2000, Monica Moorehead and Gloria LaRiva.

Founded in 1959 as a Stalinist spinoff of the Socialist Workers Party, the WWP is a small, disciplined party dedicated to leading a workers' revolution. It has run presidential tickets since 1980, rotating the top spot among its leaders. It added campaigns to its political repertoire in order to reach a wider audience for its views on national policies.

The first WWP candidate was one of its founders. Deirdre Griswold grew up in Buffalo, New York, in a family of socialists. Following in her steelworker father's footsteps, she dropped out of college to work in a variety of low-level jobs while devoting herself to political activism and union work. In 1970 she became editor of *Workers World*, the WWP weekly newspaper. She and her running mate campaigned actively, speaking in over seventy cities around the country and appearing on many radio shows. Griswold was the only actual candidate to show up when five left-wing parties held their own debate in New York City on October 9, 1980. In November she got 13,300 votes in eighteen states.

In 1984 the WWP ran Larry Holmes and Gloria LaRiva as its presidential ticket. However, several states would not put them on the ballot because they were both too young to be president. The WWP put Holmes' wife, Gavrielle, on the ballot in Ohio and Rhode Island with a different running mate because they met the age requirements, but campaigned for its real ticket, not the surrogates. Gloria LaRiva has been a frequent candidate. She was the WWP's vice presidential candidate four times and ran for numerous state and local offices for the California Peace and Freedom Party. In 1988 she helped change the ballot access law in her birth state of New Mexico as a plaintiff in a case to put the WWP on the general election ballot. The U.S. District Court found unconstitutional a New Mexico law requiring that all parties provide five hundred signatures of voters declaring that they were members of the party. The WWP didn't run a campaign in 1992, but did put Gloria LaRiva on the New Mexico ballot as its presidential candidate to hold the spot for future races. Even without a campaign, the WWP ticket got 181 votes.

Monica Moorehead was the WWP's most successful candidate. Born in Tuscaloosa, Alabama, in 1952, her family moved to Hampton, Virginia, in time for her to attend one of the few integrated high schools in Virginia. She became politically active after she refused to play "Dixie" in her high school band, progressing from selling the Black Panthers' newspaper to corresponding with Panthers in prison to working for prisoners' rights. After college she taught grammar school, joined the WWP in 1975, and was elected to its National Committee in 1979. In 1996, she and running mate Gloria LaRiva got 29,083 votes from twelve states. In 2000 they received only 4,795 votes from four states. Although their 1996 campaign budget was less than ten thousand dollars, they were still paying off the debt ten years later.

The Worker's League (WL) formed from a 1966 split in the SWP, but didn't abandon its Trotskyist roots. It ran Helen Halyard in 1992; she got 1,432 votes in Michigan (her home state) and 1,618 votes in New Jersey. Halyard has run for numerous offices as the WL candidate. In 1996 the Workers League founded and was absorbed by the Socialist Equality Party, which continued to run candidates, but not another woman.

The Most Successful Female Minor Party Candidate

The only woman ever to appear on the ballot in all fifty states plus DC was Lenora Branch Fulani, who headed the ticket of the New Alliance Party (NAP) in 1988 and 1992. Both times she ran with another woman. Their success in getting on the ballot was due to the rather unusual nature of the NAP. Founded in New York City in 1979, the NAP was the creation of Dr. Fred Newman, who encouraged participation in radical politics as part of his psychotherapy practice. Some alumni of his group moved to other states, where they started their own practices employing Newman's theories. The result was a cultlike group of a couple of hundred people dedicated enough to work full time for little or no pay, joined by a few hundred more supporters who worked part time for little or no pay.

Born and raised in Chester, Pennsylvania, Fulani joined Newman's therapy group in the early 1980s, while a graduate student in psychology at the City University of New York, and quickly became its primary public persona. Bold and articulate, she ran for numerous offices in New York before becoming the NAP's second presidential candidate in 1988. NAP had learned from its 1984 campaign what it needed to do in each state to get on the ballot. Wherever possible, NAP members took over small, single-state parties with their own ballot lines (e.g., the Solidarity Party in Illinois). It also had lawyers among its members ready and willing to go to court. The ability of the NAP's supporters to move from state to state in order to gather 1.5 million signatures on state petitions made Fulani, in her words, "a major minor candidate."

Although Newman had declared himself to be a Marxist, and even a Trotskyist at one time, the NAP's own political philosophy was muddled. It said publicly that it was black-led, pro-gay, and progressive, but it often attacked liberal political candidates and left-leaning groups. It supported almost any black leader who had a following, such as Nation of Islam minister Louis Farrakhan, who is not pro-gay or progressive, even when such support brought widespread criticism. Its members often joined other groups in order to disrupt them or take them over. In 1988 Fulani said her primary purpose in running was to take votes away from Democratic candidate Michael Dukakis. In 1992, Fulani ran in the New Hampshire Democratic primary to continue her attacks on Democrats.

NAP also gathered signatures for the 1992 general election, eventually putting Fulani on the ballot in every state except California, Oklahoma, and Florida. To get the coveted ballot line of the California Peace and Freedom Party, Fulani entered its primary, receiving almost 51 percent of the 8,289 votes cast. However, the P&F primary result was overruled at its nominating convention. There delegates refused to give her the nomination, reflecting the sour experiences many of them had had with the NAP.

The NAP was also very successful in raising money. For the 1988 campaign it raised $2,013,323.42, for which it received $922,106.34 in federal matching funds. For 1992, it raised $4,137,281, for which it received $2,011,929.42 in primary matching funds. NAP said over two hundred volunteers collected all this money by knocking on doors and soliciting donations on street corners, mostly in New York and California. Much of the money was spent for services provided by organizations created by NAP.

It was less successful in winning votes. In 1988 217,219 people voted for the NAP ticket. In 1992 only 73,714 did so.

Fulani liked running for president and probably would have run again if Newman had not disbanded the New Alliance Party in 1994. Instead, NAP members became heavily involved in what became the new Reform Party. They helped Ross Perot get on the ballot as a presidential candidate in 1996 and worked in his campaign. On March 19, 1996, Fulani filed her last statement of candidacy for president with the Federal Election Commission. This time she listed her party affiliation as "none."

The Other Minor Party Candidates

The only clearly right-wing party to run a woman for president was the American Party, which ran Diane Beall Templin in 1996. This party evolved from the American Independent Party created by Alabama governor George Wallace when he ran for president in 1968. After he returned to the Democratic Party in 1972, his creation broke into two competing parties. While both ran tickets in most presidential elections, both steadily declined in votes received and in the number of states providing those votes. With a budget of less than three thousand dollars Templin and her running mate obtained 557 votes from Colorado and 1,290 from Utah. She didn't get any votes from her home state of California, where she was an attorney and real estate broker and had previously run for office. In 2004 Templin once again was the candidate of the American Party but didn't qualify for a single ballot line.

Two other women have run for president as minor party candidates whose political views defy classification. Isabel Masters has made a career out of running for president. Born in 1918, she took up campaigning as her *second* career after many years as a secondary school teacher. In 1981 a "divine revelation [told her] to seek the presidency." She declared herself a candidate for president in 1984 but did not get on a ballot. The self-described "International Evangelist" succeeded in getting on the Republican Party primary ballot of Oklahoma, her home state, in 1988, 1992, and 1996. Her most successful year was 1992, when she was also on the primary ballot in Kansas, where she lived at the time. In 1992 and 1996 she headed her own Looking Back Party in November, but was only on the Arkansas ballot. Some of her six children shared her interest in politics. Two were her running mates. In 1992 she and Walter Masters received 327 votes from Arkansas and 12 votes from California (his state of residence). In 1996, she and Shirley Jean Masters did a little better, getting 749 votes from Arkansas, 2 from California, plus 1 vote from Maryland. Daughter Cora taught political science in the

District of Columbia and married DC mayor Marion Barry. Masters filed statements of candidacy with the FEC for the Republican Party nomination for 2000 and 2004 although she neither raised nor spent any money. As late as 2006, now retired and living in Florida, Masters was resisting the FEC's efforts to "terminate her reporting obligation."

Cathy Gordon Brown was on the 2000 ballot in her home state of Tennessee as an Independent, receiving 1,606 votes. She never filed a statement of candidacy or any reports with the FEC—only required if her receipts or disbursements were over five thousand dollars. But she did tell ABC News that "I always wanted to be the first woman president."

No woman headed a minor party ticket in 2004, although the usual plethora of minor parties were on the ballot in at least one state that year.

The Major Party Candidates

Between 1964 and 2004, twenty-two women were on the ballot in Democratic primaries and fourteen ran in Republican primaries—some more than once. Some states, such as New Hampshire, make it very easy to get on the ballot and consequently attract a lot of candidates; others make it hard. Most of the women, like most of the men, were only on the ballot in one state. One of these was Caroline Pettinato Killeen, who was on the New Hampshire Democratic Party primary ballot in 1992, 1996, and 2004. A retired Catholic nun from Scranton, Pennsylvania, she acquired the title of "Hemp Lady" from her many campaigns for the legalization of marijuana. Her best showing was in 1996 when she got 391 votes.

In addition to those already discussed, seven women were on major party primary ballots in more than one state. The most successful Republican woman in getting on the ballot was Tennie Rogers, whose name was on more state primary ballots than Senator Margaret Chase Smith's had been in 1964. A retired teacher and registered nurse, she got 7,677 votes in nine Republican Party primaries in 1992. A strong supporter of "Christian Family Values," Rogers got into politics when her uninsured car was hit by an insured driver and she lost her driver's license for a year. She became militantly opposed to mandatory insurance laws as an example of oppressive state regulation and ran for president to campaign against them (even though these laws are matters of state policy, not national). Although a California resident, she was not on that state's ballot. She later moved to Oklahoma, which had given her 674 votes in 1992. But she only got 47 votes (in New Hampshire and Mississippi) in 1996. She tried again in 2000—spending sixty-six dollars without getting on a single ballot.

The closest equivalent Democratic woman was Elvena E. Lloyd-Duffie, who was on the 1996 Democratic primary ballot in five states. An accountant and native of Arkansas, she got 92,324 votes in a year in which there were very few Democratic challengers to incumbent Bill Clinton. Only three other women have been on more Democratic primary ballots or received more votes (Chisholm, McCormack, and Braun).

Fewer women have run in Republican primaries than in Democratic primaries, but that is also true of men. Two women have run in the Democratic primary and also as a minor party candidate (McCormack and Fulani); one Republican has done so (Masters). Mary Jane Rachner was on the North Dakota and New Hampshire Republican primary ballots in 1988 and the Minnesota Democratic primary ballot in 1992. A retired teacher living in St. Paul, Minnesota, she told the press that she ran for president because the spirits of her late mother and grandmother told her to.

Most women who have run in the major party primaries have not been taken seriously as candidates. However, two women who did not appear on any primary ballots were. In 1987 Congresswoman Pat Schroeder (CO) explored the possibility of running in the 1988 Democratic primaries. Starting in June, by September she had only raised $872,462. Convinced that she couldn't raise the money to make a serious effort, she withdrew. In 1999 former Secretary of Transportation Elizabeth Dole also raised her finger to test the political winds. After receiving $5,461,958 in contributions she decided the Republican climate was too chilly. Instead, she successfully ran for U.S. senator from North Carolina in 2002. Despite withdrawing early from the 2000 presidential campaign, she received 231 write-in votes in the New Hampshire Republican primary.

The Twenty-first Century

The first presidential election of the twenty-first century saw not one female minor party candidate get her name on a general election ballot, but nine women did for a Democratic primary and one did for a Republican Party primary ballot. The most prominent of these was Carol Moseley Braun, former Democratic U.S. senator from Illinois. As a professional politician with a long track record in elected and appointed offices, she was taken seriously as a candidate. Her campaign took place primarily in 2003 because she dropped out on January 15, 2004. She was endorsed by the Political Action Committee of the National Organization for Women and the National Women's Political Caucus on the symbolic date of August 26, 2003—the eighty-third anniversary of the Nineteenth Amendment. However, by the start of the 2004 primaries she had only raised $627,869 in campaign funds—not enough money to run a serious race. After coming in third in DC's nonbinding primary in January she announced her withdrawal. However, her name was already on the ballot in several states, resulting in over a hundred thousand votes.

Changes in Public Opinion

In 1959 James Farley, chairman of the Democratic National Committee during the New Deal and legendary political boss, published an article in the popular magazine *This Week,* with the provocative title "Why We'll Never Have a Woman President." Even though he admitted that women "are physically stronger than men" and their "mental equals," he still believed that women would never make the grade because 1) women couldn't get "the broad, varied training now needed for the world's most demanding job"; 2) "women tend to be more emotional and subjective than men"; and 3) "she wouldn't command respect" as commander in chief.

Maurine Neuberger, wife of the Democratic senator from Oregon, promptly wrote a letter of disagreement, which Republican senator George Aiken of Vermont put into the *Congressional Record* of May 20, 1959. Perhaps as a sign that the times sometimes change faster than expert opinion, less than two years later she was elected senator from Oregon, and in 1964, Senator Aiken placed the name of Margaret Chase Smith into nomination at the Republican Convention.

At the time that Farley wrote, only 58 percent of respondents to the Gallop Poll were willing to vote for "a well-qualified woman of your own party for president." The positive responses would stay between 55 and 60 percent throughout the 1960s. Ironically, men were more likely to answer yes than women, as did more older people than younger ones. When this question was first asked in 1937, only a third of the respondents said they were willing to vote for a woman. After World War II almost half said yes.

When in 1972 a similar question was asked by the National Opinion Research Center, over 70 percent of both sexes said they were willing to vote for a woman for president. By then the emerging women's liberation movement was changing attitudes toward women, and public support for a wide variety of women's rights had increased significantly. Young people in general and women in particular had changed. In 1972 women high school graduates were more approving than equivalent men, and women college graduates were much more approving. Only among the lesser educated were men more supportive than women.

After that great leap upward the percent of respondents willing to vote for a qualified woman from their own party for president continued a slow but steady increase until it hit the 90 percent level in 1990. It has generally stayed above the 90 percent level, though responses have varied with the wording of the questions.

Some have argued that responses to questions like this don't really reflect what voters would do in the privacy of a voting booth. Many people hold generic prejudices which they won't admit to a pollster because they know these views are socially unacceptable. Their answers also change when the question evokes an image of a specific woman.

When Rep. Geraldine Ferraro was nominated for *Vice* president by the Democratic Party in 1984, Republicans were much less likely than Democrats to say that they were willing to vote for a woman for *president*. Republican voters, particularly those who voted for Carter in 1980 but voted for Reagan in 1984, were 10 percent less likely to say they would vote for a woman for president in 1985 than were willing to say so in 1983.

The image of Hillary Clinton running for president had a similar effect. A December 2006 *LA Times*/Bloomberg poll, done when speculation about a Clinton candidacy was much in the news, found that only 4 percent of registered voters admitted that they would not vote for *any* woman for president. When broken down by party, 6 percent of Republicans, 4 percent of Democrats, and 3 percent of Independents said they would not do so. There was also a gender gap; 5 percent of men but only 3 percent of women would not vote for a generic female candidate for president.

However, when specific women are matched against specific men, the responses bear little resemblance to the generic answer to the generic candidate. An Annenberg Survey done in the middle of 2004 found that if Hillary Clinton were running against President George W. Bush she would do no worse than Senator Kerry—who became the Democratic candidate that year. Similarly, Senator Elizabeth Dole ran almost as well against Kerry as Bush did. In this survey, a substantial number of the 7 percent of total respondents who said they were "very unlikely" to vote for a generic woman for president, would vote for Clinton or Dole when matched against Bush or Kerry. To sum up, despite some lingering antiquated attitudes about putting a woman into the country's highest office, partisanship is much more important than gender.

Sources

I'd like to thank the following people for helping me locate the information in this chapter and/or providing it directly: Sarah Chilton, Judy Baston, Michael Myerson, Jack Radey, Syd Stapleton, Brian Shannon, Gwendolyn Mink, Gretchen Kafoury, Jill Norgen, Elizabeth Martinez, Janet Spikes, Charlene Mitchell, Stoney McMurray,

Yolanda Retter, Gloria La Riva, Deirdre Griswold, and Larry Holmes. Information on campaign receipts, expenditures, and public funding for 1976 and later is available from the Federal Election Commission. Some is online at www.fec.gov. The following web resources were also useful, though the information on them is not always reliable: www.politics1.com and http://en.wikipedia.org.

ABC News 20/20 Downtown. 2000. The also-rans; Twelve presidential candidates not mentioned in most news broadcasts. November 6. (Brown)

Bennetts, Leslie. 1980. Goal of Workers World candidate is to spread the socialist message. New York Times, August 28, B8. (Griswold)

Bernstein, Phyllis. 1975. Anti-abortion candidate for president. New York Times, November 30, 126. (McCormack)

Carroll, Maurice. 1978. The unlikely beginning of the Right to Life Party. New York Times, November 25, 25.

CBS News/New York Times Poll. 2006. A woman for president. February 5. http://www.cbsnews.com/htdocs/pdf/020306woman.pdf.

Chisholm, Shirley. 1973. The good fight. New York: Harper and Row.

Ciment, James, and Immanuel Ness, eds. 2000. The encyclopedia of third parties in America. Armonk, N.Y.: Sharpe Reference. (Fulani, Johnson, McCormack, Moorehead)

Collier, Barnard. 1968. Crowd here cool to communists. New York Times, October 1, 64. (Mitchell)

Connors, Cathy. 1996. A third [sic] African-American Woman runs for president of the U.S. Amsterdam News (New York), Ethnic NewsWatch. March 2, 87:9:34. (Moorehead)

Cruz, Tania, and Eric K. Yamamoto. 2003. A tribute to Patsy Takemoto Mink. Asian-Pacific Law & Policy Journal 4, no. 2 (Summer): 569–97.

Dionne, E. J. Jr. 1980. 5 parties of the left conduct a presidential debate. New York Times, October 12, 34. (Griswold)

Farley, James A. 1959. Why we'll never have a woman president. This Week, January 18, 8, 9, 16.

Ferree, Myra Marx. 1974. A woman for president? Changing responses: 1958–1972. Public Opinion Quarterly 38, no. 3 (Fall): 390–99.

Fox, Mary Virginia. 1975. Lady for the defense: A Biography of Belva Lockwood. New York: Harcourt Brace Jovanovich.

Freedland, Jonathan. 1992. On the bottom of the ballot; Not for Bush or Clinton or Perot? Check out these candidates. Washington Post, October 31, D1.

Fulani, Lenora B. 1992. The making of a fringe candidate. New York: Castillo International.

Gottlieb, Martin. 1991. Minor candidate's fund-raising success turns spotlight on party. New York Times, December 31, A-16. (Fulani)

Grann, David. 1999. What you don't know about Lenora Fulani could hurt you: Coming soon to a presidential campaign near you. New Republic, December 13, 20.

Hafetz, David. 2004. Last of the true believers. *New York Times*, May 2, late ed., 14:1:4. (Griswold)

Harrington, Maureen. 1996. Other Arkansan ready for race. *Denver Post*, November 4, 2nd ed., A-10. (Hollis)

Honan, William H. 1968. If you don't like Hubert, Dick or George, How About Lar, Yetta or Eldridge? *New York Times Magazine*, October 27, SM 110.

Hypothetical showings of Hillary Clinton, Elizabeth Dole, suggest that women's chances of winning the presidency are better than some polls say, Annenberg data show. 2004. *National Annenberg Election Survey '04* press release, June 18. http://www.annenbergpublicpolicycenter.org/downloads/political_communication/naes/2004_03_women-for-president_6-18_pr.pdf.

Kihss, Peter. 1968. Communists name Negro woman for president. *New York Times*, July 8, 3. (Mitchell)

Koplinski, Brad. 2000. *Hats in the ring: Conversations with presidential candidates.* North Bethesda, MD: Presidential Publishing. (Chisholm and Mink)

Kupferberg, Seth M. 1972. Socialist fish in a capitalist sea. *Harvard Crimson*, November 3. (Jenness)

Lawless, Jennifer L., and Richard L. Fox. 2005. *It takes a candidate: Why women don't run for office.* New York: Cambridge University Press. (For public opinion on voting for a woman for president, see chart on 23.)

Los Angeles Times/Bloomberg Poll, Study #539. 2006. Clinton, McCain face obstacles on the road to nomination. December 13. http://www.latimes.com/media/acrobat/2006-12/26874703.pdf.

Lynn, Frank. 1980. Right to Life's political dilemma. *New York Times*, July 20, LI-14. (McCormack)

———. 1980. Right to Life Party won't slate Reagan. *New York Times*, August 27, A17. (McCormack)

Nelson, Jill. 1992. Fulani for president: Do ends justify means? *Ms.* 2, no. 6 (May): 86.

Norgren, Jill. 2002. Lockwood in '84. *Wilson Quarterly* (Autumn): 12–20.

———. 2007. *Belva Lockwood: The woman who would be president.* New York: New York University Press.

Owen, Penny. 1995. Woman plans 2nd presidential bid—Tulsan says she stands for Christian values. *Daily Oklahoman* (Oklahoma City), August 13. (Rogers)

Schmidt, Patricia L. 1996. *Margaret Chase Smith: Beyond convention.* Orono, ME: University of Maine Press.

Schroeder, Pat. 1998. *24 Years of house work . . . and the place is still a mess.* Kansas City, MO: Andrews McMeel.

Selbin, Eric. 1988. It's my party and I'll try if I want to: Third party alternatives to Bush and Dukakis. *Utne Reader*, September–October, 10–12. (Kenoyer and Fulani)

Smallwood, Frank. 1983. *The other candidates: Third parties in presidential elections.* Hanover, N.H.: University Press of New England. (Griswold and McCormack)

Smith, Tom W. 1985. Did Ferraro's candidacy reduce public support for feminism? *GSS Social Change Report No. 22*, November.

Smith, Margaret Chase. 1972. *Declaration of conscience*, ed. William C. Lewis, Jr. New York: Doubleday.

Sullivan, Bartholomew. 1996. Ark. woman says she has chance against Clinton. *Commercial Appeal* (Memphis), May 21, 1st ed., Metro: 2B. (Lloyd-Duffie)

Underhill, Lois Beachy. 1995. *The woman who ran for president: The many lives of Victoria Woodhull*. New York: Penguin Books.

Vallin, Marlene Boyd. 1998. *Margaret Chase Smith: Model public servant*. Westport, Conn.: Greenwood Press.*

Waldron, Martin. 1972. A female Trotskyite nominee stumping in Texas. *New York Times*, January 2, 57. (Jenness)

Woodlee, Yolanda, and Linda Wheeler. 1996. Cora Barry's mom eyes Oval Office. *Washington Post*, February 8, J01. (Masters)

CHAPTER SIX

~

Ruth Bryan Owen:
Florida's First Congresswoman*

In November of 1928 the voters of Florida's Fourth Congressional District, in a state that had not yet ratified the Nineteenth Amendment, elected Ruth Bryan Owen to represent them in Congress. She was one of three women, all named Ruth, elected to Congress that year. Two were the daughters of famous political men.†

Owen was born in Illinois, the oldest child of two lawyers, William Jennings Bryan and Mary Elizabeth Baird Bryan. As a Member of Congress from Nebraska for two terms and the candidate of the Democratic Party for president three times (1896, 1900, 1908), Bryan gave his daughter inside lessons on politics and campaigns. In 1908, at age twenty-three, she was responsible for his campaign correspondence, acquiring an intimate knowledge of the personal relationships involved in politics.

Ruth inherited from her father his oratorical skills, but not his love for the law. After two years at the University of Nebraska she married an artist and promptly had two children. She divorced him in 1909 and married a British Army officer in 1910. This spousal switch cost her her American citizenship, as a 1907 law specified that all married women took the citizenship of their husbands.

For many years Ruth traveled the world with her husband, bearing two more children and working as a volunteer nurse in a military hospital in

*Published in the *Florida Association of Women Lawyers Journal* (Spring 2000): 15.
†The other two "Ruths" were Ruth Hanna McCormick (R-IL), daughter of Mark Hanna (R-OH) and wife of former Senator Medill McCormick (R-IL), and Ruth Baker Pratt (R-NY).

Figure 7.   Ruth Bryan Owen (date unknown), courtesy of the Library of Congress.

World War I. As a result of injuries suffered during that war Major Owen became an invalid and the family moved to Florida, where Ruth's parents had retired. For several years she earned money on the lecture circuit and involved herself in community activities.

She did not run for Congress until 1926, after her famous father's death, and did not win on her first try. She did win her second race, after her husband's death, despite only token support from the Democratic Party organization and outspoken opposition from many voters who did not believe women belonged in politics. She won because she took her campaign directly to the voters, bypassing the organization, a tactic she had learned while campaigning with her father, who also faced hostility from his own party in many states.

Her Republican opponent did not readily accept his loss to a woman. He challenged Ruth's election on the ground that she had not been a citizen for seven years when elected, as required by Article I, Section 2 of the U.S. Constitution. Since Section 5 provides that "each House shall be the judge of the elections, returns and qualifications of its own members," the House Elections Committee held hearings.

Ruth argued her own case before the Committee. While she had not been vocal as a feminist, she effectively combined a feminist appeal with a traditionally feminine one. She told them that the 1907 law only applied to women, but not to men who married aliens. While the 1922 Cable Act made it possible for women like herself to be "renaturalized" it was difficult to do so. She had finally accomplished this in 1925.

Why had it taken so long? Because she had to care for and support her husband and family, and these duties were demanding. The new law was so exacting that it was three years after passage before she could meet its requirements without neglecting her family obligations. The Committee voted to seat her as a Member, and on June 6, 1930, the House concurred, by 66 to 30.

In 1930 Owen won reelection unopposed, but in 1932, she ran into a new kind of opposition: a special interest campaign to repeal Prohibition.

After the 1928 election, opponents of the Eighteenth Amendment began a major campaign for what would become the Twenty-first Amendment. One of their leaders was Pauline Morton Sabin, who resigned as the Republican National Committeewoman from New York to found the Women's Organization for National Prohibition Reform (WONPR). By the 1932 election it had grown to 600,000 members, of all political parties, and was targeting candidates for Congress who supported Prohibition.

Like her father, Ruth Bryan Owen was a strong "dry." Since Florida was a Democratic state, WONPR found a "wet" man to oppose her in the party primary. With Repeal as the main issue, Owen lost by two-to-one.

She wasn't out of office for long. In April of 1933, the new Democratic President, Franklin Delano Roosevelt, appointed her as Minister to Denmark (a rank lower than Ambassador). She served successfully until 1936 when she married a Danish Captain of the King's Guard. This gave her dual citizenship as a Dane, so she resigned her post.

Although Ruth never ran for office again, her political interests were passed on to her daughter, Helen Rudd Owen. In 1958 and 1960 she ran for Congress in California as Rudd Brown, but in a Republican district where she was defeated. Ruth Bryan Owen Rohde died in 1954, and was buried in Denmark. The Cable Act was amended several times until women's citizenship requirements were finally the same as men's.

Suggested Readings

Black, Ruby A. 1930. The Case of Ruth Bryan Owen. *Equal Rights*, April 5, 67–69.

Brown, Dorothy. 1986. *Setting a course: American women in the 1920s*. Boston: Twayne.

Chamberlin, Hope. 1973. Ruth Bryan Owen: Democrat of Florida. In *A minority of members: Women in the U.S. Congress*, 76–81. New York: Praeger.

Lemons, J. Stanley. 1973. *The woman citizen: Social feminism in the 1920s*. Urbana: University of Illinois Press; see 63–69, 235–37.

Miller, Kristie. 1999. Ruth Bryan Leavitt Owen Rohde: Speaker, author, diplomat, first woman envoy. In *Women in world history*, ed. Anne Commire and Deborah Klezmer, 13:425–28. Waterford, CT: Yorkin Publications.

New York Times. 1929. House will consider 5 contests for seats. November 29, 12.

———. 1930. Mrs. Owen defends her citizenship. January 19, 10.

———. 1930. Vote to seat Mrs. Owen. March 2, 25.

———. 1930. Agreed on Owen seating: House committee drafts report rejecting Florida contest. March 23, N1.

———. 1932. Wet rival leads Bryan's daughter; Repeal proponent ahead in Florida primary though Mrs. Owen favored referendum. June 8, 2.

———. 1932. Wets pile up lead in Florida primary; Mrs. Owen and Yon trail in congressional race. June 9, 2.

———. 1932. Ruth Bryan Owen, defeated for renomination, will quit. June 10, 1.

Root, Grace. 1934. *Women and repeal: The story of the Women's Organization for National Prohibition Reform*. Authorized by Mrs. Charles H. Sabin. New York: Harper and Brothers Publishers.

U.S. House of Representatives, Committee on Elections. 1930. *Arguments and hearings in the contested election case of William C. Lawson v. Ruth Bryan Owen*, no. 1. January 17.

Young, Louise M. 1980. Ruth Bryan Owen Rohde. In *Notable American women: The modern period*, ed. Barbara Sicherman and Carol Hurd with Ilene Kantrov and Harriette Walker, IV: 591–93. Cambridge, Mass.: Belknap Press of Harvard University Press.

~

CHAPTER SEVEN

Marion Martin of Maine:
A Mother of Republican Women*

The woman most responsible for creation of the National Federation of Republican Women in 1937 was Marion E. Martin of Maine. In 1944 she estimated that she could mobilize one million Republican women through the clubs in her federation. At its height the NFRW had 400,000 members, which made it the largest women's political organization in the country.

Martin spent her life in politics, where she was known for her thorough preparation and distinctive hats. She inherited her commitment to public service from her mother, who had worked for numerous causes and thought her daughter would make a fine legislator. In 1930 Martin was elected to the Maine House. She served two terms in the Maine House and two in the Senate.

To better do her job Martin took courses at the University of Maine between legislative sessions. When she found herself chairing the Senate's legal affairs committee—the first nonlawyer to do so—she commuted to Yale to take classes in the law school. There, one of her professors recruited her to work for the Republican National Committee.

After the 1936 Democratic landslide there were only eighty-nine Republicans in the U.S. House, sixteen in the U.S. Senate, and six Republican governors. In only a few years the Republican Party had gone from the majority party to one that could barely qualify as serious opposition. The new RNC

---

*Slightly revised from the version published in the *Maine Sunday Telegram* (May 14, 2000) City Edition, C:3.

Figure 8.   Marion Martin in 1968. She was Maine's Commissioner of Labor from 1947 to 1972. Photo courtesy of the Maine State Archives and the Maine Department of Labor.

Chairman, John D. M. Hamilton, decided to rebuild it into a "loyal opposition," with regular funding, professional staff, and an ongoing program. In 1937 he asked the new national committeewoman from Maine to become the assistant chairman for women's activities with the task of organizing Republican women.

Republican women's clubs had been campaigning for their party for over fifty years, but they went their own way and did not coordinate their work. After meeting with the other national committeewomen, Martin put together the National Federation of Women's Republican Clubs (NFWRC), with herself at its head and invited the existing clubs to join. Within a year clubs with 100,000 members had affiliated.

For the next ten years Martin nursed the Federation, traveling widely, writing pamphlets, and creating a structure through which every Republican woman who wanted to work could find a place in the party. She saw the clubs as a training ground for Republican women, teaching them political skills even while it put them to work for Republican candidates. She also used her position to lobby for women, urging Republican governors to appoint them to state offices, pushing state parties to give them more seats at national conventions, and urging women to run for office. By 1946, her federation had 400,000 members in its constituent clubs.

In the November elections that year the Republican Party gained control of both houses of Congress for the first time since 1928. The new RNC Chairman, Carroll Reece, fired Marion Martin. According to one report he "walked into Miss Martin's office" and said, "You have enemies on the committee. I want harmony here; I will appreciate it if you would sever your connection with us as rapidly as possible." While Martin never publicly gave a reason for her sudden departure, she appeared to be a casualty of the GOP's faction fights.

Respected in both parties, Martin was proposed to President Truman for appointment to the Federal Communications Commission, which had to be bipartisan. However, the director of the Democratic Women's Division, India Edwards, vetoed her because she didn't want Truman's first female appointee to be a Republican.

Instead Martin returned to Maine, where she served her state as commissioner of labor from 1947 to until her retirement in 1972. She earned a reputation for her innovative approach to labor problems, and for championing programs to benefit women.

After Martin was fired, the NFWRC began to cut the umbilical cord to the RNC. In 1952, it reorganized and renamed itself the National Federation of Republican Women (NFRW), with its own elected president and board of directors.

Suggested Readings

Baer, Denise. 1991. National Federation of Republican Women. In *Political parties and elections in the United States: An encyclopedia*, 2 vols. ed. Sandy Maisel, 683. New York: Garland Publishing, Inc.

Kanes, Candace A. 2004. Marion Ella Martin. In *Notable American women: A biographical dictionary completing the twentieth century*, ed. Susan Ware and Stacy Braukman, V: 415–16. Cambridge, Mass.: Belknap Press of Harvard University Press.

New York Times. 1987. Marion E. Martin dies at 86; Began G.O.P. women's clubs. January 11.

Rymph, Catherine E. 2006. *Republican women: Feminism and conservatism from suffrage through the rise of the New Right*. Chapel Hill: University of North Carolina Press.

Williams, Clare B. (assistant chairman, RNC). 1962. *The history of the founding and development of the National Federation of Republican Women*. Washington, D.C.: Republican National Committee.

CHAPTER EIGHT

~

Gender Gaps in Presidential Elections*

It is a popular misconception that the gender gap between the voting preferences of men and women began in 1980, or at least that that was the first
time that anyone noticed (Sigel 1999, 5). On the contrary a good deal of the
political commentary on women in the twentieth century was devoted to
real and speculative analyses about how women voted, or might vote, differently than men.

The 8 percent gender gap in 1980 was larger than any previously measured, but it was not the first. Prior to 1980 there were two presidential candidates for whom women voted at notably greater rates than did men: Herbert Hoover and Dwight Eisenhower.

The election of 1928 could well be called the "year of the woman voter."
Throughout the 1920s, most women had been relatively apathetic about politics, enthused by only a few local candidates and none of the national ones.
But Hoover was so popular that he became known as "the woman's candidate" (McCormick 1928, 22; Smith 1929, 126; Barnard 1928, 555). Some of
his popularity derived from his role as food administrator during the Great
War, and some from the importance of Prohibition in the election of 1928.
Hoover was "dry," Smith was "wet," and it was commonly assumed that
women wanted Prohibition to be enforced.

---

*Revised from a letter to the editor published in *P.S.: Political Science and Politics* 32, no. 2 (June
1999): 191–92.

Figure 9.   Top left: Hoover-Curtis-Pratt ribbon from the election of 1928. Top right: Harding-Coolidge ribbon from the election of 1920. Photographed by Jo Freeman from the collection of the late Marshall Levin. Bottom: Poll in suburban Philadelphia, election day, 2004. Photograph by Jo Freeman.

In anticipation of the election, women registered to vote in record numbers and the Republican Party's Women's Division was "besieged by unprecedented numbers of women who wanted to participate in the campaign" (Morrison 1978, 84). Hoover was endorsed by the National Woman's Party, the only major-party presidential candidate to be endorsed by a specifically feminist organization prior to 1984.

When the dust settled, both private and public commentators were impressed with the significant increase in the number of woman who voted—especially for Hoover. While scientific polling did not yet exist, straw polls recorded a gender gap. Robinson's review of these polls concluded that the Hearst poll was the most accurate; it had predicted that 60 percent of women and 56 percent of men would vote for Hoover (Robinson 1932, 92). Private reports to the Republican National Committee and to Franklin Delano Roosevelt estimated larger differentials, some that women were 10 percent more likely than men to vote for Hoover. Indeed these observations repeatedly emphasized the strong, conspicuous support of women for Hoover. Women were credited or blamed for the fact that Smith got a majority in only five Southern states and one border state, and even lost New York, while the Democratic candidate for governor won (Summary of reports in the FDR and Hoover presidential libraries; Morrison 1978; Lichtman 1979, 163, 291–93; Harvey 1995, 253; New York Times, November 8, 1928, 9:2–3).

Attention to women faded in the election of 1932, dominated as it was by the Depression, and fewer observations were recorded. However, when Gallup surveyed expected voters in 1936, he asked those who had voted in 1932 to declare their choice. Of those who said they had voted, 63 percent of the men had been for FDR, but only 57 percent of the women. Only 35 percent of the men said they voted for Hoover, compared to 41 percent of the women (AIPO [Gallup] Poll #53).

This differential voting pattern faded to less than 2 percent in presidential elections until 1952. Polls of voters done before and after that election found women were 5 percent more likely to vote for Eisenhower than were men, though both gave him a majority. Republican women gleefully claimed that women had elected him president (Priest 1953), and this belief soon became "firmly enshrined among American political lore" (Shelton 1955, D:1). Lou Harris's analysis of the Roper/NBC polls found a difference in male and female votes of 9 percent for those with high incomes, 6 percent for those with middle incomes, and 3 percent for those with low incomes, with women in all three groups more likely to vote for Ike. Harris attributed this to more women than men blaming the Democratic party for the Korean War, inflation, and corruption in Washington (Harris 1954, 112–13, 116, 222). By 1956 the press was once again paying attention to the woman voter. The

New York Times sent reporters into several states to find out why women favored Eisenhower (*New York Times*, Oct. 9, 1956, 22:3; Oct. 14, 1956, 49:2; Oct. 22, 1956, 1:3, 20:3; Oct. 23, 1956, 1:3; Oct. 26, 1956, 16:1; Brown 1956; French 1956). In the 1956 election the gender gap increased to 6 percent, though more men as well as women voted for Eisenhower than in 1952.

The election of 1960 saw women once again fade from political sight. Some of this was due to the ongoing campaign of the DNC to downplay the idea that there was a woman's vote, and some was due to the rise of new issues. The gender gap dropped to between 2 and 3 percent in 1960—too small to be statistically significant but implying that women still voted more frequently for the Republican candidate. The GOP women's division proudly declared that in the last three presidential elections a majority of women voted for the Republican Party, and a majority of Republican votes came from women (WD-RNC 1962). In 1964 as in 1960 the gender gap of 2–3 percent was too small to be significant, but it was notable because, for the first time, women were more likely than men to vote for the Democratic presidential candidate. In 1968 43 percent of both men and women said they voted for Nixon. But men were 4 percent more likely to vote for George Wallace (16 percent to 12 percent) while women were more likely to vote for Humphrey (45 percent to 41 percent) (Lynn 1979, 409). In the same polls, the traditional relationship between socioeconomic status (SES) and party preference disappeared. High-SES white women were 3 percent more likely to vote Democratic than low SES white women (Ladd and Hadley 1978, 240). In 1976 the gender gap was back to 5 percent, but now women favored the Democratic candidate (Lynn 1979, 409).

What's notable about this history is not merely that there was a gender gap prior to 1980, but that the pattern shifted in the 1960s. Previously the Republican Party had been the beneficiary of woman suffrage; subsequently the Democratic Party was. Furthermore, this change correlates with different attitudes by the national parties toward women and women's rights. While partisan differences were not large prior to 1980, they were present. Historically, it was the Republican Party that was the party of women's rights, and the Democratic Party that was the home of antifeminism. After the new feminist movement rose in the 1960s and 70s, the parties switched sides (Freeman 1987).

References

Barnard, Eunice Fuller. 1928. Madame Arrives in Politics. *North American Review* 226 (November): 551–56.

Bonk, Kathy. 1988. The selling of the gender gap: The role of organized feminism. In *The politics of the gender gap: The social construction of political influence*, Vol. 12 of

Sage Yearbooks in Women's Policy Studies, ed. Carol M. Mueller, 82–101. New-bury Park: Sage Publications.

Brown, Nona B. 1956. Women's vote: The bigger half? *New York Times Magazine*. October 21, VI:28, 63–67.

Freeman, Jo. 1987. Whom you know vs. whom you represent: Feminist influence in the Democratic and Republican Parties. In *The women's movements of the United States and Western Europe: Feminist consciousness, political opportunity and public policy*, ed. Mary Katzenstein and Carol Mueller, 215–44. Philadelphia, Pa.: Temple University Press.

French, Eleanor Clark. 1956. Key political force—The ladies. *New York Times Magazine*. March 11, VI:14, 32, 34.

Harris, Louis. 1954. Women: A new dimension in politics. In *Is there a Republican majority? Political trends, 1952–1956*. New York: Harper & Brothers, 104–17.

Harvey, Anna L. 1995. *The legacy of disenfranchisement: Women in electoral politics, 1917–1932*. PhD diss., Princeton University.

———. 1998. *Votes without leverage: Women in American electoral politics, 1920–1970*. Cambridge and New York: Cambridge University Press.

Ladd, Everett Carll, and Charles D. Hadley. 1978. *Transformations of the American party system*. 2nd ed. New York: Norton.

Lichtman, Allan J. 1979. *Prejudice and the old politics: The presidential election of 1928*. Chapel Hill: University of North Carolina Press.

Lynn, Naomi. 1979. American women and the political process. In *Women: A feminist perspective*. 2nd ed., ed. Jo Freeman, 404–29, table 3. Palo Alto, Calif.: Mayfield Publishing Co., based on Gallup Opinion Index, December 1976, report No. 137.

McCormick, Anne O'Hare. 1928. Enter women, the new boss of politics. *New York Times Magazine*. October 21, 3, 23.

Morrison, Glenda E. 1978. Women's participation in the 1928 presidential campaign. PhD diss., University of Kansas.

Priest, Ivy Baker. 1953. The ladies elected Ike. *American Mercury* 76 (February): 23–28.

Robinson, Claude E. 1932. *Straw votes: A study of political prediction*. New York: Columbia University Press.

Shelton, Isabelle. 1955. Spotlight pinpoints the woman voter, though '56 campaign is still off stage. Women's World column, *Sunday Star* (Washington, D.C.). May 15, D-1.

Sigel, Roberta. 1999. Gender and voting behavior in the 1996 presidential election: Introduction. *PS: Political Science and Politics* 32, no. 1 (March): 126–28.

Smith, Helena Huntington. 1929. Weighing the women's vote. *Outlook and Independent* 151 (January 23): 126–28.

Women's Division, Republican National Committee (WD-RNC). 1962. *Win with womanpower*. 16-page pamphlet.

Pro-Life demonstration at the 1976 Democratic Convention in New York City

Pro-Choice demonstration at the 1996 Republican Convention in San Diego

Figure 10.   Top: Pro-life demonstration at the 1976 Democratic Convention in New York City. Photograph by Jo Freeman. Bottom: Pro-choice demonstration outside a meeting of the Platform Committee before the 1996 Republican National Convention in San Diego. Photograph by Jo Freeman.

CHAPTER NINE

~

Feminism and Antifeminism in the Republican and Democratic Parties

By the end of the twentieth century feminism had become highly identified with the Democratic Party and antifeminism with the Republican Party. This development was neither planned nor predictable. When the women's liberation movement emerged in the mid-1960s its founders had no desire to become closely identified with any political party; many of them viewed both parties as representatives of a status quo which they disdained and the rest preferred bipartisan activity. Furthermore, the parties with which feminism and antifeminism became identified are the opposite of their historical affiliations. Over a period of thirty years not only did feminism become highly partisan in nature but the parties switched sides.

The original identification of feminism with the Republican Party and antifeminism with the Democrats was not a strong polarization. Not only was there much overlap in the party affiliations of both sides, but the antifeminists in the Democratic Party were largely social reformers who had worked with the feminists in pursuit of female suffrage. After ratification of the Nineteenth Amendment they eschewed the label "feminist," primarily because it was used by the militants of the National Woman's Party (NWP) with whom they disagreed on the Equal Rights Amendment (ERA) and protective labor legislation. Although they shared with the antifeminists of today some beliefs, such as a woman's need for protection due to her lesser physical strength, different emotional makeup, and special responsibilities for the welfare of the family, they never doubted that women were still men's equals.

At its founding in 1916, the NWP had chosen to follow the British example of blaming the party in power for any legislative failures. Woodrow Wilson was a Democrat, and his repeated failure to support suffrage until circumstances forced him to do otherwise forever tainted the Democratic Party in its eyes. The Congress which sent the Suffrage Amendment to the states for ratification was a Republican Congress and twenty-nine of the first thirty-six states to ratify it had Republican legislatures. In 1928 the NWP even endorsed Herbert Hoover for president despite the fact that he had not personally expressed support for the ERA. His running mate, Senator Charles Curtis of Kansas, was the chief ERA sponsor in the Senate and his Democratic opponent, New York governor Alfred E. Smith, was an ardent supporter of protective labor legislation. Most Democrats left the NWP as a result (Becker 1981).

After almost two decades of struggle, Republican feminists succeeded in getting an endorsement of the ERA into their national party platform in 1940. Democratic feminists didn't succeed until 1944, and did so then largely because protective labor laws had been suspended when women were needed in wartime industries. ERA opponents remained active in the Democratic Party and replaced the ERA with modified language in the Democratic platform in 1960. The ERA disappeared from the Republican Party platform in 1964 because the party wanted a short platform that year and thus left out issues it considered no longer relevant. Both parties left it out of their 1968 platforms; by then the NWP was so weak it couldn't muster much support and awareness of gender issues was very low. Indeed the 1968 Democratic Party platform did not so much as mention women, while the Republican Party platform expressed concern for discrimination on the basis of sex (among other things) (Freeman 2000).

However, by 1972 the women's liberation movement had captured public attention and put feminist issues back on the national agenda. Although there was some opposition to the ERA from a few new feminists in the late 1960s, the issue of protective labor legislation was largely mooted by court decisions on the "sex" provision of Title VII of the 1964 Civil Rights Act. The National Organization for Women (NOW), founded in 1966, made passing the ERA a priority. After a two-year campaign, the ERA was sent by Congress to the states on March 22, 1972; it was expected to be ratified quickly. Thus the ERA was not an issue for either the Democratic or the Republican parties that year.

A new organization, the National Women's Political Caucus (NWPC), was founded in 1971 to bring more women into the parties and into politics. Capitalizing on the greater interest in women and the greater numbers of women at the 1972 national nominating conventions, it was equally successful in influencing how the parties treated women that year. In the previous two decades women had fluctuated between 10 and 17 percent of the delegates. At the 1972 conventions women were almost 40 percent of the Democratic delegates and 30 percent of the Republican delegates (Lynn 1984). As a result of feminist lobbying both parties put support for the ERA back into their platforms. Neither platform committee was willing to include a plank supporting women's right to reproductive freedom—the Supreme Court decision legalizing most abortions wouldn't be issued until January 23, 1973. Feminists were partially successful in various fights over credentials and rules. After George McGovern, senator from South Dakota, won the Democratic nomination, he acknowledged women's importance by appointing the first woman to chair the Democratic National Committee (DNC). Jean Westwood served until McGovern was badly defeated in November. In 1974 newly selected president Gerald R. Ford appointed Mary Louise Smith to be the first woman to chair the Republican National Committee. She served until 1977. Neither national committee has had another female chair, though after the Democrats' devastating defeat in 1984 two of the six candidates for DNC chair were women (Sharon Pratt Dixon of DC and Nancy Pelosi of California).

Congressional passage of the ERA and the Supreme Court decision on abortion provoked grassroots movements against each of them. Begun separately, these movements eventually merged as the participants in each sought common cause against feminists, liberals, and seculars. Abortion in particular prompted partisan realignment, as pro-choice and pro-life voters switched to parties that conformed to their views, and candidates often switched views in order to be elected by their parties. The beginning of this switch could be seen at the 1976 conventions, though at that time the primary issue was the ERA. Abortion would rise to prominence in 1980 and stay there; the ERA lost salience once the 1982 deadline for ratification passed.

By the 1976 conventions the stage had been set for major battles over women's issues in both parties, but they were very different battles. In the Democratic Party feminists fought for power independently of other struggles going on within the party. In the Republican Party feminists fought for the ERA as part of the contest between Ronald Reagan and Gerald R. Ford to head the party's ticket. In the Democratic Party, feminists lost their battle but won the war. Feminists in the Republican Party did the opposite (Freeman 1976a).

In the intervening years, the NWPC had decided to institutionalize its party activities into two task forces, based on the lists of potential supporters its convention efforts had generated. The Democrats were organized first, largely because the party planned a miniconvention in 1974 to adopt a party charter. With its adoption, Democratic Party affairs would no longer be governed by a hodgepodge of tradition, convention decisions, and state, local, and national rules. The Republican Women's Task Force (RWTF) was organized in 1975. Although nominally composed of several hundred Republican women, throughout most of its subsequent history the work was done and the decisions made by a dozen women active in the liberal wing of the party, often independently of the NWPC. Since the NWPC was overwhelmingly Democratic, the RWTF became a cohesive subgroup within it, creating tensions which eventually resulted in its elimination. The Democratic Women's Task Force (DWTF) was less cohesive, had a rotating leadership, and was always subservient to the NWPC leadership (Burrell 1977; Feit 1979).

In the Democratic Party, keeping the ERA was not an issue, and a compromise was reached on abortion to oppose a proposed constitutional amendment eliminating it. The fight at the 1976 convention was over "50–50"— whether the rules should be amended to require that delegates to the quadrennial nominating conventions be half women. While Democratic women debated at daily meetings of a women's caucus whether or not to take this issue to the floor of the convention, a compromise was reached between the feminists and the campaign of Jimmy Carter. Carter sensed victory and didn't want a divisive floor fight. They agreed that 50–50 would not be demanded now, but might in the future (Freeman 1976b). As a result, the rules for the December 1978 midterm convention were changed to require equal division, and at that convention the Democratic National Committee amended the 1980 "call" to also require it.

As it had for Democratic women, the political environment for Republican women changed between 1972 and 1976, but it was a shift to the right. The person most identified with the defeat of the ERA in the states is Phyllis Schlafly, who as late as 1971 did not find it objectionable. However, in February 1972 she devoted an entire issue of her newsletter, the *Phyllis Schlafly Report*, to condemning the ERA for its detrimental impact on the family. Schlafly had long been active in the right wing of the Republican Party, whose ranks had been augmented in the 1950s when the National Federation of Republican Women expanded its numbers by recruiting many women active in right-wing causes (Rymph 2006). Until the ERA came along, Schlafly's concerns were primarily in the areas of foreign affairs and military policy. These activities and her publications gave her a wide base among conservative Republicans, which she mobilized against the ERA. The response was strong enough to prompt her to form STOP ERA in October 1972 with herself as chair.

Schlafly brought her supporters to the 1976 Republican convention for the purpose of removing the ERA from the platform. She also supported Reagan's quest for the Republican nomination for president. By 1976 Reagan opposed the ERA (having changed his mind); Ford supported it (and always had). All of the key RWTF members at the 1976 convention were tied to the Ford campaign personally or professionally. Feeling that Ford's reelection was the single most important contribution they could make to the women's movement, the RWTF chose to ignore abortion and possible rules changes in favor of working only to keep the Equal Rights Amendment in the Republican Party platform. Nonetheless, the ERA actually lost in the relevant platform subcommittee by one vote. This so shook up the Ford campaign that they ordered their delegates on the full committee to vote for it. It still won only by 51 to 47. The platform took "a position on abortion that values human life" after a 1:30 a.m. effort to remove all mention of abortion from the platform led by Rep. Millicent Fenwick (R-NJ).

In 1980 there was a good deal of tension between feminists and the leaders of both parties. At both conventions feminists had poor relations with the dominant candidate's campaign, but this resulted in their virtual exclusion from the Republican convention while at the Democratic convention it was merely a stimulus to alternative routes of influence.

Most of the Republican feminists who had been active in the 1972 and 1976 conventions did not go to the 1980 convention. Some had received political appointments from the Carter administration and thus were legally prohibited from participating in politics. Others were just discouraged by what they expected to be a hostile atmosphere. The ERA was easily removed from the Republican platform in the subcommittee. The RWTF recruited former RNC chair Mary Louise Smith, whose Republican credentials were too solid to be dismissed, to talk to the Reagan campaign. Consequently, the anti-ERA language of the subcommittee was modified to oppose not the ERA itself but federal pressure on the states that had not ratified. A strong statement in support of a Human Life Amendment was put into the platform.

By 1980 most feminists who were not personally tied to the Democratic Party were disaffected from it. They blamed the Carter administration for not doing enough to get the ERA ratified and to maintain women's right to get an abortion. NOW's Board and PAC had voted to oppose the nomination and reelection of President Jimmy Carter in December 1979, leading the Carter campaign to assume that they were supporting challenger Senator Ted

Kennedy. Although NOW was only part of the feminist coalition active at the 1980 Democratic convention, the DNC refused to allot hotel space for the usual women's caucus meetings. Instead women met at a nearby labor union hall. About 20 percent of Democratic delegates identified themselves as feminists in the first 50–50 convention, giving the feminist coalition a great deal of clout even though they were outsiders. The coalition decided to demand a platform plank that "the Democratic Party shall offer no financial support and technical campaign assistance to candidates who do not support the ERA." This won in a voice vote on the floor. Another measure added support of government funding for abortions for poor women to the support for the 1973 Supreme Court decision already in the platform. It won overwhelmingly in a floor vote. However, Democratic incumbent Carter lost to Republican challenger Ronald Reagan in November, mooting any possibility of putting these provisions into practice.

By the end of 1980, it was clear that the Democratic Party and the Republican Party were rapidly moving in opposite directions on any issue that could be identified as feminist. Feminists in the Democratic Party had a veto on any platform proposals or candidates for president they did not like, and antifeminists had a similar veto in the Republican Party. For the first time in many years, a significant difference appeared in the way men and women voted in November. Women were 8 percent more likely to vote Democratic, and men were more likely to vote Republican.

Because of their veto power, Democratic candidates for president in 1984 went out of their way to court feminists. Jesse Jackson dropped his opposition to abortion so he could be a credible candidate from the Democratic left (Bill Clinton would change his position for 1992). All of the candidates spoke at the NWPC convention in July, and courted NOW after it announced that it would endorse one of them. After NOW endorsed front-runner Walter Mondale his campaign put a NOW vice president on the platform drafting committee with authority to veto any proposal or language that NOW did not like. An incipient women's caucus, run by the DNC Women's Division, decided to focus its efforts on persuading Mondale to choose a woman as his running mate. The women put together a short list; Mondale chose New York Congresswoman Geraldine Ferraro.

After Mondale lost badly to incumbent President Reagan, party insiders blamed the feminist pressure to run a woman for vice president. However, polls showed that Ferraro's presence really hadn't made a difference one way or the other. If Mondale had not been so far behind before the conventions were held, he most likely would not have made such a novel choice. Candidates who feel victory is near rarely take risks. It's candidates who feel they have nothing to lose who try to do something different, in hopes that a long shot will pay off in the end. This time, it didn't.

Although the Reagan campaign never felt Mondale was nipping at its heels, the Republican Party did make a special effort to reach out to women. At the convention this influence could be seen not in the content so much as in the quantity of attention paid to women. Although the Republican Party has never required that half of its delegates be women, 48 percent were female in 1984, as were 52 percent of the alternates. One-third of the major speakers were women and for the first time the Republican convention had a large booth in the press area solely to provide information on women. Women and women's issues occupied a larger portion of the platform than ever before, though the content was dictated largely by Phyllis Schlafly and the Moral Majority. When anything was proposed in a platform subcommittee that might appeal to feminists, it was denounced and handily voted down. When Republican feminists tried to speak about their concerns for the platform, they were harshly quizzed about the finances of Ferraro's husband (Freeman 1985).

The RWTF had, for all practical purposes, disbanded. Because the Reagan administration's attitude toward feminist organizations was that they were extensions of the Democratic Party, many Republican women who were sympathetic to feminist issues would have nothing to do with the NWPC. Instead they formed the Pro-Choice Republicans and joined the Republican Mainstream Committee. These would continue to host events and hold press conferences at Republican conventions for many years, but would never have any power in the national party (Melich 1996).

Some Republican feminists returned to the Republican convention in 1988 to ask that all mention of abortion be dropped from the platform. However, most of the earlier Republican feminists were no longer involved with the party, or were part of the Bush team and more interested in avoiding divisiveness than in making policy. Thus it was mostly a new group of women, and men, who tried to remove the plank that said "the unborn child has a fundamental right to life which cannot be infringed." Nominee-to-be George H. W. Bush probably agreed with removal, since he had been pro-choice before becoming Reagan's running mate. But he said nothing and support of the Human Life Amendment remained in the Republican platform, along with opposition to "public revenues for abortion . . . [or] organizations which advocate or support abortion." Indeed, the 1988 platform was essentially the one that had been drafted by the Right in 1984. Support for child care was one of the few new issues (Freeman 1988b).

The activities of feminists at the 1988 Democratic convention were driven by an overriding desire to elect a Democratic administration in

November. For feminists, the Reagan administration was a disaster, as the only women he listened to were those who opposed everything they wanted. They swallowed their pride and made no demands. They held their tongues even when Democratic candidate Michael Dukakis chose as his running mate an opponent of federal funding of abortions. But by now feminists were getting pretty much everything else that they wanted. The Democratic platform had feminist planks and feminists had important positions in the campaign. Publicly at least, the parties had completely polarized on feminist issues; the Democratic Party was the feminist party and the Republican Party was the antifeminist party.

By the 1992 conventions each party's positions on women had become institutionalized to the point where they were not seriously questioned within either national party and where the differences were clearly evident to the voting public. Although the party platforms and the speeches at the conventions devoted many words to many issues, each party's vision can be summed up in a slogan. The Republicans articulated theirs clearly in the phrase "family values." While their platform did not define this slogan, both the document and the speeches indicated that it stood for programs and policies which strengthen the traditional two-parent, patriarchal family in which the husband is the breadwinner, the wife is the caretaker, and children are completely subject to parental authority. The Democrats incorporated into their platform the feminist view that "the personal is political" and put on the public agenda issues which were once deemed to be purely personal. The most controversial of these was abortion; the most recent was sexual harassment. In between were a plethora of concerns ranging from wife abuse and incest, to ending discrimination against gays, lesbians, and others living nontraditional lifestyles, to proposals to reduce the conflict between work and family obligations.

Abortion was still the reigning issue. No longer seen as just a "women's issue," or even a debatable one, it had become a deep moral conflict on which elections could be won or lost and on which deviation from each party's official line was tantamount to treason. Democratic convention chair Ann Richards denied the request of the Democratic governor of Pennsylvania, Robert P. Casey, to speak against what he claimed was the platform's support of "abortion on demand." She herself set the tone when she began her own opening remarks Monday night by declaring "I'm Pro-Choice and I vote." Virtually every speaker in the four-day marathon pledged fealty to choice and received thunderous applause. Nonetheless, the National Abortion Rights Action League (NARAL) and Planned Parenthood lobbied for the Freedom of Choice Act, by which Congress would limit the states' ability to impose restrictions on abortion. At the Republican convention, Phyllis Schlafly's STOP ERA was reincarnated as the Republican National Coalition for Life. Although not a member of the platform committee this time, Schlafly and her minions worked closely with the Bush campaign to "Keep Our Winning platform," as their lapel stickers declared. An attempt to remove all language concerning abortion was squashed. The right-wing conservatives were so dominant in so many states that former RNC chair Mary Louise Smith could not be elected a delegate from her home state of Iowa.

The ease with which feminists and antifeminists could have their respective positions adopted by the two major parties was facilitated by major transformations within each party. The underlying cause was a change in the social base of each party. Traditionally, the Republican Party had been the party of the middle class and the Democratic Party the party of the working man. Before World War II people with more education were more likely to be Republicans. The GI Bill sent the children of the working class to college, making them part of the educated middle class. They filled the ranks of the ballooning professions, but kept the political faith of their parents. As a result the relationship between party preference and education became curvilinear: the most and the least educated people were more likely to be Democrats while those in the middle were more likely to be Republicans.

It was the college-educated children of the working class that led the reform movement in the Democratic Party. This reform movement began in the early 1950s, but blossomed in the 1960s when the civil rights movement illuminated minority underrepresentation. The Democratic Party's support for civil rights stimulated a racial and regional realignment; by 1980 African Americans had replaced Southern whites as a key Democratic constituency. That year also saw the beginning of the modern-day "gender gap," as fewer women than men voted for Republican Ronald Reagan. In the six decades before 1980, when there was a national gender gap it was because more women were voting Republican.

The Democratic Party has always been a pluralistic party, in which representing an important group entitled one to a say in party policy. The reform movement within the Democratic Party changed the nature of that representation from geographic entities to demographic entities. The party morphed from a coalition of state parties and local machines into one of national constituencies. Organized labor retained its traditional clout, but over time it was joined by organized minority groups, women, gays and lesbians, and others who won acceptance within the party by their ability to elect delegates, raise money, and conduct quadrennial struggles over platform planks and rules changes (Freeman 1986).

The Republican Party began in 1854 as the party of progress but soon developed a conservative wing. Dividing on issues of national defense, foreign policy, and economics, the original conservatives were not culturally conservative. Many of those who won the party's nomination for Goldwater in 1964, including Goldwater himself, were pro-ERA and pro-choice. But these were not priority issues for those conservatives. They were priority issues for evangelicals, especially Southern evangelicals. When the Democrats' support for civil rights led to white flight, Southern Democrats joined the Republican Party, bringing their conservative cultural values with them.

This shift was encouraged by more traditional Republicans in the expectation that the evangelical voters would give the party victory at the polls. In the 1970s several well-known ministers were recruited by hard-right Republicans looking for troops. They in turn persuaded their deeply religious followers to overcome their repugnance to party politics as well as their traditional Democratic voting habits. Politicized by the legalization of abortion, evangelical Christians began to move into the Republican Party in 1980 to support Ronald Reagan. Pat Robertson's 1988 presidential campaign organized them to become delegates to the 1988 convention. Not warmly received by more traditional Republicans who found them rather déclassé, their persistence, organization, and numbers compelled their reluctant acceptance. As their numbers and influence inside the GOP grew, they drove out the party's liberal wing—the political descendants of the original abolitionists and progressives—whose voters clustered in the Northeast. Most of these eventually joined the Democratic Party, or at least voted for Democratic candidates. By 1992, the Christian right had the same hegemony over social issues within the Republican Party that the liberal constituency groups did inside the Democratic Party. They not only wrote the platform, but the party line.

References

This chapter is heavily based on my coverage of feminist and women's activities at the Democratic and Republican conventions. I've been to every Democratic convention since 1964 and every Republican convention since 1976. Some of my published stories are cited below.

Becker, Susan D. 1981. *The origins of the Equal Rights Amendment: American feminism between the wars*. Westport, Conn.: Greenwood Press.

Burrell, Barbara C. 1977. A new dimension on political participation: The Women's Political Caucus. In *A portrait of marginality: The political behavior of American women*, ed. Marianne Githens and Jewel Prestage, 241–58. New York: McKay.

Feit, Rona F. 1979. Organizing for political power: The National Women's Political Caucus. In *Women organizing: An anthology*, ed. Bernice Cummings and Victoria Schuck, 184–208. Metuchen, N.J.: Scarecrow Press.

Freeman, Jo. 1976a. The Republican Convention: What's half elephant, half woman and all establishment? *Majority Report* (September 4–17): 6–7.

———. 1976b. Something did happen at the Democratic National Convention. *Ms*, October, 113–15.

———. 1976c. Republican politics—Lets make a deal. *Ms*, November, 19–20.

———. 1980a. Republicans: Feminists avoid a direct showdown. *In These Times* 4, no. 32 (July 30): 5.

———. 1980b. Feminist coalition faces down the Carter campaign. *In These Times* 4, no. 33 (August 27): 2.

———. 1985. The women's movement & the 1984 Democratic & Republican Conventions: The search for a radical flank. *off our backs* (February): 11–13, 20.

———. 1986. The political culture of the Democratic and Republican parties. *Political Science Quarterly* 101, no. 3 (Fall): 327–56.

———. 1987. Whom you know versus whom you represent: Feminist influence in the Democratic and Republican parties. In *The women's movements of the United States and Western Europe: Feminist consciousness, political opportunity and public policy*, ed. Mary Katzenstein and Carol Mueller, 215–44. Philadelphia, Pa.: Temple University Press.

———. 1988a. Women at the 1988 Democratic Convention. *off our backs* 18, no. 9 (October): 4–5.

———. 1988b. Feminist activities at the 1988 Republican Convention. *off our backs* 18, no. 10 (November): 10–11.

———. 1993. Feminism vs. family values: Women at the 1992 Democratic and Republican conventions. *off our backs* 23, no. 1 (January): 2–3, 10–17.

———. 2000. *A room at a time: How women entered party politics*. Lanham, Md.: Rowman & Littlefield.

Lynn, Naomi B. 1984. Women and politics: The real majority. In *Women: A feminist perspective*, ed. Jo Freeman, 402–22. Palo Alto, Calif.: Mayfield Publishing Co.

Melich, Tanya. 1996. *The Republican war against women: An insider's report from behind the lines*. New York: Bantam Books.

Rymph, Catherine E. 2006. *Republican women: Feminism and conservatism from suffrage through the rise of the New Right*. Chapel Hill: University of North Carolina Press.

5Q/5♂ LEADERSHIP THAT WORKS

Figure 11.   Top: Republican Party Platform Committee votes the week before the 1984 Republican Convention. Equal division by gender has been required since 1944. Photograph by Jo Freeman. Middle: Bumper sticker from the personal collection of Jo Freeman. Bottom: Geraldine Ferraro and Walter Mondale salute the women's caucus at the 1984 Democratic National Convention. Photograph by Jo Freeman.

CHAPTER TEN

~

Gender Representation in the Democratic and Republican Parties*

In the late twentieth century, group representation acquired a "bad rep" in the United States. Yet for most of U.S. political history since the mid-nineteenth century, political parties paid particular attention to representing identifiable groups when putting together their slates. This was especially true in cities heavily populated by the descendants of earlier waves of immigration. A place at the political table was one part of the American dream. When I was a graduate student at the University of Chicago between 1968 and 1973, it was common knowledge that ethnicity was second only to loyalty when the Democratic machine run by Mayor Richard J. Daley picked people to run for public office. The rule then was that the Democratic ticket for the top city offices generally had to have at least one Irishman, one Jew, and one Pole. African Americans were rarely considered for these offices, though they did get a couple of state legislative and congressional seats in

---

*This chapter was originally prepared as a lecture for the Nordic American Studies Association, held in Trondheim, Norway, on August 7, 2003. I revised it into a paper and prepared the tables while I was at the Centennial Center of the American Political Science Association in the spring of 2004. I'd like to thank Elizabeth M. Cox, Eric Eisinger, and Sarah Chilton for their help with the research. Although some of the state party rules are online, most are not. I read them in the DNC and RNC headquarters in Washington, DC. I'm indebted to Ann Lewis, Phil McNamara, Erica DeVos, Christy Agner, and Geneva C. Jones at the DNC and Brian Marshall and Dyllan Rankin at the RNC for arranging access and assisting in locating the information in the tables. I was able to find most of the relevant state law online, but not all state codes are organized for online access in a way that made it possible to find out what I needed to know. I read the last dozen or so state codes at Boalt Hall Law Library at the University of California at Berkeley when I was on campus to give a lecture in the spring of 2005.

majority black districts. Women of any ethnicity weren't even on the maybe-list, though a deserving woman might be given a lower-level position after years of faithful party service—if she had the right connections. Since Chicago in those years was solidly Democratic, slating by the machine was tantamount to election, except in a few small areas of the city (Porter and Matasar 1974).

Although women weren't run for public office by the big city machines, they weren't ignored. Indeed, "making a place" for women was a well-estab-lished tradition within the parties if not by them. This tradition began with women's enfranchisement and expanded over the decades. It was strongly promoted by women working inside the major political parties who saw it as "an opening wedge" to greater influence (Blair 1929, 218–19).

Beginnings

Women got suffrage slowly, in bits and pieces, in different places over many decades. By the end of the nineteenth century four Rocky Mountain states had given women equal suffrage with men: two by territorial legislatures, and two by popular referenda. Colorado was the leader in bringing women into the parties.

Woman won suffrage in Colorado in 1893 largely as a result of the Pop-ulist Movement. The People's Party was stronger in Colorado than in any other state. As part of its effort to break the dominance of the Republican Party, it campaigned for and won suffrage for Colorado women. This at-tracted national attention and made Colorado something of a test tube for the participation of women in politics. At the urging of its women the Pop-ulist Party proposed that there be one man and one woman from each dis-trict on its governing committees (Sumner 1909, 58). While only partially successful, this idea was quickly picked up by women in the Democratic and Republican parties. It was erratically applied. Not until 1906 did the state conventions of these parties adopt equal representation as official policy. Im-patient with implementation, party women in Colorado appealed to the leg-islature. They backed their appeal with organization, having both Republi-can and Democratic women's clubs with membership in the thousands. In 1910, Colorado became the first state to require equal representation on party committees by law (Meredith 1934, 10–11).

Although only a few state parties followed Colorado's lead before 1920, the idea that for every committeeman there should be a committeewoman became known as "the Colorado Plan." Ellis Meredith, a Colorado suffragist and Populist who became a Democrat when the two parties fused, made equal representation one of her causes. She took it with her when she became director of publicity for the new women's bureau of the Democratic National Committee (DNC) created in December of 1916. By 1918, when both national committees were deciding how to incorporate women, the Colorado Plan had become the model. It soon became known as "50–50." For the next fifty years its attainment was high on the priority list of both Democratic and Republican women (Vaile and Meredith 1927, 1134).

Women's first success was in the national committees, their second in the state and local committees, and last of all at the national conventions. This reflected the respective importance of these bodies, with the least important being the most willing to accept women on an equal basis with men. By the time women achieved equal, or almost equal, representation at the national conventions, these bodies no longer made major decisions.

The National Committees

Party committees are the official governing bodies of the major political parties. While there are committees at many levels, the most important committees are the state central committees and their executive committees. In the nineteenth century each state party sent one representative to its national committee. Apart from running each party's presidential campaigns, the national committees weren't very important. They sustained the party between the quadrennial nominating conventions, but since most elections were state and local elections, there wasn't much to do. Within each state, the most important party committee is usually the county committee. Currently there are roughly three thousand counties, though there were fewer in earlier times. There may also be party committees for a wide variety of legislative districts. These vary from state to state, and can change over time. Depending on state politics they may be more important than the county committees.

Each state was authorized to send one woman as well as one man to the national committee by the Democrats at their 1920 national convention and by the Republicans at their 1924 national convention (*New York Times*, June 26, 1920, 2:6; Democratic Congressional Wives Forum [DCWF] 1960, 27; Republican National Committee [RNC] 1924, 90, 93). Prior to this formal expansion, each party's national committee appointed some women as associate members, the Democrats in 1919 and the Republicans in 1923 (DCWF 1960, 31; Good 1963, 15; *Literary Digest*, July 4, 1923, 15). At the 1952 Republican national convention the Eisenhower forces compelled the addition to the Republican National Committee (RNC) of those state party chairmen from all but solidly Democratic states (i.e. the South) (RNC 1952, 278–98, Rules 22 and 23). Although this was intended to reduce the weight of Southern committee members, women protested strongly that since the state chairs were male, it would reduce their representation as well. Nonetheless the *New York Times* reported that "as a battle of the sexes it was rather one-sided. The women made the speeches and the men got the votes" (*New York Times*, July 11, 1952, 1:4). In 1968, RNC membership was extended to all state party chairs, appeasing the South, but not the women. Women's demand that state vice-chairmen, all of whom were women, be added to the national committee was denied (Saloma and Sontag 1973, 95). A similar effort at that year's Democratic National Convention to add state chairmen and state Young Democratic presidents to the DNC was defeated by 1,349.25 votes to 1,125.75 (*National Party Conventions*, "1968").

The loss that Republican women protested was merely symbolic. Important decisions weren't made by either national committee. In 1950, Florence J. Harriman, who represented the District of Columbia on the DNC from 1924 to 1955, described it as "rather a farce. . . . We're just figureheads. That's all. . . . The National Chairman and the Vice Chairman runs it all" (Harriman oral history 1950, 29). Being a national committeewoman was not a route to influence but a reward for contributing money and service.

Although the formal organization of the national committees has not remained constant, custom or rules of both parties since the early 1920s have required that at least one woman be a vice chair or assistant chair of each national committee, usually with jurisdiction over party women. In the days when the national parties had women's divisions, its head was the top party woman, regardless of whether or not she was also a vice-chairman. Between 1940 and 1960 there was always one, but only one, woman vice-chairman of the DNC, while the Republicans had two out of four, neither of whom headed the RNC Women's Division. After 1937 the woman in charge of women on the RNC usually held the title of assistant to the chairman or assistant chairman and was paid for her services. In 1940 she became an ex officio member of the RNC Executive Committee. In 1971 her title was changed to co-chairman (Good 1963, 52–54).

State Party Committees

National leaders in both parties urged that the state parties adopt 50–50, but the receptivity of party men to this suggestion varied enormously. In 1922, after Emily Newell Blair was given the task of organizing the DNC Women's Division, she wrote the three thousand Democratic county chairmen for the names of the women on their committees. Only seven replied, and one answered "None, thank God" (Blair 1940, 15). To change this attitude, DNC Chairman Cordell Hull wrote all of the state chairmen, urging them to put women on their committees, even if that meant changing the state law. Only a few states passed statutes, but Blair reported early in 1924 that "in more than thirty States women have representation on state committees, and down through the county and ward to the precinct committees" (*New York Times*, March 16, 1924, IX:18:2).

During the 1920s the drive for 50–50 statutes was led by Republicans, in part because they controlled most of the state legislatures. Several states passed laws similar to Colorado's; some also required that the vice-chairmen of each committee be female, or of the opposite sex than the chairman, or that half the officers be female. Where 50–50 was not required by state law, it was often required by party rule. In 1927, the League of Women Voters found that "equal representation on the general party committees is now the prevailing though not universal practice, by party rule rather than by law" (National League of Women Voters 1927, 4).

In 1929 Blair assessed the effects of 50–50 as mixed. States which had not adopted it by law or rule showed no increase in the number of women on party committees; without a "special place" women did not get in at all. However, in 1928 Eleanor Roosevelt observed that "women who have gone into politics are refused serious consideration by the men leaders" and recommended that women organize women to back women political bosses (Roosevelt 1928, 78). Blair concluded that showing such prowess only caused a backlash: "as soon as women used their knowledge to their own advantage against some men on the committees, they found themselves replaced by women who did not have such knowledge" (Blair 1929, 220, 224, 227).

Despite these less than glowing assessments, party women in states that did not have 50–50 labored to get it. After Republican women in Illinois failed to add it to the state primary law they persuaded both parties to require it by rule on some committees (*Republican Women of Illinois* 1931, 4). The New York legislature passed several laws to permit parties to require 50–50 that the courts repeatedly invalidated. At the 1938 state constitutional convention delegates changed the state constitution to keep the courts from doing so again (New York Constitution, Article XIII, §1).

In 1933, when Molly Dewson took over the DNC Women's Division, she found Democratic women's "political participation was casual and spotty" (Dewson 1949, 1:54). Believing that 50–50 was the best way available for women to get responsibility in the party organizations, Dewson made it a priority. The Women's Division produced a study of state election laws and drew up model legislation which it urged Democratic women to have passed in their states. In August 1935 DNC Chairman Jim Farley sent a letter to all Democratic county chairmen giving his support for the plan, and asking theirs (*Democratic Digest* 1935, 31).

Without national pressure, state parties often ignored women's demands for representation. But even with it, they wrote laws or rules than ran short of equal representation. Some states defined the primary duties of the vice chair, or co-chair, as supervision of the party's women's clubs, and used the pronoun "she" to distinguish it from the supposedly generic "he." Others specifically made the female leader of a party unit subordinate to the male leader, even to the point of total exclusion from the ruling executive committee. When rules did require women on the executive committee, it was not in equal numbers with men (Segal 1971, 9896–97). In the 1950s the RNC held an annual campaign school for its state chairmen; the women vice-chairmen were not invited (Summers 1954).

There was a significant increase in states with some form of 50–50 during the 1920s and 1930s, but little increase afterwards. A study done in 1947 found that the Republican Party provided for equal representation on all party committees only in the states where it was required by law, and on some party committees in another twenty-one states. "In only eight states—Arizona, Georgia, Maryland, Mississippi, Nevada, North Dakota, Virginia, and Wisconsin—has no systematic effort been made to secure equal representation in either party, either by statute or by party regulation" (Fisher 1947, 89–90). More progress was reported in 1960 by a Democratic Party survey that showed 50–50 was required on all committees in twenty-one states, on some in nineteen, and on none in ten (DCWF 1960, 42). Those were the last systematic surveys done of 50–50 laws and rules before the present one.

During the 1970s, when the federal Equal Rights Amendment was being debated and ERAs were added to some state constitutions, Washington state Democrats challenged the 1927 law which mandated 50–50 on their state central committee as a violation of the state ERA (among other things). The state supreme court rejected their challenge, finding that "mandated equality" did not violate the state ERA or the First Amendment right to freedom of association (*Marchioro v. Cheney* 1978).

The National Conventions

Delegates to each party's quadrennial nominating convention are selected by each state party. Although a few women delegates had represented the full suffrage states before 1920, in that year women's participation jumped.

It jumped again in 1924, declined in 1928, then remained fairly stable until 1972. Unlike the national committees, the national conventions made important decisions for most of the twentieth century. Equal representation was occasionally proposed but not seriously considered. Through 1968 women were never more than 15 percent of Democratic delegates or 18 percent of Republican delegates. Since the Democrats permit divided votes and women were somewhat more likely to be given a partial vote than were men, their proportion of total delegates was slightly higher than their proportion of the total vote. Women were more likely to be selected as alternates, sometimes as much as 29 percent. Republican conventions traditionally have fewer delegates and more alternates than do Democratic conventions; women often found their place as alternates. Some states tried harder than others to choose women, though only the Florida parties required equal division. (See table 10.1.)

Women did better in gaining equal representation on the convention committees. There are usually four convention committees: Credentials, Platform (or Resolutions), Rules, and Permanent Organization. How important a committee is varies with the politics of each convention. Originally each state was entitled to send one representative to each committee; from the 1924 convention on at least one woman was on each committee at each party convention, with an occasional exception (DCWF 1960, 30). In 1936 Molly Dewson arranged for women to be appointed alternates to the Platform Committee so they could vote when their male delegate was not present (Dewson 1949, II:129). The 1940 convention voted to double the size of the next Platform Committee by permitting each state to send one man and one woman; in 1944 there were forty-two women on the Democratic Platform Committee (Blair 1940, 38; DCWF 1960, 30).

In the Republican Party, Maine national committeewoman Marion Martin led a similar movement. In December of 1936 the RNC voted for equal representation on future Resolutions Committees, but it was not enforced. The composition of the convention committees was not in the permanent rules; each convention passed a new resolution, though a perfunctory one. Beginning in 1944, Republican conventions voted that each state could send one man and one woman to the Resolutions Committee (Good 1960, 25–26, 41–42; DCWF 1960, 30; RNC 1944, 32, 36–37). The 1944 Resolutions Committee had thirty women; several state delegations had no women to send. In 1959 the DNC voted for equal representation on all committees at the 1960 convention. The Republican convention voted in 1960 to require equal representation on all committees beginning in 1964 (CQ Weekly Report, September 25, 1959, 1307; Good 1960, 41).

Table 10.1. Percentage of Female Delegates at the Republican and Democratic Conventions

	Republican Convention	Democratic Convention
1916	.5	1.0
1920	2.7	7.4
1924	10.9	14.0
1928	6.4	10.6
1932	7.5	11.6
1936	6.1	15.0
1940	7.8	11.4
1944	9.5	11.8
1948	10.2	12.6
1952	10.5	12.6
1956	15.7	11.2
1960	15.1	10.1
1964	17.8	14.3
1968	16.7	13.3
1972	29.8	39.9
1976	31.5	33.7
1980	35.9	49.8
1984	48	49.5 (1951/3942)
1988	36.4	48.8 (2055/4214)
1992	42	49.7 (2146/4319)
1996	32.8 (602/1836)	49.9 (2157/4320)
2000	34	48.2 (2108/4372)
2004	44	49.8 (2170/4353)

Sources:

1916–1932: Breckinridge, Sophonisba Preston. *Women in the twentieth century: A study of their political, social and economic activities.* New York: McGraw-Hill, 1933. Reprinted by Arno Press, New York, 1972, 289.
1936–1944: Fisher, Marguerite J. and Betty Whitehead. "Women and national party organization." *American Political Science Review* 38 (October 1944): 896.
1948–1956: Democratic Congressional Wives Forum (DCWF). *History of Democratic women.* 43-page pamphlet prepared under the auspices of the Democratic National Committee, 1960.
1960–1980: Lynn, Naomi. "American women and the political process." In *Women: A feminist perspective,* 3rd ed., ed. Jo Freeman, 410. Palo Alto, Calif.: Mayfield Publishing Co., 1984.
1984–2004: Democratic data from Elizabeth Wainright, deputy director for delegate tracking, Office of the Secretary of the Democratic National Committee. Republican data from a variety of sources: 1984 from the Republican Women Information Services at the convention, run by the National Federation of Republican Women; 1988 from Rob Fairbank, delegate tracker for the 1988 convention; 1996 from Lisa Ziriax, communications director of the National Federation of Republican Women; 1992 and 2000 are averages from delegate surveys done for news organizations; 2004 is from an RNC press release, which also averaged delegate surveys done for news organizations. Repeated requests to the RNC for more exact delegate counts for 1984, 1992, 2000, and 2004 were ignored.

Notes: At Republican National Conventions each delegate has one vote, so the total vote was used as the denominator in calculating the percentage of women. The Democrats frequently allowed delegations to split their votes so the total number of delegates had to be counted to calculate the percent women. States include territories and any entity allowed to send delegates to the national conventions. These varied from convention to convention.

There are some slight differences in the data. The numbers in the DCWF pamphlet (which start in 1892) vary from those in Fisher and Whitehead. Elizabeth Cox re-counted both women and total Democratic delegates from the *Proceedings* of each quadrennial convention from 1916 through 1964. I used her numbers to calculate the Democratic percentages for those years.

Data from delegate polls done by various media were obtained by the author at the conventions and are reported in the stories she wrote on those conventions.

Equal representation did not mean that women would be half of the voting delegates on the committees; it meant that each state had the right to send one female and one male delegate to each one. States which had no women delegates, or did not appoint one, simply lost a vote; this happened to several states in every convention. For some conventions the Democratic rules allowed delegations to select two members of the same sex for each committee "for which one of each sex was not available." As late as the 1968 convention, twenty-two Republican and thirteen Democratic delegations did not have the four women necessary for full representation on the convention committees (Segal 1971, 9896). In 1996, I was observing the Rules Committee at the Republican National Convention when a young man from West Virginia moved to change Rule 17 to allow each state to send two delegates of either sex to the convention committees. He said his state didn't have four women in its delegation and thus was deprived of representation. The woman chair quickly called for a vote, and without any discussion the motion was defeated in a voice vote by about two to one.

The slow movement toward equal representation of women took place between the suffrage movement and the women's liberation movement that emerged in the late 1960s. The latter, like the former, would catalyze greater participation by women in the political process but not in isolation from other changes that were going on. In the Democratic party these changes can best be characterized as a revolution; in the Republican Party they were more of a coup d'etat.

The Democratic Revolution

The Democratic Party traces its origins to Thomas Jefferson's and Andrew Jackson's Democratic-Republican Party—and even deeper to the antifederalists who opposed ratification of the U.S. Constitution. It has always been a coalition of outsiders even when it has been the dominant party (Freeman 1986). Workers, immigrants, the South, and small farmers have at different times been part of the Democratic Party's electoral base. The revolution in the Democratic Party was a result of conflicts between constituent groups in the coalition over the issue of representation. It was precipitated by the 1964 challenge by the Mississippi Freedom Democratic Party (MFDP) when it contested the seats of that state's all-white delegation. While the compromise that was offered (and rejected) only gave the MFDP two at-large votes, the issues it raised about participation and representation in the context of the civil rights movement transformed the Democratic Party. The 1964 compromise also provided that future delegations must assure participation by all the voters in the state, regardless of race, color, creed, or national origin. In 1968 the MFDP's successor was seated in place of the regular Mississippi delegation and Georgia's votes were split between the white regular and integrated insurgent delegations. Credentials challenges in another thirteen states were decided in favor of the regulars (*National Party Conventions*, "1964," "1968").

The 1968 Democratic convention was marked by turmoil and dissension, inside and outside. In 1968 state and local party leaders chose most of the delegates to the nominating convention, not the candidates. When the delegates met in Chicago, 67 percent of their votes went to Vice President Hubert Humphrey on the first ballot even though he had not run in a single primary. Because so many active Democrats felt "frozen out" of the candidate selection process, the Democratic Party created a commission to write national rules—rules which would provide guidelines for resolving the waves of disputes over who represented each state. One commission led to another, and in 1974 the Democrats held a non-nominating convention to adopt a national party charter. This became the governing document of the Democratic Party, to which all state rules and practices must conform.

The imposition of national rules that would supersede those of the state parties was the first revolutionary act. The second revolution superimposed onto traditional geographic representation a requirement for demographic representation, specifically for minorities, youth, and women in "reasonable" representation to their proportion of the population. Blacks had increased their importance to the Democratic Party when 90 percent voted for Johnson over Goldwater in 1964, a shift from about two-thirds in prior elections. Youth weren't yet voting, but were fighting the war in Viet Nam and protesting loudly. Persons between eighteen and twenty-one would be added to the electorate in 1971 with the addition of the Twenty-Sixth Amendment to the Constitution. Women were also organizing and speaking out. The National Women's Political Caucus (NWPC) was founded in 1971 as a bipartisan organization, but its Democratic Women's Task Force (DWTF) was always larger and more influential than its Republican equivalent. The DWTF had many personal connections to the party commissions writing and interpreting the new rules (Shafer 1983; Freeman 1987, 222).

In preparation for the 1972 convention most of the state parties tried to comply with the new delegate selection guidelines. I lived in a state whose major city—Chicago—did not. Mayor Richard J. Daley's complacency about his own powerful place in the Democratic Party was not disturbed by such trivial things as national rules. His machine would elect the delegates he selected, virtually all of whom were male.

Less than half of the states held primaries in 1972, but these elected almost two-thirds of the delegates. Some states had both delegate selection primaries and presidential preference primaries; some did not. In Illinois there was no presidential preference primary; individuals ran for delegate, either committed to a specific candidate or uncommitted. In Chicago the Daley Democrats ran uncommitted so that Daley could decide how they would vote at the convention. When I heard in the fall of 1971 that Shirley Chisholm—the first black woman to be elected to Congress—was going to run for the Democratic Party's nomination for president I decided to run for delegate in order to put her name on the ballot in Chicago's First Congressional District. There were only four of us in Illinois running for delegate committed to Chisholm, all in different districts. I came in ninth out of twenty-four in my district; the top eight winners were all Daley machine Democrats. The next day I read about an impending challenge of Daley's delegation by others who had run for delegate in Chicago. They were committed to a variety of candidates—mostly Senators Ted Kennedy and George McGovern—whose names appeared on the ballot beside theirs, but all lost to Daley's uncommitted candidates in every district in Chicago. I quickly joined in. Because the Daley delegation did not comply with the rules for demographic representation, the Credentials Committee awarded those fifty-nine seats to our challenge delegation, which fully reflected the minority, female, and youth populations of each district. Daley contested this decision in court, but the Supreme Court quickly declared that the national party rules were supreme (*Cousins v. Wigoda* 1975). Mayor Daley of Chicago did not attend the 1972 Democratic convention.

This convention was more demographically representative than any that had gone before. Women and blacks trebled their representation among the delegates to 40 and 15 percent, respectively. The number of delegates under thirty went up tenfold. Along with this diversity came eighty-two challenges to the state delegations (*National Party Conventions*, "1972"). Conflict and controversy at the convention, coupled with defeat in the election, led to a backlash. Party regulars who felt excluded blamed "quotas" for the defeat. A new commission rewrote the rules to emphasize good intentions rather than good results. They still required affirmative action, but if a state party submitted and followed an approved plan, it was not held responsible for inadequate results. Midway through the 1976 selection process, the number of black, female, Latino, and under-thirty delegates was running 15 to 35 percent less than in 1972. New, complex restrictions prohibited the challenge of delegations on the basis of composition alone. Mayor Daley and his cohorts took back their traditional seats at the 1976 convention.

The NWPC and the Caucus of Black Democrats didn't want this to happen again. They proposed stronger rules with "goals and timetables" for achieving specific results. Women especially wanted equal representation at the conventions from 1980 on.

The Rules Committee wouldn't agree to this, but there was enough support for a minority report, which would result in a floor fight. Jimmy Carter, the nominee-in-waiting, didn't want a contentious convention, so after several days of debate by women—delegates and nondelegates—meeting at the 1976 convention, agreement was reached to "promote" equal division at future conventions. In 1978, when the Democrats wrote the rules for selecting delegates to the 1980 convention, equal representation by gender was required for each state. The NWPC ran workshops all over the country to encourage women to run for delegate. In 1980 the DNC proposed amendments to the national charter requiring 50–50 on all national party bodies—convention delegates and committee members—and also on the Democratic state central committees. These were adopted by a voice vote at the 1980 convention and have been the rule ever since.

The Republican Coup d'Etat

The Republican Party took a different route. It was founded in the 1850s as a radical, progressive party. Throughout the nineteenth and early twentieth centuries it was the party of African Americans. It also ran ten to twenty years ahead of the Democrats in supporting women's rights and bringing women into the political process. However, over the decades that it was the dominant party (1860–1932) it also developed a strongly conservative section; these two tendencies almost split the Republican Party in 1912. The party survived, while conservatives continued to fight progressives for dominance within. Feminists within the Republican Party found their home in its liberal wing, but the conservatives were better organized.

The conservatives recovered from a devastating defeat in 1964 by developing direct mail techniques to raise massive amounts of money and by appealing to traditional Democrats with conservative social values. They were not opposed to the greater participation of women, or equal representation on party committees, or initially opposed to women's rights, but they were determined to take control of the Republican party. When they discovered that there was significant grassroots opposition to the proposed Equal Rights Amendment and also to the Supreme Court's decision legalizing most abortions, they quickly adopted these issues. Both issues became litmus tests in both parties, but for the opposite positions. Some conservative Republicans even worked to defeat liberal Republicans holding office, reasoning that it was worth the risk of electing Democrats to remove liberals from the Republican Party. Eventually the conservatives stigmatized the word "liberal" and drove Republicans who supported liberal social policies, such as abortion, into the far corners of the Republican party. Republican feminists, who long ago ceased to call themselves feminists or liberals, went undercover or left (Freeman 1987, 240).

Like the Democrats, the Republican Party established a committee (on Delegates and Organization) to review its rules after its 1968 convention. Its chairwoman was Rosemary Ginn, a feminist from Missouri, and its July 1971 report said that each state should "endeavor to have equal representation of men and women in its delegation to the Republican National Convention." Balancing demands from feminists and conservatives, it also added to the Republican rules clauses asking each state to "take positive action to achieve the broadest possible participation by men and women" while adding that "these rules are not intended to be the basis of any kind of quota system" (RNC 1971). However, without enforcement procedures, nothing changed (Melich 1996, 69).

The Republican Party did not write a national charter. Its rules, which are voted on at each national convention, generally defer to the state parties. The 1971 language put into the rules has remained to this day. Republican women have never organized to ask for equal representation of women at the national nominating conventions. Indeed, leaders of the Republican Women's Task Force of the NWPC said in 1976 that they considered such a requirement to be an "illegal quota" (Freeman 1979). Generally, since 1972 women have been about one-third of the delegates, but a greater percentage of the alternates. However, the convention hasn't had a contested vote on anything significant since 1976, so who sits in the delegate seats has little impact on matters of political importance.

What Happened

The Democratic revolution and the Republican coup d'etat were part of other changes taking place in American society as a result of the sixties social movements and were also part of a partisan realignment that was shifting the social base and the issue priorities of each party. In the 1970s the Democrats supplanted the Republicans as the Party more committed to women's rights. The first party platforms where this was strikingly apparent were passed by the 1980 conventions; that year was also the first presidential election where women were significantly more likely than men to vote for the Democratic candidate. Ironically, in the very year in which women were required by their party charter to be 50 percent of all national party bodies, they became roughly 60 percent of the national Democratic electorate.

These changes turned what had been a politically neutral issue before the 1970s—making a place for women—into a politically loaded one. The parties different responses reflected not so much their different attitudes toward women as their different political cultures. Essentially, the Democratic Party is, and always has been, pluralistic, while the Republican Party is homogenous (Freeman 1986). The components of the Democratic Party coalition have changed over time, but its nature has stayed the same. This made the party readily responsive to claims that it was unrepresentative. Women were one of the groups whose claim for representation was seen as legitimate; "gender balance" was seen as the solution. The charter also requires "goals and timetables" to achieve representation for minority groups plus youth, "as indicated by their presence in the Democratic electorate." Discrimination against many other groups is specifically prohibited.

The Republicans saw such group representation as a form of "quotas" which interfered with individual decisions to choose or be chosen. While its quadrennial rules also prohibit discrimination due to a variety of demographic characteristics, they stop short of the Democratic mandate for representation and defer to the states to decide whom to represent and how.

Current Practices

The Republican Party retreated from the practice of 50–50, but didn't abandon it. The national committee is still composed of one man and one woman from each state plus the state chairs—most of whom are men. The national committee is required to have "a chairman and a co-chairman of the opposite sex" plus four men and four women vice-chairmen. But equal division is no longer required on the RNC committees. The tradition continues of letting each state send one man and one woman to sit on the convention committees, but there are no mandates on the composition of the state delegations.

The charter increased the size of the Democratic National Committee to three times the size of the Republican National Committee; the sizes of state delegations vary with population. The number of Democratic delegates to their party's nominating convention is roughly twice those of the Republicans. While 50–50 is required, it has never been perfectly achieved. Places are provided for party and elected officials, who are more likely to be male. Similarly the requirement of 50–50 for committees has been interpreted to mean *all* committees collectively, not each committee individually.

However, since both the national committees and the national nominating conventions now ratify decisions already made, who casts the votes has only a symbolic meaning. The method by which the parties choose their presidential candidates continues to evolve; it is never quite the same from one election to the next. But it can safely be said that the convention delegates play no part in choosing the major party nominees, and haven't in many, many years.

The biggest change in 50–50 requirements is in the state party committees. Surveys of state party rules were made most recently in 1960 for the Democrats and 1947 for the Republicans. There were only ten states in which there was no 50–50 requirement at all (eight in 1947; the two states added in 1959 did not require 50–50). In 2003 and 2004 I reviewed the state party rules in the offices of the DNC and the RNC. While the language varies enormously, the Democratic charter mandate is not followed by the party rules in four states; various ways are used to get around it. In the Republican Party twenty-one states require gender representation on the state central committees, but not always 50–50. The rules of several state parties don't require 50–50 but do require that the chairman and vice-chairman be of the opposite sex (even when the word used is chairman). Party rules are less likely to require gender representation in the precinct, county, and legislative district committees than in the state central committees, and least likely to require it in the ruling administrative committee. (See tables 10.2 and 10.3.)

A review of state law reveals that many states have repealed their sections specifying the composition of party committees; others have kept composition requirements but removed provisions for gender representation. Colorado no longer follows the Colorado Plan. Its law on political parties now says that two persons shall be elected from each unit without specifying gender. Some state laws limit the election to one person per party unit (e.g., North Dakota, South Carolina), which makes it difficult for even the Democrats to engineer gender balance. Illinois, Louisiana, and California have different laws for the different parties, which authorize the Democrats to require gender representation, but not the Republicans. Oregon's and New York's gender representation requirements are optional. Some state laws require that the chair and vice chair be of the opposite sex, and that both represent their unit to the next higher committee; some that only the chairman represent the given unit. Only a few have changed the wording to "chairperson" (e.g., South Dakota). Many states simply defer to party rules on organization. (See table 10.4.)

There are not as many states today as there were before 1960 which require or even encourage equal representation in their state party rules or state

Table 10.2. Republican State Parties with Gender Representation Requirements in State Party Rules, Constitution, or Bylaws in 2004 (states are the fifty states plus the District of Columbia)

	SCC	GC	Int. Com.	Precinct
AL	No	No	No	—
AK	No	No	Yes+	Yes+
AZ	No	No	—	—
AR	Yes+ 2VC/OS	No	Yes+ 2VC/OS	—
CA	No	No	—	—
CO	No	No	No	No
CT	No	—	No	No
DE	No	No	No	—
DC	VC/OS	No	No	—
FL	Yes+	—	Yes	Yes
GA	No	No	No	No
HI	No	No	No	No
ID	Yes+	No	Yes+	—
IL	No	No	—	—
IN	Yes VC/OS	—	Yes VC/OS	No
IA	No	No	No	No
KS	—	No	—	No
KY	No VC/OS	Yes+	Yes+ VC/OS	No VC/OS
LA	—	No	—	—
ME	Yes+	No	No	No
MD	No	No	No	No
MA	Yes	No	No	—
MI	Yes+ VC/OS	—	VC/OS	—
MN	No	No	—	—
MS	No	No	—	—
MO	Yes+ VC/OS	No	—	—
MT	Yes+	No	Yes VC/OS	Yes
NE	Yes+ VC/OS	No	Yes VC/OS	—
NV	No	No	—	—
NH	No	No	No	No
NJ	Yes VC/OS	No	—	—
NM	No	No	No	No
NY	Yes	No	—	—
NC	No	No	No	No
ND	No 2VC/OS	No	—	—
OH	Yes	Yes	—	—
OK	Yes+ VC/OS	Yes+	Yes VC/OS	Yes+ VC/OS
OR	No	No	No	No
PA	Yes+ VC/OS	No	—	—
RI	No	No	No	No
SC	No	—	Soft VC/OS	No
SD	Yes+	No Alt/OS	Yes+ VC/OS	Yes
TN	Yes VC/OS	No	Yes+ VC/OS	—
TX	Yes VC/OS	—	No	No

Table 10.2. (*Continued*)

	SCC	GC	Int. Com.	Precinct
UT	No	No	—	—
VT	Yes	No	No	No
VA	No	No	No	No
WA	Yes+	No	No	—
WV	Yes+	No	—	—
WI	No	No	No	—
WY	Yes+	No	Yes	Yes

Abbreviations

SCC = State Central Committee or equivalent (sometimes called the Executive Committee)
GC = Governing Committee of the State Central Committee (also called Executive Committee)
Int. Com. = County Committees and various district committees
Precinct = lowest-level committee, whatever it is called
Yes = gender representation is required in the state party rules
Soft Yes = rules encourage but do not require 50–50
+ = officers, elected officials, county chairs, reps of other groups, but not by gender
No = rules cover committee composition, but do not mention gender representation
— = rules do not mention committee composition
VC/OS = requires vice chair of the opposite sex of the chair
2VC/OS = requires two or more vice chairs equally divided by gender
Alt/OS = alternate of the opposite sex

law. But what of the practice? No one keeps track of the sex of county chairmen, or of the other units of party representation below the state. Data on the number of women who have headed state parties is available from 1968 for the Republicans and 1976 for the Democrats. The Republicans had three women state chairs in 1968 and 1976; the Democrats had two in 1976. In August of 2004, the Democrats had nine women heading state parties and the Republicans had eight. Only the year before both parties had fourteen women chairing their state parties. (See table 10.5.)

One of the Democratic women was African American and one was Hispanic. Diversity has increased in both parties, even without any rule specifying the sex of state chairs. It hasn't quite reached the national committees despite the long tradition of representing women. Only one woman has headed either party's national committee: Democrat Jean Westwood (Utah) served for six months in 1972, and Mary Louise Smith (Iowa) chaired the RNC in 1975–1976. Each was chosen by her party's titular head, and lasted as long as he did.

Furthermore, while the rules may specify gender balance, or even a heavy gender representation, that doesn't tell you where the power lies. Very little political power comes from position in formal party committees. Most comes from a variety of factors, such as personal connections and the ability to contribute to the success of a party's candidates. Traditionally, men have had more of these but women are catching up.

Table 10.3. Democratic State Parties with Gender Representation Requirements in State Party Rules, Constitution, or Bylaws in 2004 (states are the fifty states plus the District of Columbia)

	SCC	GC	Int. Com.	Precinct
AL	Yes	Yes	Yes+ VC/OS	—
AK	Yes+ VC/OS	Yes+	Soft Yes	No
AZ	No	Yes+	—	—
AR	Yes VC/OS	—	No VC/OS	—
CA	Yes VC/OS	Soft Yes+Alt/OS	—	—
CO	Yes+ VC/OS	No	No	No
CT	Yes+ VC/OS	No	No	No
DE	Soft Yes+VC/OS	—	No	—
DC	Yes+	No	—	—
FL	Yes+VC/OS	Yes+	Yes C/OS	—
GA	Yes+VC/OS	No	No	—
HI	Yes+	No	Soft Yes	Soft Yes
ID	Yes+	No	—	—
IL	Yes+	—	No	No
IN	Yes+	—	Yes VC/OS	Yes
IA	Soft Yes+	—	Soft Yes	Soft Yes
KS	Yes+VC/OS	Yes+	Yes+VC/OS	Yes
KY	Yes+VC/OS	—	Yes+VC/OC	Yes+
LA	Yes VC/OS	Yes+	Yes+VC/OS	—
ME	Yes+VC/OS	No	Soft Yes	Soft Yes
MD	Yes 2VC/OS	No	No	—
MA	Yes	No	No	No
MI	Yes+VC/OS	Yes+	No VC/OS	No VC/OS
MN	Yes	Yes	Yes	Yes
MS	Yes VC/OS	No	No	No
MO	Yes VC/OS	Yes+	Yes	Yes
MT	Yes+VC/OS	Yes+	Yes VC/OS	Yes
NE	Yes+	No	Yes+VC/OS	Yes
NV	Yes VC/OS	No	—	—
NH	No	No	No	No
NJ	Yes	No	Yes VC/OS	—
NM	Yes+VC/OS	No	No	No
NY	Yes 2VC/OS	Yes	Yes	Yes
NC	Yes+VC/OS	No	Yes+VC/OS	Soft Yes VC/OS
ND	No VC/OS	No	No 2VC/OS	—
OH	Yes 2VC/OS	No	No	—
OK	Yes+VC/OS	—	Yes+VC/OS	Yes+VC/OS
OR	Yes VC/OS	No	No	No
PA	Yes VC/OS	No	No	—
RI	Yes 2VC/OS	Yes+	No	—
SC	Soft Yes VC/OS	VC/OS	Soft Yes VC/OS	—
SD	Yes VC/OS	Yes+VC/OS	Yes+VC/OS	Yes

Table 10.3. (Continued)

	SCC	GC	Int. Com.	Precinct
TN	Yes VC/OS	—	—	—
TX	Yes VC/OS	—	—	No
UT	No	Yes+	No	—
VT	Yes+	No	—	—
VA	Yes+	No	No	—
WA	Yes+	No	—	—
WV	Yes+	—	Yes	—
WI	Yes VC/OS	Soft Yes	Soft Yes	Soft Yes
WY	Yes+VC/OS	No	Yes VC/OS	Yes

Abbreviations

SCC = State Central Committee or equivalent (sometimes called the Executive Committee)
GC = Governing Committee of the State Central Committee (also called Executive Committee)
Int. Com. = County Committees and various district committees
Precinct = lowest-level committee, whatever it is called
Yes = gender representation is required in the state party rules
Soft Yes = rules encourage but do not require 50–50
+ = officers, elected officials, county chairs, reps of other groups, but not by gender
No = rules cover committee composition, but do not mention gender representation
— = rules do not mention committee composition
VC/OS = requires vice chair of the opposite sex of the chair
2VC/OS = requires two or more vice chairs equally divided by gender
Alt/OS = alternate of the opposite sex

Table 10.4.   State Laws on Political Parties with Gender Representation Requirements in 2004 (states are the fifty states plus the District of Columbia)

	SCC	GC	Co. Com.	Leg. Com.	Precinct
AL	—	—	—	—	—
AK	—	—	—	—	—
AZ	No	No	No	No	No
AR	No	—	No	—	—
CA	Yes+/No	—	No	—	—
CO	No	No	No	No	No
CT	—	—	—	—	—
DE	—	—	—	—	—
DC	—	—	—	—	—
FL	No	No	Yes+Opt	—	Yes
GA	No	—	No	—	—
HI	—	—	—	—	—
ID	Yes+	—	No	No	No
IL	Yes/No	—	No	No	No
IN	No	—	—	—	No
IA	—	—	—	—	—
KS	—	—	—	—	Yes
KY	—	—	—	—	—

Table 10.4. (Continued)

	SCC	GC	Co. Com.	Leg. Com.	Precinct
LA	Yes/No	—	No	No	No
ME	—	—	—	—	—
MD	No	No	No	—	—
MA	Yes	—	—	—	No
MI	Yes	—	No VC/OS	No VC/OS	—
MN	No	No	—	—	No
MS	No	No	No	—	No
MO	Yes VC/OS	—	Yes VC/OS	Yes	—
MT	Yes VC/OS	—	Yes VC/OS	—	Yes VC/OS
NE	—	—	—	—	—
NV	No	—	No	—	—
NH	—	—	—	—	—
NJ	Yes	—	Yes VC/OS	Yes	—
NM	—	—	—	—	—
NY	Yes Opt	—	Yes Opt	—	—
NC	—	—	—	—	—
ND	No	—	—	No	No
OH	Yes	No	No	—	—
OK	—	—	—	—	—
OR	No	No	Yes Opt	—	Yes Opt
PA	—	—	—	—	—
RI	No	—	No	No	No
SC	No	—	No	—	No
SD	No	—	Yes+	—	Yes
TN	Yes	—	—	—	—
TX	Yes VC/OS	—	No	No	No
UT	—	—	—	—	—
VT	Yes+	—	No	No	No
VA	—	—	—	—	—
WA	Yes VC/OS	—	No VC/OS	No	No
WV	Yes+	—	Yes	Yes	—
WI	No	—	Yes	—	Yes
WY	Yes+	—	Yes	—	Yes

Abbreviations

SCC = State Central Committee or equivalent (sometimes called the Executive Committee)
GC = Governing Committee of the State Central Committee (also called Executive Committee)
Co. Com. = County Committees
Leg. Com. = Various legislative district committees (e.g., Congress, State Senate, Assembly)
Precinct = lowest-level committee, whatever it is called
Yes = gender representation in party committees is required in the state party law
Soft Yes = law encourages but does not require 50–50
Opt = law specifies gender representation, but makes it optional
+ = officers, elected officials, county chairs, reps of other groups, but not by gender
No = law covers committee composition, but does not mention gender representation
— = law does not mention committee composition
Yes/No = law has different requirements for the two major parties, though not always by name
VC/OS = requires vice chair of the opposite sex of the chair

Table 10.5.   Number of Women and Men State Party Chairs

	Democrats		Republicans	
	W	*M*	*W*	*M*
1968	—	—	3	47
1972	—	—	2	52
1976	2	53	3	51
1980	7	49	8	46
1984	4	53	9	45
1988	10	46	9	46
1992	7	49	9	46
1996	14	42	7	48
2000	15	41	—	—
2003	14	42	14	41
2004	9	47	8	47
2007	6	49	—	—

Source: Geneva C. Jones of the DNC, and Brian Marshall and Dyllan Rankin of the RNC. The RNC couldn't find the numbers for 2000 and my requests for 2007 numbers were ignored.
Notes: States include the fifty states, the District of Columbia, Puerto Rico, and other bodies which send delegates to the national nominating conventions. At different times these were Guam, the Virgin Islands, the Canal Zone, American Samoa, and Democrats Abroad.

Conclusion

What then do we make of almost a century's experience with rules requiring gender representation in the governing bodies of U.S. political parties? Is it more than just window dressing? The studies of 50–50 are so few and far between that what little we do know comes more from impressions and anecdotes. They tell us that 50–50 might bring women in, but equal representation by itself does not bring much influence. Yet women have clung to 50–50, demanded it when they could, and given it up only when they had to. Were they naive? I think the answer lies in one's expectations. Gender representation of women did not bring direct, short-term benefits, except perhaps to a few individuals. But it did contribute to indirect, long-term changes. It gave more women exposure to and experience in party politics than would have attained these absent 50–50. And it got men used to having women around. When other social changes—specifically the feminist movement of the late twentieth century—opened the doors to women's greater participation in all aspects of society, and made female leadership acceptable, political women were ready, and political men were almost ready. The decades of experience with 50–50 did not make women's greater political participation possible, but did make it easier.

References

Blair, Emily Newell. 1929. Women in the political parties. *Annals of the American Academy of Political and Social Science* 143 (May): 217–29.

———. 1940. Advance of Democratic women. *Democratic Digest* 17, no. 4 (April): 15, 38.

Cousins v. Wigoda. 1975. 419 U.S. 477, 95 S.Ct. 541, 42 L.Ed.2d 595.

Democratic Congressional Wives Forum (DCWF). 1960. *History of Democratic women.* Forty-three-page pamphlet prepared under the auspices of the Democratic National Committee.

Democratic Digest. 1931. Chairman Farley asks fifty-fifty. August, 31.

Democratic National Committee and Democratic Congressional Committee, Women's Division. 1945. *Democratic women march on.* Twenty-page booklet.

Democratic National Committee, Commission on Delegate Selection and Party Structure. 1973. *Democrats all.* Washington, D.C.: Democratic National Committee.

Dewson, Mary W. 1949. *An aid to the end.* Unpublished autobiography in two volumes. (Copies are at the FDR Library, Hyde Park, N.Y., and the Schlesinger Library, Cambridge, Mass.)

Fisher, Marguerite J. 1947. Women in the political parties. *Annals of the American Academy of Political and Social Science* 251 (May): 87–93.

Freeman, Jo. 1979. Women map delegate selection plans. *Congressional Quarterly Weekly Report* (August 4): 1615.

———. 1986. The political culture of the Democratic and Republican parties. *Political Science Quarterly* 101, no. 3 (Fall): 327–56.

———. 1987. Whom you know vs. whom you represent: Feminist influence in the Democratic and Republican parties. In *The women's movements of the United States and Western Europe: Feminist consciousness, political opportunity and public policy*, ed. Mary Katzenstein and Carol Mueller, 215–44. Philadelphia, Pa.: Temple University Press.

———. 2000. *A room at a time: How women entered party politics.* Lanham, Md.: Rowman & Littlefield.

Good, Josephine L. 1963. *The history of women in Republican National Conventions and women in the Republican National Committee.* Fifty-four-page pamphlet. Washington, D.C.: Republican National Committee, April.

Harriman, Florence (Daisy). 1950. *The reminiscences of Florence Jaffray Harriman.* Oral history interviews with Allan Nevins, Dean Albertson, and John D. Kennedy in April 1950. Oral History Research Office, Columbia University, New York.

Marchioro v. Cheney. 1978. 90 Wn.2d 298; 582 P.2d 487.

Melich, Tanya. 1996. *The Republican war against women: An insider's report from behind the lines.* New York: Bantam.

Meredith, Ellis. 1934. Again—and yet again—organize. *Democratic Digest*, May, 10–11.

National League of Women Voters, Committee on the Legal Status of Women. 1927. *The legal and political status of women in the United States: A summary of the out-*

standing facts in the present situation. Fifteen-page pamphlet. Washington, D.C.: League of Women Voters.

National Party Conventions, 1831—. Washington, D.C.: Congressional Quarterly. Updated every four years to add the most recent conventions.

Porter, Mary Cornelia, and Ann B. Matasar. 1974. The role and status of women in the Daley organization. In *Woman and politics,* ed. Jane S. Jaquette, 85–108. New York: Wiley.

Republican National Committee. 1924. *Official report of the proceedings of the 18th Republican National Convention held in Cleveland, Ohio, June 10, 11, & 12, 1924.* New York: The Tenny Press.

———. 1944. *Official report of the proceedings of the 23th Republican National Convention held in Chicago, Illinois, June 26, 27, & 28, 1944.* Washington, D.C.: Judd & Detweiler.

———. 1952. *Official report of the proceedings of the 25th Republican National Convention held in Chicago, Illinois, July 7, 8, 9, 10, & 11, 1952.* Washington, D.C.: Judd & Detweiler.

———. 1971. *The delegate selection procedures for the Republican Party II: Progress report (of the) DO Committee.* Washington, D.C.: Republican National Committee, July 23.

Roosevelt, Eleanor. 1928. Women must learn to play the game as men do. *Redbook 1,* no. 6 (April): 78–79, 141–42.

Saloma, John S. III, and Frederick H. Sontag. 1973. *Parties: The real opportunity for effective citizen politics.* New York: Vintage Books.

Segal, Phyllis N. 1971. Women and political parties: The legal dimension of discrimination. Unpublished paper inserted into *Congressional Record 117,* April 6, 9896–97, by Rep. Martha Griffiths (D-MI).

Shafer, Byron E. 1983. *The quiet revolution: The struggle for the Democratic Party and the shaping of post-reform politics.* New York: Russell Sage Foundation.

Summers, Eileen. 1954[?] Women long way from top. *Washington Post,* in "Papers of Katie Louchheim," oversize container no. 3, Library of Congress.

Sumner, Helen L. 1909. *Equal suffrage: The results of an investigation in Colorado made for the Collegiate Equal Suffrage League of New York State.* New York: Harper and Bro. Reprint. New York: Arno Press, 1972.

Vaile, Anna Wolcott, and Ellis Meredith. 1927. Woman's contribution. In *History of Colorado,* ed. Leroy Hafen and James H. Baker, 3:1075–1147. Denver: Lewis Historical.

What do we mean when we say 50–50? 1931. *Republican Women of Illinois,* February, p. 4.

PART III

PROMOTING POLICY

Figure 12.   Clockwise from top: Executive committee of the National League of Women Voters, left to right: Elizabeth Hauser, Katherine Ludington, Ruth Morgan, Belle Sherwin, and Maud Wood Park, 1924 (image no. LC-USZ62-122140 from the National League of Women Voters Collection at the Library of Congress); Three women work at the card index files at the headquarters of the National Woman's Party in Washington, DC, 1920 (image no. LC-USZ62-112771 from the National Photo Company Collection at the Library of Congress); Alice Paul, chairman, and officers of the National Woman's Party: Sue White, Mrs. Benigna Green Kalb, Mrs. James Rector, Mary Dubrow, and Elizabeth Kalb in front of their Washington headquarters holding a banner with a Susan B. Anthony quote, 1920 (image no. LC-USZ62-95442 from the National Photo Company Collection at the Library of Congress); Subcommittee of the Women's Joint Congressional Committee working on passage of the Sheppard-Towner Maternity Relief Bill: Mary Stewart, Mrs. Ellis Yost, Mrs. Maud Wood Park, Jeannette Rankin, Mrs. Florence Kelley, Lida Hafford, Mrs. La Rue Brown, Adah Bush, Betsy Edwards, Mrs. Raymond Morgan, Mrs. Arthur Watkins, Mrs. Milton P. Higgins, and Amy Maher, 1921 (image no. LC-USZ62-63740 from the Library of Congress).

CHAPTER ELEVEN

~

"Equality" vs. "Protection": Setting the Agenda after Suffrage

The thing that marks the Woman's Party off from the other groups in the woman's movement in America . . . is an attitude toward women and toward the work for their emancipation. . . . It, alone, of all the national organizations of American women, holds beyond any possibility of compromise that women are the equals of men; it repudiates both privileges and disabilities based on sex in every sphere of human activity, and it possesses both a program of action designed to remove the remaining forms of the subjection of women, and the spirit to see this program through.

—*Equal Rights*, official organ of the
National Woman's Party, September 18, 1926[1]

It is with great regret that some of us recognize that the small group of women in the National Woman's Party who were in favor of suffrage and who worked with us for suffrage, should have taken this doctrinaire position which makes more difficult the passage and maintenance of legislation aimed to improve the conditions of their working sisters, which was one of the primary reasons why many women wanted to vote and many wanted to have them vote.

—Secretary of Labor Frances Perkins to
Florence A. Armstrong, July 10, 1944[2]

I have never approved of the National Woman's Party. I think they are a perfectly useless organization. . . . where laws are unequal they should be eliminated, but if the National Woman's Party would devote a little more time to working in the states to do this and a little less time on a national amendment which will not mean much when achieved, I think it will not take long to eliminate these laws.

—Eleanor Roosevelt, 1952[3]

The Woman Suffrage Movement was not a united movement. It had two distinct branches with different strategies and different goals which were not abandoned even after suffrage was attained. The moderate branch was by far the larger and is given most of the credit for the Nineteenth Amendment. Although dominated by the National American Woman Suffrage Association (NAWSA), it was in fact a coalition of groups that arose during the Progressive Movement of the late nineteenth and early twentieth centuries to pursue a variety of social reforms. Once convinced that female suffrage would aid their accomplishment, reformers worked with NAWSA president Carrie Chapman Catt, who mobilized the ratification campaign through NAWSA's state chapters. Even before final ratification Catt successfully urged her followers to disband the organization and form a nonpartisan, nonsectarian League of Women Voters (LWV), which would encourage women to work within the parties and to support a broad range of social reforms.[4]

Under the banners of the Congressional Union and the National Woman's Party (NWP), both led by their founder, Alice Paul, the militant feminists had used civil disobedience, colorful demonstrations, and incessant lobbying to get the Nineteenth Amendment out of Congress. Unlike NAWSA, the NWP never considered disbanding. It viewed suffrage as a step along the way to full equality, not an end in itself. Once the Nineteenth Amendment was ratified, the NWP decided to focus its attention on the eradication of all legal discrimination against women.

Reformers and feminists shared a common desire to improve the status of women. But they also had fundamental disagreements on the roles and nature of woman, as well as differences in strategy on how to achieve those goals they shared. The NWP favored absolute equality of opportunity. Women would never achieve economic independence as long as laws treated them like children in need of protection. The reformers accepted fundamental differences in physiology and family role as incontrovertible. They noted that the female labor force was largely young, unmarried, and transitional. Labor unions did not want to organize women because they were not permanent workers and did not earn enough to pay dues. Thus collective bargaining did not offer the same protection for women workers that it potentially could for men. Only legislation could save them from gross exploitation by industrial capitalism.

The Reform Agenda

Shortly after the 1920 elections, at the invitation of the LWV, women formed the Women's Joint Congressional Committee (WJCC) to coordinate their work. Initially composed of ten women's organizations, claiming a combined membership of ten million, the "Women's Lobby on Capitol Hill" would become known as the "most highly organized and powerful lobby ever seen in Washington."[5] The "Women's Joint," as it was customarily called, was extremely successful in its first five years in persuading the Republican Congress to pass numerous social reform bills and an additional constitutional amendment. Three were considered major legislative achievements: the Sheppard-Towner Maternity Act (1921); the Cable Act, equal nationality rights for married women (1922); and the Child Labor Amendment (1924). The WJCC also lobbied for appropriations for the Children's Bureau and the Women's Bureau in the Department of Labor.[6]

However, after Congress sent the proposed Child Labor Amendment to the states in June of 1924, it encountered unexpected opposition. Three Southern states quickly rejected it and Massachusetts legislators, who had generally supported industrial regulation, sidestepped the issue by submitting it to a popular referendum that November. During the campaign it was attacked by manufacturers and farm and patriotic organizations. The final blow was rendered by the Roman Catholic Church, which claimed it would destroy parental control over their children. Voters rejected the amendment by three to one and set the stage for New York's refusal to ratify the following year. By 1930 only six states had ratified, though a total of twenty-eight did so eventually.[7]

Prior to the New Deal, most of the laws that reformers wanted had to be passed on the state level. Women's state legislative activity was conducted by women's legislative councils, usually with the state League as its nucleus. In 1924 the League reported that 420 state laws had been enacted with its support since suffrage. Most of these laws (130) were in the realm of child welfare, though the next largest number (86) were to remove legal discriminations against women. However, the League also concerned itself with laws to improve social hygiene, education, efficiency in government, the condition of women in industry, living costs, anti-lynching, and the repression of vice. A subsequent count in 1930 for the League's tenth anniversary showed further progress at a slower rate. The League claimed that in the previous ten years it had helped pass a total of 130 laws in thirty-two states specifically aimed at women, particularly enhancing their rights to hold property, retain guardianship, run for public office, and serve on juries. But a survey by NWP attorney Burnita Shelton Matthews for the same period identified only 89 laws in twenty-four states which equalized women's rights. Regardless of the actual count, women's local lobbying activities had clearly crested by the end of the decade. The League could only identify eighteen state legislative councils in 1930, and many of those were informal coalitions.[8]

Although the WJCC achieved some of its legislative goals in the late 1920s, its successes were few compared to those of its first four years.[9] The reasons for this decline are many. The most popular explanation at one time was that when politicians discovered that women did not vote as a bloc, they no longer felt compelled to listen to them.[10]

This attempt to lay failure at the feet of organized women was argued more as ideology than as fact. By 1920 a sufficient number of women had voted in many states long enough for political analysts to know that they voted pretty much like everyone else in their communities. Women's turnout *was* lower than men's. Professionals estimated that women cast 30 percent of the vote in 1920, 35 percent in 1924, and 45 percent in 1928—a year when women were highly mobilized by the issues and the candidates.[11]

Historical hindsight illuminates the role of larger social trends. The Woman Suffrage Movement was an integral part of the Progressive Movement that flourished before World War I. This movement, like all social movements, eventually stimulated a vicious backlash about the time its proponents were running out of energy and the country was tired of constant challenges. This backlash was fed by postwar red-baiting and a series of Supreme Court decisions which gutted much Progressive legislation. Although remnants of the Progressive Movement survived into the twenties, it was unable to institutionalize many of its proposals in the newly conservative political climate. The pursuit of world peace siphoned off the energies of many prewar activists, and conflict over the reality of Prohibition discouraged others. If anything, women's organizations were among the strongest and most successful of the remaining Progressive groups. What is surprising is not that they eventually wilted after repeated defeats due to concerted conservative attacks in a hostile atmosphere, but that despite this they sowed the seeds of future welfare legislation. These seeds would eventually flower in the policies of the Roosevelt Administration.[12]

The Feminist Agenda

In pursuit of its goal to remove all sex-based discriminatory laws, NWP members lobbied for state laws to equalize jury service, allow a married woman to chose her domicile separate from her husband's, the right of women to hold office, and equal guardianship and property rights. They also fought many laws that the reformers wanted, especially those limiting the hours women could work, prohibiting night work by women, or excluding them from some occupations. NWP attorneys analyzed each state's discriminatory laws and drew up bills to eliminate them. "Blanket" equal rights bills aimed at removing all legal disabilities and discriminations with broad sweeping language were also prepared. Wisconsin was the only state to pass one, in 1921, and it contained an exemption for "the special protection and privileges which [women] now enjoy for the general welfare." The enforcement of this bill was discouraging. Prior to its passage, state law restricted legislative employees to members of the male sex. When this practice was contested after passage of the Equal Rights Act, the Wisconsin attorney general upheld it on the grounds that the long hours legislative employees worked fell under the exemption. As late as 1929, Milwaukee advertised that male applicants for the position of municipal reference librarian would be given preference, and the school board in Portage stated that female teachers would be paid five dollars less than men for the same position.[13]

In 1925 NWP legislative secretary Emma Wold wrote that there is no reason for "great rejoicing among women seeking equality." One prominent member summed up the discouragement of many when she said that "if Equal Rights for men and women are to be secured during our lifetime, they must eventually be obtained through the only logical and permanent method, the amendment of the National Constitution."[14]

By 1923 Alice Paul was convinced that attacking state laws one by one and state by state was intolerably slow and unreliable. It was time to switch strategy. The vehicle chosen to obtain legal equality was the Equal Rights Amendment. She wrote the original version of the ERA: "Men and women shall have equal rights throughout the United States and every place subject to its jurisdiction." It was publicly proposed at a major conference held in Seneca Falls, New York, on July 21, 1923, on the seventy-fifth anniversary of the original Declaration of Principles, and was officially introduced into Congress later that fall.[15] It was strongly opposed by the LWV, the Women's Bureau, and most other women's organizations. The WJCC formed a special subcommittee devoted to its death. Their opposition was based on the one fact about the ERA on which everyone could agree: that it would abolish protective labor legislation for women.

The Conflict

Protective labor legislation was a generic label for a host of state laws applicable to women only which restricted the number of hours they could work, the amount of weight they could lift, occasionally required special benefits such as seats and rest periods, and sometimes prohibited their working at night or in certain occupations. When originally proposed in the nineteenth century to curb sweatshop conditions caused by the Industrial Revolution, they applied to members of both sexes, but they were easier to pass when limited to women and minors. The American Federation of Labor (AFL) also preferred that these laws apply only to women. It felt unions were a better protection for men than the government. The first effective law, restricting the hours of women and minors in the mills to ten a day, was passed by Massachusetts in 1874. By 1900, fourteen states had similar laws, and even more states had a variety of other protective measures. By the mid-1960s every state had some form of protective labor legislation.[16] The next battle was over minimum wage laws that applied to women only. The Supreme Court's 1923 decision in *Adkins v. Children's Hospital* was the first time the Court struck down a sex-specific law. Five justices took the feminist position, concluding that the minimum wage law was "simply and exclusively a price-fixing law, confined to adult women, . . . who are legally as capable of contracting for themselves as men."[17]

The NWP was not originally opposed to all sex-based legislation. It intended the ERA to serve as a means of eradicating laws which restricted women, not those, like hours limitations, that reformers had sought to protect them. Before becoming involved in suffrage, Alice Paul had worked in a settlement house and helped organize a labor union; she was not unsympathetic to the plight of the working-class woman. Initially she told members working on state laws to avoid conflict with protective labor legislation, and the Blanket Equality Bill the NWP prepared specifically exempted "laws regulating the employment of women in industry." But within the NWP a feminist core argued that protection was simply another form of sex discrimination. Lawyer and future Maine legislator Gail Laughlin finally persuaded Paul that permitting *any* sex-based legislation would permit *all* sex-based legislation that might "appeal to the caprice or prejudice of our legislatures."[18]

After *Adkins* and the introduction of the ERA in 1923 both sides hardened. Each devoted itself to undermining the position of the other. For example, in 1932, at the urging of Republican NWP members, President Hoover issued an executive order denying Federal agency heads the right to use sex as a job qualification. In 1934 the Women's Bureau persuaded President Roosevelt to reverse this decision by arguing that appointments of women to the civil service had declined as a result.[19] Organizations in the WJCC testified against the ERA at every congressional hearing. In those states where the NWP had active members, they lobbied against any increase in protective laws. The battle was particularly harsh in New York, where both reformers and several dedicated NWP members made their homes. The animosity created between the two camps during the twenties ensured the NWP's exclusion from the Roosevelt administration in the thirties.[20]

By the 1930s both sides had reached a stalemate. Even when the two antagonists agreed, they were not very successful. Section 213 of the National Economy Act, which prohibited husbands and wives from working for the federal government at the same time, was opposed by all women's organizations, but their combined efforts neither kept it from being passed in 1932 nor compelled its repeal in 1937. Between 1932 and 1937 1,600 married women were dismissed from the federal government. Women's organizations could not even get the Democratic Party to adopt a plank opposing Section 213 in its 1936 platform.[21]

This weakness reflected the disintegration of the social reform movement. Some key women's organizations, such as the Women's Trade Union League (WTUL), completely disappeared when their founders died or retired. Others, such as the LWV, turned their energies to other problems. While the Women's Bureau continued to work for protective laws and against the ERA, it needed stronger allies, and found them in labor unions and liberal organizations such as the American Civil Liberties Union (ACLU) and Americans for Democratic Action (ADA).

At the same time, support for the ERA expanded beyond the NWP to include the National Federation of Business and Professional Women's Clubs (BPW); the General Federation of Women's Clubs (GFWC); Soroptimists; and organizations of women lawyers, dentists, osteopaths, real estate agents, accountants, and physicians.[22]

Over time, the division of opinion on the ERA more and more became one of class, or more specifically, occupation. Women in or associated with women working in industry, particularly unionized industries, opposed the ERA because they supported protective labor legislation. Business and professional women supported the ERA and saw protective labor legislation as a barrier to their effectively competing against men in their professions. Indeed it was the attempt of protectionists to bring women in business establishments (primarily clerical and retail sales workers) under the protective umbrella which pushed the clubs of the National Federation of Business and Professional Women from neutrality to support for the ERA. From the businesswomen's perspective, these positions were not industrial ones and their occupants were potential executives and managers who should not be protected from promotions and the responsibilities that went with them.[23]

To a lesser extent the division was also one of party. By the 1930s the women who actively supported protective labor legislation were mostly, though not exclusively, Democrats. Although they overlapped only slightly with Democratic Party activists, and could not keep the ERA out of the Democratic Party platform in 1944, they and the unions with which they worked closely did exercise some influence within the Democratic Party and virtually none in the Republican Party.[24]

With some notable exceptions (e.g., Emma Guffey Miller), NWP members were Republicans. While somewhat disdainful of both parties, Alice Paul and her followers had once worked for progressive causes and still retained some ties to the progressive wing of the Republican Party. They could get audiences with high-level officials in the Republican administrations of the 1920s, but had no access to the Democratic administration of FDR. Furthermore, the NWP's opposition to government protection of women was much more compatible with Republican opposition to any regulation of labor. Equally important, the professional and business women who became the ERA's primary supporters were more likely to be Republicans, the Members of Congress who sponsored the ERA were Republicans, and conservative organizations like the National Association of Manufacturers, which opposed any law regulating industry, supported the ERA.

In 1940 "protection" was still more popular than "equality." But this would soon change as the growing European conflict shifted national priorities from social and economic concerns to international affairs. Democratic ideals and slogans about equality took on a different meaning when the audience was international than when it was local.[25] During World War II protective labor laws would be suspended so that women could work in the war industries. After the war ended the battle between "protection" and "equality" would be renewed, but on new and different terrain.

Notes

1. Editorial in *Equal Rights* 13, no. 3: 252.
2. Martin 1976, 458.
3. Quote on the National Woman's Party in ER's letter of March 12, 1952, to Gertrude W. Fairbanks, Katherine St. George papers, Manuscript Department, Cornell University Library.
4. Lemons (1973, 50) uses the term "social feminism" for this branch. He adopted it from William L. O'Neill (1969, ch. 2), but it was not widely used until Lemons put it into the title of his book. As historian Nancy Cott has pointed out (1987, 3), the term *feminism* was not used in the nineteenth century; it first appeared in the 1910s. Members of the moderate branch of the suffrage movement considered themselves to be "reformers." By the 1920s "feminist" was a pejorative

term to the reformers. Therefore I will refer to members of this branch of the post-suffrage women's movement as reformers and save "feminists" for those who defined themselves as such.

5. The first ten organizations were the National League of Women Voters (LVW), the General Federation of Women's Clubs (GFWC), the National Consumers League (NCL), the National Federation of Business and Professional Women's Clubs (BPW), the American Association of University Women (AAUW), the American Home Economics Association (AHEA), the National Congress of Mothers and Parent-Teachers Associations (PTA), the National Council of Jewish Women, the National Woman's Christian Temperance Union (WCTU), and the National Women's Trade Union League (WTUL). The coalition expanded to twenty-one organizations between 1924 and 1927 and contracted to nineteen thereafter. Quote from the *Journal of the American Medical Association*, found in Breckinridge 1933/1972, 259–60.

6. Johnson 1972, 51–53; Lemons 1973, 56–57; Breckinridge 1933/1972, 261–62.

7. Chambers 1963, 33–46; Goldmark 1953, 114–19; Johnson 1972, 50–51; Lemons 1973, 144–46, 219–21; O'Neill 1969, 233–35. The National Council of Catholic Women, which was not a member of the WJCC, endorsed the Child Labor Amendment, as did the American Legion and the American Federation of Labor.

8. Lemons 1973, 119; Breckinridge 1933/1972, 266–70. Johnson 1972, 49, cites the League as claiming 175 laws passed in thirty-five states plus the District of Columbia during this period. The NWP's count, including the District of Columbia, appears in a "Report of Legislative Work from 1921 to 1929" by Burnita Shelton Matthews, *Equal Rights* (January 4, 1930): 379–81. The League's count probably includes protective laws, which the NWP opposed. Scott 1970, 187–88, describes the activities of organized women in the South. The decline in state legislative activity may not have been uniform. Gordon 1986, 107–11, showed that New Jersey feminists achieved their greatest legislative successes between 1924 and 1930, primarily due to the efforts of the NWP. The state legislative councils also served as an entry into the political arena. Ivy Baker Priest, treasurer of the United States under Eisenhower, reported that the opportunity to be on the Utah Legislative Council while a housewife in the thirties provided that boost to her: Priest 1958, 94.

9. Breckinridge 1933/1972, 261–66.

10. Breckinridge 1933/1972, 268; Blair 1925, 513–22. This view has also been offered by contemporary scholars. See Chafe 1972, 37; Lemons 1973, 57. However, Cott 1990, 156, reports that "suffragists rarely if ever portrayed a future voting 'bloc' of women."

11. Michelet 1929, 13.

12. Chambers makes this point in his book, aptly named *Seedtime of Reform*, 1963.

13. Becker 1981, 19; *Equal Rights* (March 24, 1923): 34; "Unequal Opportunity in Wisconsin," September 14, 1929, 251. However, in 1931 the Supreme Court ruled that the Wisconsin law precluded taxing a couple at the higher joint rate rather than on their separate incomes. *Hoeper v. Tax Commission of Wisconsin*, November 30,

1931 (284 U.S. 206, 52 S.Ct 120, 76 L.Ed. 248, 1931); *Equal Rights* (December 12, 1931): 359–60; (March 12, 1932): 43; Mimeographed letter to general membership, March 21, 1921, on "blanket" equal rights bill, Reel 7, NWP Papers; Putnam 1924.

14. Emma Wold, "Equal Rights in the Legislatures of 1925," *Equal Rights* (October 24, 1925): 295; Jane Norman Smith in *Equal Rights* (November 28, 1925): 333–34; quoted in Becker 1981, 130. In 1929, *Equal Rights* ran a series of articles on bills to achieve equality currently before the state legislatures. Successes were rare. Of several dozen bills introduced into one dozen state legislatures, the only new laws that year were Maine and New York acts that a married woman could have her own domicile. See *Equal Rights* (January 26, 1929): 407; (February 23, 1929): 22; (March 2, 1929): 27; (March 9, 1929): 35, 37; (March 16, 1929): 43, 46; (March 23, 1929): 51; (March 31, 1929): 59; (April 20, 1929): 83; (April 27, 1929): 90.

15. Becker 1981, 19; *Equal Rights* (July 28, 1923): 189, Reel 156, NWP papers.

16. O'Neill 1969, 248; Baker 1964, 90–96. As originally used by its proponents, "protective labor legislation" referred to all laws that protected industrial workers, not just those that applied to women only. After World War II, it was more likely to be used as a capsule description of those laws which applied to women only.

17. *Adkins v. Children's Hospital*, 261 U.S. 525, 552–53 (1923). Chief Justice (and former president) William Howard Taft and Associate Justice Oliver Wendell Holmes wrote stinging dissents, arguing that woman suffrage did not eliminate the differences between men and women. Idem 567 and 569–70.

18. Paul 1972, 406; Goldmark 1953, 181; Laughlin quote in Cott 1984, 56–59. Even Alva Belmont, the very wealthy suffragist who financed the NWP, had contributed money to the Women's Trade Union League: Cook 1992, 536.

19. Harrison 1982, 242–45.

20. Becker 1981, 220–21; O'Neill 1969, 240–41; Gordon 1986, 62, 103, 169, for New Jersey; Dye 1980 and Lehrer 1987 focus on the battles in New York. *Equal Rights* (November 12, 1927): 318; "Women Protest Night Work Ban" (November 15, 1930): 323–24; "The Barring of Women by law from Night Work" (November 29, 1930): 340–41; "Decisions of the Courts on Legislation Barring Women from Night Work" (December 6, 1930): 349–50; "Women's Work Bill an Outrage" (May 2, 1931): 104; "Rhode Island Workers Oppose Night Work Ban" (January 9, 1932): 387. Although the number and scope of protective laws generally increased, the NWP slowed the pace. See Jane Norman Smith's table in *Equal Rights* (March 26, 1932): 99, and her claim in "Labor Laws for Women on the Wane" that in 1931 the AFL campaigned for a forty-eight-hour week for women in thirteen states and lost in all.

21. Ware 1981, 79–82. The 1936 GOP platform stated the party's opposition to legislation which discriminates against women in Federal and State governments.

22. Lemons 1973, 204.

23. Lemons 1973, 199–200.

24. Freeman 2000, 207.

25. Ware 1981, 125–26.

References

Adkins v. Children's Hospital. 1923. 261 U.S. 525.

Baker, Elizabeth. 1964. *Technology and women's work*. New York: Columbia University Press.

Becker, Susan D. 1981. *The origins of the Equal Rights Amendment: American feminism between the wars*. Westport, Conn.: Greenwood Press.

Blair, Emily Newell. 1925. Are women a failure in politics? *Harpers*, October, 513–22.

Brandeis, Elizabeth. 1957. Organized labor and protective labor legislation. In *Labor and the New Deal*, ed. Milton Derber and Edwin Young, 193–238. Madison, Wisc.: University of Wisconsin Press.

Breckinridge, Sophonisba P. 1933. *Women in the twentieth century*. New York: McGraw-Hill. Reprint, Arno Press, New York, 1972.

Chafe, William. 1972. *The American woman: Her changing social, economic and political roles 1920–1970*. New York: Oxford University Press.

Chambers, Clarke A. 1963. *Seedtime of reform: American social service and social action 1918–1933*. Minneapolis: University of Minnesota Press.

Cook, Blanche Wiesen. 1992. *Eleanor Roosevelt*. Vol. 1, *1884–1933*. New York: Viking.

Cott, Nancy F. 1984. Feminist politics in the 1920s: The National Woman's Party. *Journal of American History* 71 (June): 47.

———. 1987. *The grounding of modern feminism*. New Haven, Conn.: Yale University Press.

———. 1990. Across the great divide: Women in politics before and after 1920. In *Women, politics, and change*, ed. Louise A. Tilly and Patricia Gurin, 133–76. New York: Russell Sage Foundation.

Dye, Nancy Schrom. 1980. *As equals and sisters: Feminism, the labor movement and the Women's Trade Union League of New York*. Columbia, Mo.: University of Missouri Press.

Freeman, Jo. 2000. *A room at a time: How women entered party politics*. Lanham, Md.: Rowman & Littlefield.

Goldmark, Josephine. 1953. *Impatient crusader: Florence Kelley's life story*. Urbana, Ill.: University of Illinois Press.

Gordon, Felice D. 1986. *After winning: The legacy of the New Jersey suffragists, 1920–1947*. New Brunswick, N.J.: Rutgers University Press.

Harrison, Cynthia Ellen. 1982. Prelude to feminism: Women's organizations, the federal government and the rise of the women's movement, 1942–1968. PhD diss., Columbia University.

———. 1988. *On account of sex: The politics of women's issues, 1945–1968*. Berkeley: University of California Press.

Johnson, Dorothy. 1972. Organized women as lobbyists in the 1920s. *Capitol Studies* 1, no. 1: 41–58.

Lehrer, Susan. 1987. *Origins of protective labor legislation for women: 1905–1925*. Albany: SUNY Press.

Lemons, Stanley J. 1973. *The woman citizen: Social feminism in the 1920s*. Urbana, Ill.: University of Illinois Press.

Martin, George. 1976. *Madam Secretary: Frances Perkins*. Boston: Houghton Mifflin.

Michelet, Simon. 1929. *Election of 1928*. Twenty-page pamphlet. Washington, D.C.: National Get-Out-the Vote-Club.

National Woman's Party Papers. 1913–1974. Microfilm, University Publications of America.

O'Neill, William L. 1969. *Everyone was brave: The rise and fall of feminism in America*. Chicago: Quadrangle Books.

Paul, Alice. 1972–1973. *Conversations with Alice Paul: Woman Suffrage and the ERA*. Interviews by Amelia Fry, November 1972 and May 1973. Suffragists Oral History Project, Bancroft Library, University of California, Berkeley.

Priest, Ivy Baker. 1958. *Green grows ivy*. New York: McGraw-Hill.

Putnam, Mabel Raef. 1924. *The winning of the first bill of rights for American women*. Milwaukee: Frank Putnam.

Scott, Anne Firor. 1970. *The Southern lady: From pedestal to politics 1830–1930*. Chicago: University of Chicago Press.

Ware, Susan. 1981. *Beyond suffrage: Women in the New Deal*. Cambridge, Mass.: Harvard University Press.

∽

CHAPTER TWELVE

How "Sex" Got into Title VII: Persistent Opportunism as a Maker of Public Policy*

The Civil Rights Act of 1964 was a milestone of federal legislation. Like much major legislation it had "incubated" for decades but was birthed in turmoil. On June 19, 1963, after the Civil Rights Movement of the fifties and early sixties had focused national attention on racial injustice, President Kennedy sent a draft omnibus civil rights bill to the Congress.[1] On Saturday, February 8, 1964, while the bill was being debated on the House floor, Howard W. Smith of Virginia, chairman of the Rules Committee and staunch opponent of all civil rights legislation, rose up and offered a one-word amendment to Title VII, which prohibited employment discrimination. He proposed to add "sex" to that one title of the bill in order "to prevent discrimination against another minority group, the women."[2] This stimulated several hours of humorous debate, later called "ladies day in the House," before the amendment was passed by a teller vote of 168 to 133.

In only a few hours Congress initiated a major innovation in public policy, one which rippled throughout the country for several years. Prior to its passage only two states—Hawaii and Wisconsin—had passed laws which prohibited sex discrimination in employment. Within four years, fifteen states and the District of Columbia did so and within ten years all but a few states included "sex" among the prohibited discriminations in their fair employment practices laws.[3] Although the agency created by the act to enforce

---

*Revised from the version published in *Law and Inequality: A Journal of Theory and Practice* 9, no. 2 (March 1991): 163–84.

Figure 13.   Celebrating the addition of "sex" to Title VII of the 1964 Civil Rights Act. From left to right: Rep. Martha W. Griffiths (D-MI); May Craig, journalist and member of the National Woman's Party; Rep. Howard W. Smith (D-VA), who introduced the "sex" amendment; Rep. Katherine St. George (R-NY), chief House sponsor of the Equal Rights Amendment. Exact date unknown, but probably on or shortly after February 8, 1964 (image no. LC-USZ62-129050 from the papers of May Craig in the Library of Congress).

Title VII, the Equal Employment Opportunities Commission (EEOC), viewed the sex amendment as a "fluke" that was "conceived out of wedlock," and tried to ignore its existence,[4] fully one-third of the complaints filed in the first year charged discrimination on the basis of sex.[5] The EEOC's apathy stimulated the formation of the National Organization for Women (NOW), whose initial goal was to pressure the agency to enforce the law. Lawyers came forward to represent women who wanted to take their sex discrimination complaints to court.[6] As a consequence the federal courts voided state protective laws on the grounds that they were in conflict with the federal prohibition against sex discrimination.[7] These laws, which limited the hours women could work, the weights they could lift, and often prohibited night work and entry into some occupations considered too dangerous for women, had been actively sought during the first half of the twentieth century by an earlier generation of women activists.[8]

The popular interpretation of the addition of "sex" to Title VII is that it was "the result of a deliberate ploy of foes of the bill to scuttle it."[9] Even a political scientist as well read in the *Congressional Record* as Orfield accepted the interpretation that "bitter opponents of the job discrimination title . . . decided to load up the bill with objectionable features that might split the coalition supporting it."[10] This view, appealing on the surface, has little evidence to support it. It ignores several factors apparent to anyone who has tried to influence a Congressional vote: 1) The potential beneficiaries of the amendment—women—had experienced lobbyists on the Hill who were very interested in the bill. 2) The Southern Members of Congress who opposed the bill had conceded defeat and gone home by Wednesday;[11] the vote occurred on a Saturday—which is not any Member's favorite day to be in Washington. 3) More Members voted on the amendment (301) than for any other counted vote that day (the other votes ranged from 178 to 240). 4) Other amendments which might "clutter up" the bill, including "sex" amendments to other titles, were voted down.

Before offering an alternative explanation which takes these factors into account, it is necessary to place the "sex" amendment into historical context. This will clarify the fact that while the prohibition of employment discrimination on the basis of sex was not a widely debated, thoroughly researched policy proposal, neither was it an "accidental breakthrough."[12]

The National Woman's Party and the Equal Rights Amendment

The National Woman's Party had been lobbying for the Equal Rights Amendment since introducing it into Congress in 1923. The NWP was originally founded by the militant branch of the suffrage movement in 1916. Once the Nineteenth Amendment was ratified, the NWP, under the leadership of Alice Paul, reorganized itself to focus attention on the eradication of legal discrimination against women through another congressional amendment.[13] The ERA was strongly opposed by the newly created Women's Bureau in the Department of Labor and virtually every other women's organization, particularly the League of Women Voters, the National Consumers League, and the Women's Trade Union League. Their opposition was based on the one fact about the ERA on which everyone could agree; that it would abolish protective labor legislation for women.

The ERA's opponents fought the National Woman's Party to a standstill throughout the 1920s and 1930s. By the 1940s, the NWP was gaining the upper hand. House and Senate subcommittees reported it favorably, the

Republican Party endorsed the ERA in its 1940 platform, and the Democratic Party followed suit in 1944. The Senate voted on the ERA for the first time on July 19, 1946, after three days of debate. Although the tally of 38 to 35 was well below the two-thirds required for a constitutional amendment,[14] expectations of favorable action in the next Congress were high because "there has been a subtle change in the public attitude toward (the ERA)." During World War II, state protective labor laws were waived by state legislatures and labor boards in order that women could work in the war industries while "WACs, WAVEs, SPARs and women Marines took over strenuous jobs, some of them on front-line assignments."[15]

ERA opponents decided to change tactics from mere opposition to a "more positive" approach. They had always agreed with the NWP that women faced discrimination in the job market, particularly in pay, but had argued that this and the discriminatory laws which truly hurt women were better dealt with through "specific bills for specific ills" rather than the broad sweep of a constitutional amendment. Calling itself the National Committee to Defeat the UnEqual Rights Amendment (NCDUERA), opponents proposed an Equal Pay Act. The idea of equal pay for equal work had been around since at least 1868 (Women's Bureau 1966). Two states had passed equal pay laws; but until 1945 there was no attempt to pass such a law on the federal level. Even with the backing of the NCDUERA, a federal equal pay act was not successful, either as an anti-ERA measure or in its own right, due to fears that it would encourage women to stay in the work force and take jobs away from returning soldiers.[16]

Renaming itself the National Committee on the Status of Women, opponents proposed a "Status Bill" which declared it to be the policy of the United States that "in law and its administration no distinctions on the basis of sex shall be made except such as are reasonably based on differences in physical structure, biological or social function." Instead of enforcement provisions, it would create a Commission on the Legal Status of Women to study sex discrimination.[17]

In January 1950, the ERA was debated on the Senate floor once again. When the Status Bill was overwhelmingly rejected by 19 to 65, Sen. Carl Hayden (D-AZ) proposed an amendment to the ERA which read "The provisions of this article shall not be construed to impair any rights, benefits, or exemptions now or hereafter conferred by law upon persons of the female sex." ERA proponents were caught by surprise, and many senators, whose support for the ERA had been on the record but never very strong, took advantage of the opportunity to vote for both the rider and the amendment. The Hayden rider passed 51 to 31 and the ERA, thus vitiated, passed 63 to 19.[18] This strategy was repeated when the ERA once again came to the Senate floor in July of 1953. This time the rider passed by 58 to 25 and the ERA by 73 to 11.[19]

The ERA never had a chance in the House. Emanuel Celler (D-NY) had been chair of the Judiciary Committee since 1949. He was a crusty liberal from Brooklyn who shared organized labor's antipathy to the ERA. No hearings were held on the ERA during his chairmanship until 1971—after a successful discharge petition by Rep. Martha Griffiths (D-MI) in 1970. Between Celler in the House and Hayden in the Senate, opponents of the ERA successfully bottled it up. Members of the NWP continued to walk the halls of Congress every year and faithfully collect endorsements from members of both houses well above the two-thirds needed for passage. But there was no serious interest in the amendment apart from the NWP and the few other women's organizations that had endorsed it in the preceding decades. Even these could do little more than pass resolutions. The NWP was a small, exclusive organization, whose aging members refused to relinquish leadership of the struggle to anyone else—even when it could no longer publish its journal *Equal Rights*.[20] Consequently, it could still get the ERA introduced into Congress, but it could not get it out.

In 1961 President Kennedy appointed Esther Peterson as assistant secretary of labor and director of the Women's Bureau. Two of the most important items on her agenda were passage of the Equal Pay Act and derailment of the ERA. To accomplish the first she organized a concerted lobbying campaign which drew upon the expertise and contacts Peterson had developed as a lobbyist for the AFL-CIO. The campaign took two years of solid work, during which there were three sets of hearings: two in the House and one in the Senate. Although the final bill was narrower than Peterson and Equal Pay advocates had wanted, and only covered 61 percent of the female labor force, by the time it was signed into law by President Kennedy on June 10, 1963, both houses had heard ample testimony on the problems faced by women in the labor force.[21]

One of Peterson's first recommendations to the new president was the creation of a national commission on women—a component of the 1947 Status Bill—which she argued would end "the present troublesome and futile agitation over the ERA,"[22] but which she also hoped would provide an alternative program of action to improve women's status.[23] To avoid the NWP lobbyists, the President's Commission on the Status of Women was created by Executive Order 10980 on December 14, 1961. Eleanor Roosevelt was named the chair and among the members was only one ERA supporter—Marguerite Rawalt, a lawyer with the IRS and a former president of the

National Federation of Business and Professional Women (BPW). The final report and recommendations of the commission, *American Women*, were issued amid much publicity on October 11, 1963, with recommendations in the areas of education, social security, child care, public and private employment, and protective labor legislation. It quickly became something of a Government Printing Office best seller. Over eighty-three thousand copies were distributed within a year and a private publisher put out a commercial version with an epilogue by Margaret Mead.

Fair Employment Practices Proposals

The roots of Title VII can be traced to the Unemployment Relief Act of 1933, which provided "that in employing citizens for the purpose of this Act no discrimination shall be made on account of race, color, or creed."[24] Most laws passed in the New Deal affecting employment contained similar provisions, or they were "read into" the acts by executive regulations. However, these were little more than statements of good intentions, as there were no enforcement mechanisms. Their ineffectiveness was highlighted by the systematic exclusion of blacks from the new jobs created by the mushrooming defense industries prior to World War II. Even before the United States entered the war, black leaders pressed President Roosevelt to sign an executive order with teeth in it that would ban discrimination in these industries. Faced with a threatened march on Washington, Roosevelt did so on June 25, 1941. Executive Order 8802 established the Fair Employment Practices (FEP) Committee with the modest powers to investigate complaints of discrimination and take "appropriate steps."[25] Although its authority was extended to all federal contractors in 1943, its enforcement power was limited to negotiation and moral suasion. It expired in June 1946.[26]

Presidents Truman, Eisenhower, and Kennedy each established FEP committees by executive order, though under different names and with different foci. The Kennedy Committee on Equal Employment Opportunity differed from its predecessors in that it required affirmative action to eliminate discrimination and had the power to terminate the contracts of noncomplying employers as well as to recommend suits to the Justice Department. Its scope was broadened to include virtually all programs and businesses receiving federal money. Nonetheless the "most effective method of achieving compliance . . . was . . . cooperation."[27]

The first FEP bill was introduced in 1942. Over the next twenty years, many more were introduced into every Congress, but only three ever reached the floor; the rest were bottled up in committee. The Senate debated FEP bills in 1946 and 1950 but they were filibustered to death when proponents could not muster the necessary two-thirds vote necessary for cloture. These were also the first two years in which the ERA was debated on the floor of the Senate, which may explain why provisions to prohibit sex discrimination in employment were proposed to the House those same two years. Early in 1946 Rep. Clare E. Hoffman (R-MI) introduced H.R. 5216, which included sex, ancestry, and union membership as protected classes. It was committed to the Labor Committee where it died.[28] On February 22, 1950, Rep. Dwight L. Rogers (D-FL) offered a floor amendment to add "sex" to the FEP bill then being debated "so the women of the country will have equal rights with men." No one spoke against it and it passed by a voice vote.[29] Although the amended bill passed the House by 240 to 177 the following day, it was a substitute for a stronger bill introduced by Rep. Adam Clayton Powell Jr. (D-NY) after an all-night session. Sponsored by Samuel K. McConnell Jr. (R-PA), it would have set up an FEP Commission with the power only to study and recommend, not to compel. Nonetheless, this was still the first time either house of Congress voted to equate race and sex discrimination.[30]

Such an equation was standard policy for the NWP. Its conservative members were not pro–civil rights. Most would have preferred no government regulation of employment. But the aging organization did not wish to see any group given rights not also given equally to women, and had no compunctions about taking advantage of any opportunity that came along to advance its cause.[31] Throughout the fifties it lobbied to have sex discrimination included in the jurisdiction of the President's Committee on Government Contracts (Eisenhower's FEPC), but it was turned down on the grounds that the addition would make enforcement difficult.[32] It was more successful in 1956, albeit temporarily, in persuading the House to include sex discrimination in the jurisdiction of the proposed Civil Rights Commission. Once again the mechanism was a floor amendment—made by Rep. Gordon McDonough (R-CA) at the request of his campaign chair, Mary Sinclair Crawford, a dean at the University of Southern California and an active NWP member. When McDonough's wife expressed opposition, NWP representative Amelia Walker asked Rep. Howard W. Smith (D-VA) to introduce it instead.[33] Smith consented, but McDonough announced his intentions to the House as soon as debate began on July 17, 1956. Smith voiced his approval, stating that "if this iniquitous piece of legislation is to be adopted, we certainly ought to try to do whatever good with it that we can."[34]

McDonough was pressured by NAACP lobbyist Clarence Mitchell to change his mind. When he refused, the opposition organized. No sooner did the clerk read the one-word amendment two days later, than Rep.

Celler tried to turn the issue into an ERA debate. Although the proposed commission's sole authority was to investigate, "sex" was not germane, he said, because "distinctions based on sex have never been considered within the purview of [the] prohibition[s of] . . . the 14th amendment." Four Democratic congresswomen agreed that adding "sex" would "destroy the real purpose of this bill and will lead to its defeat." Nonetheless, after eloquent pleas by McDonough, Rep. Katherine St. George (R-NY), chief House sponsor of the ERA, and Rep. Howard W. Smith (D-VA), the House voted in favor by 115 to 83.[35] The bill was passed by the House but by prior arrangement among the leadership was sent to the Senate too late to become law.[36] It was reintroduced and passed in the next Congress as part of the 1957 Civil Rights Act—without the sex amendment. The NWP thought the debate over the McDonough amendment was "a great help to our cause" but the request was not renewed.

Title VII

Although no one really took seriously the NWP's efforts to equate sex and race discrimination, ERA opponents were of two minds. They acknowledged that women experienced discrimination in employment and argued that specific antidiscrimination measures would be preferable to the ERA. In written testimony to the 1956 Democratic and Republican Platform Committees, Walter Reuther, president of the CIO, supported the addition of sex (and age) to the discriminations prohibited by government contractors.[37] But opponents also believed, as the President's Commission on the Status of Women concluded in 1963, that "discrimination based on sex . . . involved problems sufficiently different from discrimination based on other factors listed to make separate treatment preferable."[38]

The nature of separate treatment was not defined, nor was it to define itself over time. Even before the commission's report was released the NWP was lobbying to have "sex" added to the latest civil rights bill. It was alerted to this possibility on July 9, 1963, when President Kennedy, at the recommendation of Esther Peterson, called together over three hundred representatives of women's organizations to "discuss those aspects of the nation's civil rights program in which women and women's organizations can play a special role."[39] The NWP was included among those invited, but NWP president Emma Guffy Miller sent Nina Horton Avery in her place. Avery cornered Kennedy as he left to ask him to meet with the NWP to discuss the ERA, then departed herself. Avery reported that the word "sex" did not appear in the bill so there was no reason to stay. The NWP did not participate in the National Women's Committee on Civil Rights that was organized that evening.[40]

During the next few months both the civil rights bill and the nation experienced several dramatic and emotional shocks. Civil rights supporters marched on Washington on August 28, 1963, where they heard Dr. Martin Luther King, Jr., give his famous "I have a dream" speech. Afterwards President Kennedy met with march leaders to discourage them from trying to strengthen Title VII and other portions of the bill because doing so would kill necessary Republican support. Two weeks later four girls were killed when a black church was bombed in Birmingham, Alabama. Liberal Democrats responded by strengthening the civil rights bill, which was then in a subcommittee of the House Judiciary Committee. A major change was made in Kennedy's weak employment measure, which only covered government contractors and relied on persuasion rather than force of law. The new Title VII created an Equal Employment Opportunity Commission which had the power to investigate and, after a hearing, order violators to "cease and desist." Its scope was broadened to include all employers with over twenty-five employees. The Republicans, who thought they had a deal worked out with the Justice Department, felt betrayed and it took all of Kennedy's and Judiciary Committee Chair Celler's political skills to hammer out a compromise. The EEOC survived, but its "cease and desist" powers did not; it was left with only the power to investigate and conciliate. The bill was sent to the Rules Committee the day before Kennedy was assassinated.[41]

As a result of Kennedy's death, passage of a civil rights bill became a priority with Congress and the new administration. This emphasis was fully backed by public opinion. A December *Newsweek* poll showed that 62 percent of the people supported civil rights, and a National Opinion Research Center survey showed 83 percent in favor of equal employment opportunity. The momentum thwarted the plans of Rep. Smith to use his power as chair of the House Rules Committee to stop or at least delay the civil rights bill. Instead he subjected "this nefarious bill" to ten days of intense scrutiny through hearings in January 1964.

It was during these hearings that the idea of adding "sex" to the prohibited discriminations was publicly proposed by Smith and other members of the Rules Committee. Although Alice Paul considered such actions to be "sideshows" to the ERA, the NWP had been soliciting support for it for several weeks, and its National Council had passed a formal resolution on December 16, 1963, asking that the civil rights bill be amended. The prospects did not look good. None of the national women's organizations would help and Rep. Catherine May (R-WA) could not find one among the forty Congressional allies she queried who would support a "sex" amendment. Of those asked by the NWP, only Griffiths was enthusiastic about a "sex" amendment.[42]

The NWP asked numerous representatives to introduce a "sex" amendment from the floor. Katherine St. George (R-NY) said she opposed the entire bill, though she voted for it in the end. Rep. Julia Hansen (D-WA) would not violate an agreement among the Democratic leadership that there be no amendments. Martha Griffiths (D-MI) felt that Howard W. Smith would be the best sponsor because he would bring at least a hundred Southern votes.[43] The others agreed to back him up. Fifteen years later Catherine May told Fern Ingersoll that "Edith Green and I talked with Howard Smith—as did other women members of the House, Martha Griffiths—and asked for sex in the civil rights bill. He accepted it."[44] Smith agreed to amend only Title VII, though the NWP would have preferred a general amendment to all of the titles.[45]

In January 1964, as the civil rights bill progressed through the House, the following signaled an interest in "sex."

- On January 9, as the hearings on H.R. 7152 began, Rep. Smith and Rep. Celler exchanged their views:

  Smith: I have just had a letter this morning, which I was going to bring to your attention later, from the National Woman's Party. They want to know why you did not include sex in this bill? Why did you not?

  Celler: Do you want to put it in Mr. Chairman?

  Smith: I think I will offer an amendment. The National Woman's Party were (sic) serious about it.[46]

- On January 21, Rep. Colmer (D-MS) brought the issue up again. "One more thing," he said, "and I do this by request more or less. . . . There is nothing in here about sex, is there, although we got quite a bit of publicity a while back because that question was raised. There is no provision in here about the discrimination against women because of their sex in all this consideration, is there?"[47]

- On January 26, Rep. Smith appeared on "Meet the Press," where May Craig, White House reporter for the Portland, Maine, *Press Herald* and an NWP member, asked him if he would put equal rights for women in Title VII from the floor. "I might do that," he said.[48]

- On January 30, before the Rules Committee voted to send the civil rights bill to the House floor by 11 to 4, one Member moved that the

Rules Committee give specific clearance to an amendment to bar discrimination on the basis of sex. This was voted down by 8 to 7.[49]
- Two days later, at President Johnson's weekly press conference, a reporter asked if the president would support a ban on sex discrimination in the civil rights bill. Johnson, who had recently been campaigning for more women in government, gave a noncommittal answer.[50]

Although the three representatives (May, Griffiths, and Green) no doubt solicited support from other members of Congress, not all were working with them. On the fifth and sixth days of debate Rep. John Dowdy (D-TX) offered his own amendments to add "sex" to Titles II, III, IV, and V of the bill. A staunch opponent of civil rights who no doubt knew of Smith's plans from the Rules Committee hearings, he had not been recruited by the NWP. All of his amendments were overwhelmingly defeated, as were all but 34 of the 124 floor amendments made to the civil rights bill.[51] The House leadership of the civil rights bill, Republican Bill McCulloch (OH) and Democrat Emanuel Celler, had agreed with opponents that debate on the bill and floor amendments would not be cut off. But they had agreed between themselves "that if a proposed amendment did no violence to the bill or to the principles which underlay it, they would be flexible to preserve harmony. . . . However, if substantive changes were sought, they would be intractable."[52] Although one could argue that increasing the scope of the bill did it no violence, it was this agreement that House members approached by Catherine May and others were unwilling to violate.[53]

But violate it many did. On Saturday, February 8, 1964, Rep. Smith moved to add "sex" to Title VII. Unlike his 1956 speech, this time he played it for laughs, setting a mocking and jocular tone which led to the two-hour debate being dubbed "Ladies Day" in the House. Celler reacted as usual and denounced the amendment as an "entering wedge" for the ERA. Five congresswomen spoke in its favor, including Edna Kelly (D-NY), who had opposed the 1956 amendment. Martha Griffiths said that "if there had been any necessity to have pointed out that women were a second-class sex, the laughter would have proved it." But the women were not a united front. The administration had tried to talk Griffiths out of supporting the amendment without success, but they did persuade Edith Green (D-OR) to speak against it. After denouncing discrimination based on sex, she went on to say that racial discrimination caused far more suffering, and a bill aimed at helping Negroes should not be cluttered up. She read a letter from the AAUW opposing the "sex" amendment. The bill's leaders had also obtained a letter from the Labor Department, which quoted Esther Peterson quoting the President's Commission on the disadvantages of treating sex discrimination like race. Their efforts were insufficient. The House approved the amendment by 168 to 133.[54]

The fact that Smith played the "sex" amendment for laughs and that all the men who spoke for it were from Southern or border states and voted against the final bill, lent credence to the view that it was merely a ploy by opponents. But if that were the only—or even the primary—motive, the Title VII amendment would have met the same fate as the Dowdy "sex" amendments to the other titles, or at least some of the other attempts to "clutter up" Title VII should have passed that same day. The two Dowdy "sex" amendments on which there were counted votes earlier in the week—to Titles II and III—were rejected by 43 to 115 and 26 to 112.[55] Shortly after "sex" was added to Title VII by 168 to 133, Dowdy moved to add "age" to the prohibited discriminations. Despite a very serious debate, in which Smith was for and Celler against, this amendment was rejected by 94 to 123.[56] A motion to strike all of Title VII lost by 90 to 150.[57] Nineteen amendments were offered that day, and fourteen adopted (most of them technical ones by the bill's sponsor, Celler). The bill's managers clearly had between 112 and 133 representatives who could be counted on to be present and vote down any amendment when asked. Equally clearly there were several dozen representatives who came to the floor on a Saturday morning to vote to add "sex" to Title VII, who weren't available, or requested, to vote on any of the other amendments. The vote on the "sex" amendment was the largest counted vote that day. The overall voting pattern implies that there was a large group of congressmen (in addition to the congresswomen) who were serious about adding "sex" to Title VII, but only to Title VII. It is not consistent with an interpretation that the addition of "sex" was part of a plot to scuttle the bill.

Furthermore, if the bill's managers had perceived the "sex" amendment as a serious threat to Title VII, they had ample opportunity to scuttle it two days later when the entire civil rights bill was up for review before the final vote. At that time Rep. Robert Griffin (R-MI) tried to amend the amendment to make it applicable only to those who certified that a spouse, if any, was unemployed "when the alleged unlawful employment practice occurred." This was defeated 15 to 96.[58] Four of the 28 amendments to Title VII that were offered that day were adopted,[59] including one proposed by Rep. Frances Bolton (D-OH) making "sex" subject to the bona fide occupational qualification exception.[60] A motion for a roll call vote on the "sex" amendment was defeated, but there was a separate voice vote on "sex" right before the final roll call on February 10 which affirmed its addition.[61] That final roll call registered 290 to 130 in favor of the Civil Rights Act. If those who voiced their approval the "sex" amendment has been mostly opponents of the act, it would have been removed at that time.

After the bill went to the Senate, the National Federation of Business and Professional Women (BPW), with 150,000 members and chapters in every state, joined the campaign. Marguerite Rawalt "wrote women lawyers and BPW and Zonta members across the country, explaining the bill and Title VII, telling them whom to write, what to say." She also asked black attorney Pauli Murray to draft a supportive memorandum since Murray "could act freely, being outside the government, and could also present an argument as a victim of both race and sex discrimination." As a result, Texas BPW members wrote President Johnson asking his support, Illinois BPW members deluged Senate minority leader Everett Dirksen (R-IL) with telegrams, and Murray's memo was reproduced and distributed to the president, vice president, attorney general, and key senators.[62]

The Johnson administration did not urge that the "sex" amendment be dropped by the Senate. Indeed after the bill went to the Senate "sex" was added in other places to make the language consistent throughout. President Johnson stated that he supported the bill "in its present form" and Democratic leaders said they opposed removing "sex." When Senator Dirksen, whose support was necessary for Senate passage, said he wanted to remove the amendment, Sen. Margaret Chase Smith (R-ME), at the urging of the NWP, persuaded the Republican Conference to vote against him. He finally gave up, "in order to avoid the wrath of the women."[63]

Who Done It?

Later, savoring victory, both the NWP and Martha Griffiths claimed sole credit for the addition of "sex" to Title VII (though the NWP did give some to the Republican congresswomen). Both no doubt deserve credit, but even more credit should go to the fortuitous circumstances leading up to that fateful day. The most important of these was the Civil Rights Movement, without which there wouldn't have been a Civil Rights Act. Given the amount of time necessary to pass the relatively innocuous Equal Pay Act, and the compromises involved, it is highly improbable that an act prohibiting employment discrimination by sex alone would ever have passed Congress, let alone one creating a federal enforcement agency.

Nor was this vote taken in isolation, despite the claim by opponents that the "sex" amendment was hasty and ill-considered. Testimony about employment discrimination dominated the hearings held on the Equal Pay Act in a House Committee in March of 1962 and 1963, and in a Senate

Committee in April of 1963. In mid-October, the report of the President's Commission had been released to great publicity. President Johnson had made several public statements in January of 1964 about his intention to bring more women into government. The lobbying efforts of the NWP were weak compared to those of the civil rights forces, but they weren't nonexistent. The NWP solicited help from other women's organizations and sent letters to many Members of Congress. A member of BPW from Texas walked into the NWP headquarters to volunteer full time just when its campaign began. She distributed pamphlets prepared by an NWP attorney from statistics collected by the Women's Bureau on such topics as "The Discriminations against Women Workers Are Greater Than Those against Negro and Non-White Men."[64]

The other experienced lobbyist was Esther Peterson. While she officially opposed the "sex" amendment and supplied material against it for the House floor debate, there's no evidence that she mobilized her considerable resources against it in the Senate, even though there was adequate time to do so. Indeed, in April, Peterson drafted President Johnson's answer to a letter from Texas BPW inquiring about his stand on the "sex" provision, which expressed support for "equal opportunity for women" and the "present form" of the bill.[65]

While the initiative for adding "sex" to Title VII clearly lies with the NWP, the more important questions are who voted for it, and why. This would be simpler if there had been a roll call vote. However, there was only a teller vote. Individuals on either side passed through two tellers who counted them but did not record names. Even if all the congresswomen, except Edith Green, voted for the "sex" amendment, that would account for only 10 votes out of 168. The Southerners might have wished to undermine the civil rights bill, but many of them had concluded that passage was inevitable and gone home. Only 86 Southern Democrats were present to vote against the Civil Rights Act on Monday, February 10;[66] it's unlikely that more than that were present to vote for "sex" on Saturday, February 8. Who were the Members who came to the floor to support "sex" on Saturday and came back on Monday to support the entire Civil Rights Act?

The only evidence on who voted for "sex" on February 8 comes from Rep. Martha Griffiths, who was one of the tellers. She told an interviewer many years later that most of the pro-votes came from Southerners and Republicans.[67] The final vote on the entire civil rights bill was a roll call; the Civil Rights Act was passed by a coalition of 152 (mostly Northern) Democrats and 138 Republicans.[68] It appears that responsibility for the addition of "sex" to Title VII lies in the hands of the Republican Members of the House of

Representatives; they are the ones who voted for both the "sex" amendment and the civil rights bill. This does raise another question. Why should the Republicans, not noted for their love of federal regulation, want to do this?

The answer most likely lies in the Equal Rights Amendment, which had traditionally received much more support from Republicans than Democrats. Support for the ERA went into the Republican Party Platform earlier, and stayed in longer, than in that of the Democrats. The Senate votes on the ERA in 1946, 1950, and 1953 showed that many more Republicans than Democrats supported it.[69] Opposition to the ERA since World War II had been largely from labor unions and their supporters, whose elected representatives were to be found primarily among Northern, and liberal, Democrats. Although most everyone except the NWP thought the ERA was a dead issue, this did not deter the NWP from combing the halls of Congress every year seeking support. NWP stalwarts repeatedly asked Members to sign pledge cards, and frequently compiled lists of sponsors. Their systematic lobbying educated many Congress members about sex discrimination and built up a network of relationships with those who were sympathetic to the NWP's concerns.[70]

Nor should one assume that the Southerners' only motive in voting to add "sex" to Title VII was their antagonism toward civil rights. To judge from the sponsors, ERA sympathizers were largely Republicans and Southern Democrats: i.e., people who had a distaste for government regulation and were not attuned to the concerns of organized labor. Rep. Smith spoke in favor of a "sex" amendment in 1956 and had been an ERA sponsor since 1943; when he retired in 1966, the NWP lamented the loss of "our Rock of Gibraltar."[71] Despite the humor that Smith injected into the "Ladies Day" debate, what evidence there is does not indicate that he had proposed his amendment as a joke.[72]

Although the prohibition of sex discrimination in employment became law without the usual lengthy proceedings of major legislation, it was not as thoughtless, or as devious, as has previously been assumed. Instead it was the product of a small but dedicated group of women, in and out of Congress, who knew how to take advantage of the momentum generated by a larger social movement to promote their own goals, and a larger group of congressmen willing to make an affirmative statement in favor of women's rights. But it was casual. At a time when the division between "men's jobs" and "women's jobs" was still taken for granted, the implications of prohibiting discrimination in employment on the basis of sex had not been fully explored. If they had been, so revolutionary a proposal is unlikely to have passed. Even the President's Commission cautioned that "experience is needed in determining what constitutes *unjustified* discrimination in the treatment of women workers."[73] That is why the "sex" provision is more easily understood as a surrogate for the ERA, an issue which had been extensively discussed, if not agreed upon. Indeed, when McDonough introduced his "sex" amendment to the 1956 civil rights bill, he specifically linked it to the ERA and the "voluminous evidence of record in hearings . . . to show there has been discrimination because of sex."[74] After forty years of effort, the NWP still had not persuaded two-thirds of Congress to support the ERA, but it had apparently persuaded a majority.

Notes

1. Loevy 1990, ch. 2 and 3.
2. *Cong. Rec.* 110, February 8, 1964, 2577.
3. Women's Bureau 1975, 324–25.
4. Freeman 1975, 54.
5. EEOC 1971, 30.
6. Rawalt 1980, 454–49.
7. Freeman 1975, 186–87.
8. Lehrer 1987.
9. Whalen 1985, 238.
10. Orfield 1975, 299.
11. Whalen 1985, 110–11.
12. Orfield 1975, 299.
13. Lemons 1973, 49.
14. *Cong. Rec.* 92, July 19, 1946, 9405; Pardo 1972, 127–33.
15. *Congressional Digest* 25, December 1946, 290.
16. Harrison 1988, 39.
17. Harrison 1988, 26–29.
18. *Cong. Rec.* 96, January 25, 1950, 872–83; 1950 *Congressional Quarterly Almanac*, 539.
19. *Cong. Rec.* 99, July 16, 1953, 8954–95; 1953 *Congressional Quarterly Almanac* 386.
20. Rupp and Taylor 1987, 74–75.
21. Harrison 1988, 89–105.
22. East 1982, 7; Murray 1987, 348–49.
23. Peterson 1983, 288; Harrison 1982, 378.
24. 48 Stat. 22.
25. *Fed. Reg.* 6 1941, 3109.
26. Burstein 1985, 8; Equal Employment Opportunity Commission (EEOC) n.d., 1–3.
27. Nathan 1969, 87–89; EEOC n.d., 4–5, referring to Executive Orders 10308, 10479, 10925, 11114.

28. *Cong. Rec.* 92, January 23, 1946, 313.

29. *Cong. Rec.* 96, February 22, 1950, 2247.

30. EEOC n.d., 7–8.

31. Rupp and Taylor 1987, 153–65.

32. Rupp and Taylor 1987, 176; Pardo 1979, 161–62.

33. Letter of July 20, 1956, from NWP congressional chairman Alice Paul to Mary Sinclair Crawford; Reel 102, NWP papers.

34. *Cong. Rec.* 102, July 17, 1956, 13124–25.

35. Paul 1972, 617–68; *Cong. Rec.* 102, July 19, 1956, 13552–57.

36. *Time,* July 30, 1956, 9.

37. NWP papers, Reel 103.

38. Mead and Kaplan 1965, 49.

39. Peterson 1983, 300.

40. Telegram of July 1, 1963, from John F. Kennedy to Emma Guffy Miller; letter of July 13, 1963, from Nina Horton Avery to Emma Guffy Miller; "Report to Membership" by Nina Horton Avery; Reel 108, NWP papers.

41. Loevy 1990, 62–75; Whalen and Whalen 1985, 27–28, 34–35, 59.

42. *Newsweek* poll and Smith quote in Whalen and Whalen 1985, 91–92; NORC Survey 330 cited in Burstein 1985, 46; Zelman 1980, 60–61; House of Representatives, Committee on Rules, *Hearings on H.R. 7152,* 88th Cong. 2d Sess., January 9–29, 1964, 125, 366, 558; Loevy 1990, 96–100; Paul 1972, 615, 622, 624. The resolution is on Reel 108, NWP papers. Portions are cited by Berger 1971, 332; Brauer 1983, 43; and Rupp and Taylor 1987, 176. Reel 108 also contains a four-page, single-spaced, unsigned report on "c.r. bill progress," apparently written in late February 1964, with reports on the overtures to various Members of Congress. The author was probably Caruthers Berger, who was an attorney in the Labor Department and a member of the National Council of the NWP.

43. Bird 1968, 7.

44. May (Bedell) 1979, 144. Green [D-OR] was the only congresswoman to speak against adding "sex" to Title VII.

45. Paul 1972, 623–25.

46. U.S. House of Representatives 1964, 125.

47. U.S. House of Representatives 1964, 366.

48. Bird 1968, 3–4.

49. *1964 CQ Almanac,* 344.

50. *CQ Weekly Report,* February 7, 1964, 281; Zelman 1982, ch. 3.

51. Whalen and Whalen 1985, 123.

52. Whalen and Whalen 1985, 110.

53. Paul 1972, 625; Brauer 1983, 46, 48; *Cong. Rec.* 110, February 5–6, 1964, 1978–79, 2280–81, 2264–65, 2297.

54. Whalen and Whalen 1985, 117–119; EEOC n.d., 3213–28; *Cong. Rec.* 110, February 8, 1964, 2577–84; Zelman 1980, 64–67; Brauer 1983, 48–51; Rupp and Taylor 1987, 177–78; Harrison 1988, 177–79; *New York Times,* February 9, 1964, 1:1.

55. *Cong. Rec.* 110, February 5–6, 1964, 1978–79, 2280–81, 2264–65, 2297.

56. *Cong. Rec.* 110, February 8, 1964, 2596–99.

57. *Cong. Rec.* 110, February 8, 1964, 2599–2607.

58. *Cong. Rec.* 110, February 10, 1964, 2728.

59. EEOC n.d., Appendixes 2 and 3.

60. *Cong. Rec.* 110, February 10, 1964, 2718–21.

61. *Cong. Rec.* 110, February 10, 1964, 2804.

62. Patterson 1986, 154; Murray 1987, 356–67; Zelman 1980, 70; Bird 1968, 13; Rawalt 1980, 365, 396.

63. Zelman 1980, 70–71; Brauer 1983, 52–55; Murray 1987, 357–58; *Cong. Rec.* 110, March 26, 1964, 6239; Anita Politzer to Margaret Chase Smith, April 2, 1964; Smith to Politzer, April 9, 1964; E. G. Miller to Mary Kennedy, April 15, 1964; Alice Paul to Mary Kennedy, undated draft quoting the *Baltimore Sun* of May 25, 1964; Reel 109, NWP papers. Dirksen was an ERA supporter. Indeed, Alice Paul wrote Marjorie Longwell on August 4, 1956, praising his "uncompromising support" while a member of the Senate Judiciary Committee; Reel 103, NWP papers.

64. Berger 1971, 333; Zelman 1980, 45–47, 61, 138n17; Paul 1972, 622, 626–67. Copies of letters to Members of Congress, the NWP pamphlets, and an untitled report of Hettie Milam Cook on H.R. 7152, are in the NWP papers, Reel 108. Berger wrote the NWP arguments, but could not be public about her participation because she worked for the Labor Department. Alice Paul 1972, 628, credits her for working every night without being specific about what she did. Berger was more open about her role with Rupp and Taylor in a 1982 interview: Rupp and Taylor 1987, 177–78, 251n79.

65. Quoted in Zelman 1980, 71, 140n53.

66. Whalen and Whalen 1985, 111–12, 122.

67. Brauer 1983, 51, citing his January 11, 1979, interview with Griffiths.

68. *1964 CQ Almanac*, 606.

69. *Congressional Quarterly* II:3, July–September 1946, 568; *1950 CQ Almanac*, 539; 1953 CQ Almanac, 386.

70. Rupp and Taylor 1987, 191.

71. *NWP Bulletin* 1:7, Nov.–Dec. 1966, 3; Reel 154, NWP papers.

72. Brauer 1983, 45; Harrison 1988, 295n20.

73. Mead and Kaplan 1965, 49; my emphasis.

74. *Cong. Rec.* 102, July 17, 1956, 13124. In his papers at the University of Southern California, material on this "sex" amendment is in the folder labeled "ERA."

References

Becker, Susan D. 1981. *The origins of the Equal Rights Amendment: American feminism between the wars*. Westport, Conn.: Greenwood Press.

Bedell, Catherine May. 1979. Oral history interview with Fern Ingersoll, March 1 and 9, April 20. *Former Members of Congress*, Library of Congress.

Berger, Caruthers Gholson. 1971. Equal pay, equal employment opportunity and equal enforcement of the law for women. *Valparaiso University Law Review* 5 (Spring): 326–73.

Bird, Caroline. 1968. *Born female: The high cost of keeping women down.* New York: David McKay.

Brauer, Carl M. 1983. Women activists, Southern conservatives, and the prohibition of sex discrimination in Title VII of the 1964 Civil Rights Act. *Journal of Southern History* 49, no. 1 (February): 37–56.

Burstein, Paul. 1985. *Discrimination, jobs and politics: The struggle for equal employment opportunity in the United States since the New Deal.* Chicago: University of Chicago Press.

East, Catherine. 1982. The first stage: ERA in Washington, 1961–1972. *Women's Political Times,* September: 1, 7–10.

Equal Employment Opportunity Commission (EEOC). n.d. *Legislative history of Titles VII and XI of Civil Rights Act of 1964.* Washington, D.C.: GPO.

———. 1971. *Fifth annual report.* Washington, D.C.: Government Printing Office.

Freeman, Jo. 1975. *The politics of women's liberation: A case study of an emerging social movement and its relation to the policy process.* New York: Longman.

George, Emily R.S.M. 1982. *Martha W. Griffiths.* Washington, D.C.: University Press of America.

Graham, Hugh. 1990. *The civil rights era: Origins and development of national policy, 1960–1972.* New York: Oxford.

Harrison, Cynthia. 1982. Prelude to feminism: Women's organizations, the federal government, and the rise of the women's movement, 1942–1968. PhD diss., Columbia University.

———. 1988. *On account of sex: The politics of women's issues 1945–1968.* Berkeley: University of California Press.

Lehrer, Susan. 1987. Origins of protective labor legislation for women: 1905–1925. Albany: SUNY Press.

Lemons, Stanley J. 1973. *The woman citizen: Social feminism in the 1920s.* Urbana: University of Illinois Press.

Loevy, Robert D. 1990. *To end all segregation: The politics of the passage of the Civil Rights Act of 1964.* Lanham, Md.: University Press of America.

Mead, Margaret, and Frances Balgley Kaplan. 1965. *American Women: The report of the President's Commission on the Status of Women and other publications of the commission.* New York: Charles Scribner's Sons.

Murray, Pauli. 1987. *Song in a weary throat: An American pilgrimage.* New York: Harper and Row.

Nathan, Richard. 1969. *Jobs and civil rights: The role of the federal government in promoting equal opportunity in employment and training.* Prepared for the U.S. Commission on Civil Rights by the Brookings Institution, Washington, D.C., April.

National Woman's Party Papers, 1913–1974. 1979. Microfilmed and distributed by the Microfilm Corporation of America, Sanford, North Carolina.

Orfield, Gary. 1975. *Congressional power: Congress and social change*. New York: Harcourt, Brace, Jovanovich.

Pardo, Thomas C. 1979. *The National Woman's Party papers 1913–1974: A guide to the microfilm edition*. Sanford, North Carolina: Microfilm Corporation of America.

Patterson, Judith. 1986. *Be somebody: A biography of Marguerite Rawalt*. Austin, Tex.: Eakin Press.

Paul, Alice. 1972–1973. *Conversations with Alice Paul: Woman Suffrage and the ERA*. Interviews by Amelia Fry, November 1972 and May 1973. Suffragists Oral History Project, Bancroft Library, University of California, Berkeley.

Peterson, Esther. 1983. *The reminiscences of Esther Peterson*. Interviews by Ed Edwin, April 22–23. Oral History Research Office, Columbia University, New York.

President's Commission on the Status of Women. 1963. *Report of the Committee on Civil and Political Rights*. Washington, D.C.: U.S. GPO.

Rawalt, Marguerite. 1980. *The reminiscences of Marguerite Rawalt*. Columbia University Oral History Research Center, New York.

Rupp, Leila J., and Verta Taylor. 1987. *Survival in the doldrums: The American women's rights movement, 1945 to the 1960s*. New York: Oxford University Press.

U.S. House of Representatives, Committee on Rules. 1964. *Hearings on H.R. 7152*, 88th Cong. 2d Sess. Jan. 9–29.

Whalen, Charles, and Barbara Whalen. 1985. *The longest debate: A legislative history of the 1964 Civil Rights Act*. New York: New American Library.

Women's Bureau, U.S. Dept. of Labor. 1966. *Action for equal pay*. Washington, D.C.: GPO.

———. *Handbook of women workers*. 1975. Washington, D.C.: GPO.

Zelman, Patricia G. 1980. Women, work and national policy: The Kennedy-Johnson years. PhD diss., Ohio State University.

———. 1982. *Women, work and national policy: The Kennedy-Johnson years*. Ann Arbor, Mich.: UMI Research Press.

CHAPTER THIRTEEN

~

Congressional Passage
of the Equal Rights Amendment

Section 1. Equality of rights under the law shall not be denied or
abridged by the United States, or by any State, on account of sex.

Section 2. The Congress shall have the power to enforce, by appropriate
legislation, the provisions of this article.

Section 3. This amendment shall take effect two years after the date of
ratification.

—The Equal Rights Amendment, as passed by Congress and sent to
the states on March 22, 1972. It fell three states short of ratification.[1]

As the women's liberation movement burst into public consciousness, it liberated the Equal Rights Amendment from the congressional committees in which it had been imprisoned for decades. On February 17, 1970, two dozen members of the National Organization for Women (NOW) disrupted hearings on the eighteen-year-old-vote amendment being held by the Senate Judiciary Subcommittee on Constitutional Amendments. They demanded that hearings be scheduled on the Equal Rights Amendment.[2] On February 26, subcommittee chair Birch Bayh (D-IN) "electrified" his audience at the annual legislative conference of the National Federation of Business and Professional Women (BPW) when he announced that hearings on the ERA would be held in May. One of the largest women's organizations at that time, it had supported the ERA since 1937.[3]

After Richard Nixon became president in 1969, he appointed fourteen task forces to make recommendations to his administration. The Task Force

Figure 14. ERA rally at the Capitol on July 9, 1978, to demand an extension of the deadline for ratification. Photograph by Jo Freeman.

on Women's Rights and Responsibilities was one of them. After three months of secret meetings it submitted its report, *A Matter of Simple Justice*, to the president on December 15, 1969. The tone and content of this report were much more akin to the 1968 NOW Bill of Rights than to the 1963 *Report of the President's Commission on the Status of Women*. Unlike Kennedy's Commission, Nixon's Task Force supported the ERA.

Word of the endorsement by the President's Task Force was quickly leaked to the press. Soon another presidential body, the Citizens Advisory Council on the Status of Women (CACSW), officially endorsed the ERA—less than ten years after its parent, the President's Commission, had been created to stop it. With this endorsement the CACSW published a definitive legal analysis of the ERA, written by Justice Department attorney Mary Eastwood, and transmitted it to President Nixon. Published under the imprimatur of the CACSW, the memo was a lengthier version of one she wrote for NOW in 1967. On March 26 Rep. Martha Griffiths (D-MI) entered it into the *Congressional Record*, thus making what was originally a feminist analysis of the ERA for a feminist organization an official part of its legislative history. The memo argued that while "equal rights" did not admit of special exceptions on the basis of sex alone, only those laws which served to restrict freedom or deny rights to one sex would be voided, while those which actually conferred benefits on women would be extended to men. This interpretation mitigated some of labor's disagreements with feminists by opposing an across-the-board elimination of all sex-specific laws.[4]

Another breakthrough came in April, when the United Auto Workers (UAW) decided to support the ERA.[5] The UAW had always been more progressive on women's rights than other labor unions. In 1944 the UAW created a Women's Bureau in its War Policy Department. After World War II ended it was moved to the Fair Practices and Anti-Discrimination Department, which included "sex" in a model fair employment practices clause for union contracts. The Women's Bureau became a separate Women's Department (WD) in 1955. Always more of an internal agitator for women than an auxiliary, the WD ensured that the UAW never held the complacent attitude of other unions that protective labor legislation was all women needed, and they needed it all. The iconoclastic attitude of the women who ran the WD was rooted in the fact that several of them had lost their jobs after World War II when protective labor laws were reimposed. That happened to many other working women, of course, but no other major union provided the institutional base of a Women's Department with its support network for women unionists. As early as 1946, UAW women opposed the common practice of classifying jobs by sex because it limited their access to employment. During the fifties the UAW was persuaded to alter its policy on married women workers. Locals had commonly included clauses in their contracts with employers prohibiting the employment of married women, or limiting their acquisition of seniority. The International Executive Board came to see this practice not as a way of fairly distributing jobs, as it had been perceived during the Depression, but as a form of discrimination in violation of the UAW's fair employment practices policy. The UAW also opposed eight-hour laws for women only on the grounds that they led to excessive overwork for men and underwork, or even no work, for women. It even agreed with the National Woman's Party (NWP) that executive orders prohibiting discrimination by federal contractors should include sex. Although originally a supporter of protective labor laws, as early as 1955 the UAW acknowledged that such laws were used to deny work to women that they could do. By 1965, UAW research indicated these laws often did more harm than good.[6]

An example of this research was described by Dorothy Haener in her testimony before the Michigan Occupational Standards Commission in August of 1968. She reported that after the Civil Service Commission ruled in 1962 that state protective laws did not apply to federal employees, women's percentage of jobs in the U.S. Post Office jumped dramatically. A comparison of two states which had hours laws (Michigan and Ohio) with two which didn't (Iowa and West Virginia) illuminated the fact that the increase was due to the removal of the restriction.[7] (See table 13.1.)

The Senate hearings on the ERA held on May 5–7, 1970, were almost anticlimactical. Attendance was low and there was little press. Although Catherine East, the executive director of the CACSW, had been consulted on who should testify, her suggestions were not followed; there were no experts on constitutional law.[8] None of the women's organizations which had traditionally opposed the ERA, some of which still did, appeared to testify, though the National Councils of Catholic and Jewish Women put statements in the record. Most of the forty-two witnesses spoke in favor of the ERA; most of those who spoke against it represented unions. The presence of the UAW and the American Federation of Teachers among the ERA supporters reflected a beginning in the shift in attitudes of organized labor that would make Congressional passage possible.[9] B'nai B'rith also put a statement in the record supporting the ERA.

Table 13.1.   Problems of Discrimination Created by Restrictive Hours Regulations Applied Only to Female Employees

	Women as % of Total	Men	Women
Michigan			
1958	11.5	16,870	2,199
1967	23.9	19,488	6,122
% increase		15.5	178.4
Ohio			
1958	8.4	26,438	2,416
1967	15.9	29,481	5,559
% increase		11.5	130.1
Iowa			
1958	15.6	7,072	1,305
1967	17.9	7,646	1,671
% increase		8.1	28.0
West Virginia			
1958	25.6	3,194	1,097
1967	22.8	3,489	1,031
% increase		9.0	−6.0

Source: Appendix B of the statement of Dorothy Haener of the International Union of the United Auto Workers before the Michigan Occupational Standards Commission, August 19, 1968, on Reel 111, NWP papers.

Momentum picked up again in June. The Women's Bureau held its Fiftieth Anniversary Conference, provocatively titled "American Women at the Crossroads: Directions for the Future." It attracted over a thousand women from all over the country. To honor the occasion, the White House released the long-delayed report of the President's Task Force. Secretary of Labor–designate James D. Hodgson spoke at the conference on June 13, adding his endorsement of the ERA, and his department released the guidelines for federal contractors to eliminate sex discrimination for which feminists had been fighting for years.[10] Although this conference was not called for that purpose, women in attendance wanted to pass resolutions. The Women's Bureau dutifully printed the numerous resolutions passed by the workshops, including the ones opposing the war in Viet Nam. The ERA received a rousing endorsement, despite some opposition. Two petitions were circulated, one in favor and the other titled "Minority Report re: Protective Legislation vis-a-vis the ERA." The first received 173 signatures, and the latter only 30.[11]

Excitement at the Women's Bureau conference had been stimulated by Congresswoman Martha Griffiths' (D-MI) announcement on June 11 that she was introducing a petition to discharge the House Judiciary Committee from further consideration of the ERA. Griffiths had been chief House sponsor of the ERA since Katherine St. George (R-NY) was defeated for reelection in 1964. A long-time member of the NWP, she had a very poor opinion of the organization and did not take direction from it. However, she did respect and listen to Catherine East, Marguerite Rawalt, and Virginia Allan, who thought a discharge petition was the only way to get around Chairman Emanuel Celler's (D-NY) power to keep the ERA entombed in his committee. Both Rawalt and Allan were past presidents of the BPW. Getting the ERA out of Congress had been a personal cause for Rawalt, an IRS attorney, for decades. Virginia Allan was a businesswoman and educator from Griffiths' home state of Michigan, who had chaired Nixon's Task Force on Women's Rights and Responsibilities. Celler had been a Member of Congress since the ERA was first introduced in 1923 and was one of its most adamant opponents; as chairman of the Judiciary Committee, he had refused to hold hearings on the ERA for twenty years. A discharge petition is a seldom-used device which permits a majority of the House members (218) to bring a measure to the floor over the opposition of the committee to which it has been assigned. Because it challenges the power of committee chairs, those who sign are often sanctioned—unless they win. Between 1910 and 1970 only 835 discharge petitions were filed, of which only 24 received the requisite majority of signatures, and only two of the measures that were discharged ever became law. Griffiths won. On July 20 she filed the petition with 218 signatures.[12]

She had a lot of help. A petition to Congress was signed by those attending the Women's Bureau conference. Within four days letters were sent by Gladys O'Donnell, president of the National Federation of Republican Women, to all NFRW state presidents and by Geri Joseph, vice chair of the Democratic National Committee (DNC), to all national committeewomen and Democratic Women's Club presidents, urging them to write their representatives to sign the discharge petition. At that time BPW was holding its national conference in Hawaii where Rawalt and Allan were holding regular ERA pep talks. Every evening Griffiths phoned Rawalt with a list of those who had signed that day. Every day a Western Union clerk was brought into the conference so BPW members could send individual telegrams to their recalcitrant representatives. When Rawalt returned home she also sent a bulletin to the one hundred thousand members of the General Federation of Women's Clubs, whose Committee on the Status of Women she co-chaired, urging them to do the same. In the meantime a DC feminist consciousness-raising group with many Hill employees turned itself into the Ad Hoc Committee for the ERA after hearing Griffiths speak. They too sent mailings to lists of individuals and organizations urging them to write their representatives, and personally lobbied House members.[13]

Griffiths also had resources of her own. She had sat for several years on the powerful Ways and Means Committee where she had accumulated a lot of political favors she had not used up for home district bills. When she called in her favors, fifteen out of seventeen committee chairmen signed the petition, though Griffiths admits that many of the Southerners who chaired committees did so to "hit at Celler" who "had been strongly for civil rights for blacks, not for women." They "would never have signed otherwise." She also got the Republicans. One morning at 2:00 a.m. she phoned Rawalt to tell her that House Minority Leader Gerald R. Ford (R-MI) had finally signed. "That means the Republicans will now sign up in numbers, so the discharge petition is a sure thing."[14]

On August 10, the ERA came to the House floor for the first time in its history. It was scheduled for an hour of debate, though this "hour" took up several. The galleries were so full that the guards rotated people in and out. The antis had awakened from their complacency of the previous May. That morning all representatives received a telegram from several unions and the National Councils of Catholic, Jewish, and Negro Women urging them to vote against the ERA. The debate that day would have been amusing if the issue hadn't been so serious. Opponents objected to the amendment being voted on without "full and thorough hearings in committee," which had just been scheduled for September, and argued that Title VII had rendered it unnecessary. Under Griffiths' direction the pantheon of laws discriminating against women were reviewed by speakers ranging from all three House leaders to first termer Shirley Chisholm (D-NY), a member of the NOW Board of Directors and the first black woman to be elected to Congress. The final roll call vote showed overwhelming support for S.J. 264. It passed 350 to 15.[15]

That evening several of the women who had devoted the last few months of their lives to the ERA went to dinner at the National Lawyers Club, including Griffiths, Rawalt, East, Wilma Scott Heide of NOW, Betty Boyer of WEAL (Women's Equity Action League), Ruth Easterling of BPW, and former congresswoman Edna Kelly (D-NY). In the foyer they spotted a bust of Blackstone, the codifier of the English common law on which the American legal system is based. That codification had placed women in a distinctly inferior position to men, institutionalizing many "disabilities" which the ERA would erase. The women turned the bust of Blackstone to the wall and Rawalt put a black scarf over his head.[16]

Their jubilation was a bit premature. The House Judiciary Committee didn't hold hearings, but the Senate did, despite the fact that Majority Leader Mike Mansfield (D-MN) had placed the House bill directly on the Senate calendar. Held in September, they were presided over by the ERA's new nemesis, Sen. Sam Ervin (D-NC), who had taken up the banner left by the departure of Sen. Carl Hayden (D-AZ). He had drafted a version which did not "impair" the "validity of any law" which "exempts women from compulsory military service, or which is reasonably designed to promote the health, safety, privacy, education, or economic welfare of women, or to enable them to perform their duties as homemakers or mothers."[17]

Contrary to custom, he put on the opposition witnesses first, and gave them three days to the proponents' one. Half of the eight opposition witnesses were law professors, including Leo Kanowitz of the University of New Mexico Law School, who had published extensively on women and the law. He had once called the ERA "a potentially destructive and self-defeating blunderbuss." Ervin, who had borrowed this phrase as the title to one of his own speeches, was quite taken aback to discover that Kanowitz had changed his mind. He testified that while the ERA "would not achieve anything that could not be achieved by the courts" it would "give encouragement" and cause "no harm." Kanowitz's switch was just one sign of the realignment that was taking place between the traditional pro- and anti-ERA coalitions, in the process creating some rather strange bedfellows. Submitted for the record were statements by Teamsters president Jimmy Hoffa in support of the ERA and one by The Feminists, a New York City radical feminist group, in opposition. They damned the ERA because "it is at least useless and very likely could be detrimental to women's interests." The testimony of Harvard Law School Professor Paul Freund was less surprising, as he made the same argument he had in 1945 that the ERA would invite "confusion, anomaly and dismay." After he finished, eleven of his colleagues at Harvard Law School sent telegrams to twenty senators supporting the ERA.[18]

The Senate Judiciary Committee took no further action on the ERA, but the subcommittee had reported it favorably on July 28 and the House version was on the calendar. This brought the ERA to the Senate floor for debate in October. Its enemies were much better prepared than they had been in the House, proposing one amendment and two "riders"—unrelated measures often attached to bills because they have not been favorably reported from committee. Sen. James B. Allen (D-AL) tried to add a guarantee of "freedom of choice" school desegregation plans. This lost 17 to 57. Ervin was more successful with an amendment to exempt women from the draft, as was Sen. Howard Baker (R-TN) with a rider to permit prayer in public schools. Although 80 Senators had committed themselves as cosponsors of the ERA, the former passed 36 to 33 and the latter 50 to 20. These additions killed the ERA for the 91st Congress. Not only were they unacceptable to proponents, but if the Senate had passed the altered ERA, a conference to reconcile it with the different House version would have been necessary. The leader of the House conferees would have been the chair of the relevant committee—Emanuel Celler. Sen. Bayh tried to get around this problem by introducing a new and different version of the ERA, based on the language of the Fourteenth Amendment, but feminist groups had fought for so long for the earlier language that any changes were unacceptable and the substitute was withdrawn.[19]

During the electoral interim women regrouped into two separate but cooperative alliances. Basically there was a division of labor between the new feminists and the old, not all of whom would have used the term feminist. The Ad Hoc Committee became the National Committee for the ERA. Organized by local NOW members Flora Crater and Carol Burris, it coordinated Washington area activists from a wide variety of organizations in both branches of the new feminist movement. Its participants engaged in day-to-day lobbying, published a monthly newsletter, the *Woman Activist,* and sent out mailings. Many of them did this full time, without pay, for months on end.[20]

The other group was called Women United. It was created by Rawalt, Griffiths, and women who had worked with them, particularly Gladys O'Donnell, president of the NFRW, and Harriet Cipriani, director of women's activities for the DNC. Ostensibly a coalition of organizations, it was in fact composed of individuals because experience had taught its creators that trying to get consensus from a federation of organizations was difficult. Nonetheless, they worked through already existing organizations, acting primarily as an information clearinghouse and a catalyst by contacting organizational leaders in states whose representatives needed pressure. They designated Washington attorney Margaret Lawrence as chair, Rawalt as general counsel, and O'Donnell and Cipriani as vice chairs. The other officers were Louise O'Neil, Bernice Sandler, Virginia Allan, and Olga Madar. They solicited individual donations so they would not be dependent on organizational contributions. After an article appeared in *McCalls* with an address for Women United, enough "money rolled in" to pay for two staff workers and an office.[21]

When the new Congress convened in January of 1971 a new version of the ERA was submitted by Martha Griffiths in the House and by Birch Bayh (D-IN) and Marlow Cook (R-KY) as chief sponsors in the Senate. This version retained the substantive language, but changed the "enabling clauses" which specified how the ERA was to be put into effect. To meet those objections of Sen. Ervin which the sponsors did not feel detracted from the intent of the ERA, they added a seven-year limit on the time in which states could ratify, delayed its enforcement until two years after ratification, and altered and removed two phrases from the clause "Congress [and the several states] shall have the power, [within their respective jurisdictions], to enforce this article by appropriate legislation."[22] On January 18, 1971, Rawalt wrote Bayh and Cook that this language had been approved by NOW, BPW, General Federation of Women's Clubs, WEAL, National Federation of Republican Women (NFRW), National Association of Women Lawyers, the Ad Hoc Committee, and the DC Women's Bar association. She didn't tell them that the NWP disapproved. It wrote its own "Memorandum" in case other ERA supporters didn't know. The NWP pointed out that the "new" enabling clause was in fact the one from the 1923 version of the ERA. It had been changed in 1943 by the Senate Judiciary Committee to meet objections by the states that they were being asked to surrender all enforcement power to the federal government. The NWP was concerned that states' rights proponents in the state legislatures would be troubled by the deletion.[23] When the NWP testified to this effect at the House hearings in March and April, no one paid any attention.

What they did pay attention to was the testimony of Assistant Attorney General William Rehnquist. Although President Nixon had verbally supported the ERA at least since his 1960 campaign, other than Secretary of Labor Hodgson's speech his administration had done nothing on its behalf.

Indeed when the Justice Department agreed to testify at House hearings scheduled by Don Edwards (D-CA), chair of the Subcommittee on Civil and Constitutional Rights, word went around that the attorneys assigned to write the testimony were anti-ERA. Rehnquist had been directed to testify in its favor, but was himself opposed. In a dazzling compromise between personal preference and institutional obligation, he did both. After acknowledging the president's endorsement, his subsequent testimony was so negative that it was quoted by the opposition.[24]

The opposition didn't quote the testimony given by draft-age women on how the ERA would affect them. On February 10, 1971, at hearings by the Senate Armed Services Committee on the administration's proposal to extend the draft for two years, Carol Vance of George Washington University Women's Liberation read a statement prepared by her and Beverly Fisher demanding that young women not "be spared from making critical decisions." With the Viet Nam War still claiming thousands of lives every year, they denounced the threat of the draft as a means of intimidating women seeking equal rights.[25] This testimony was repeated during the House ERA Hearings in April[26] when they "came in one day, about 50 of them . . . in their jeans and sweaters. . . . Two or three of them had babies on their backs [and] they really did make a tremendous impression on that Judiciary Committee [with] some of the best testimony."[27] What was remarkable about this event was not just that draft-age women had faced down those "who seek to deny us this equality with the tactic of fear"[28] but that self-defined radicals were joining with "establishment" women in pursuit of a legislative goal.[29]

Three weeks after the hearings, on April 28, the subcommittee recommended the ERA to the full committee by a voice vote. But Cellar was still the chair, and he had no intention of letting the ERA out in its pristine form. When the Judiciary Committee met in June, he found his allies among the Republican members rather than the northern labor Democrats as he had in the past. In the past year several unions had shifted to support of the ERA. After the UAW, the AFT, and the Teamsters came the American Newspaper Guild, United Farmworkers, Retail Clerks, International Brotherhood of Electrical Workers, International Union of Painters and Allied Trades, International Chemical Workers Union, and the National Association of Railway Business Women. Several organizations which had traditionally opposed the ERA, such as the ADA, the AAUW, the ACLU, and the American Nurses Association, also decided to endorse it. This still left several Democratic groups in the opposition camp, including the AFL-CIO, which worked against the ERA at every opportunity, but their numbers were steadily dwindling. By 1971 the list of opponents was relying as heavily on individuals as organizations, and many of those individuals were listed as "former" chair or director (e.g., of the Women's Bureau) or "former" member (of the PCSW or CACSW).[30]

This growing crescendo of support did not deter Rep. Charles Wiggins (R-CA) from proposing an amendment in the House Judiciary Committee incorporating all of the fears of the proponents. It stated that "This article shall not impair the validity of any law of the United States which exempts a person from compulsory military service or any other law of the United States or of any state which reasonably promotes the health and safety of the people." It passed by 19 to 16 in June, with only one Republican, Robert Mc-Clory (R-IL), opposed. There was no obvious reason why the Republican members should have been so unanimously in favor of crippling the ERA, as they were its traditional supporters. NFRW president Gladys O'Donnell, one of the most active ERA advocates, was so appalled that she told the Republican National Committee this party-line vote would be used by the Democrats for political purposes. A month later she and RNC co-chair Anne Armstrong persuaded the RNC to unanimously endorse the ERA and urge its immediate passage "without nullifying amendments." Rawalt and Griffiths were so impressed with her efforts they felt that without her "we might not have succeeded when we did."[31]

Even with the Wiggins addition Celler remained adamantly opposed, and, along with two Republican members voted against sending the ERA to the House floor.[32] Any other year the crippling amendment would also have persuaded supporters to keep the ERA in committee. But after the overwhelming House vote the year before, they felt they could remove the amendment on the floor. The one person who disagreed with them was Alice Paul. She had opposed the "new, revised" ERA that Griffiths, Bayh, and Cook had introduced the previous January, and had been working "morning, noon and night" behind the scenes to keep the ERA in committee. She had secured agreement from Democratic leaders to detain it at least until Labor Day and assumed they would willingly postpone it even longer.[33] Women United sent a memo to all supporters in June urging them to assure their representatives that the NWP was alone in this opposition. It was concerned that "Congressmen are provided with the alibi that women do not agree."[34]

When Paul returned to Washington from her summer home she found dissent among the usually compliant members of her organization. Carol Burris of the National Committee tried to talk her into dropping her opposition without success, but when NWP national chair Marjorie Longwell backed Burris up, she was rather shaken. Paul had persuaded Sen. Vance Hartke (D-IN) to introduce the unaltered ERA the previous spring,[35] but she could not persuade her friends John T. Myers (R-IN) and Florence Dwyer (R-NJ) to move it as a substitute in the House. They assured her they preferred the standard version, but that Bayh "had it all tied up." Faced with this united opposition, she gave up and dropped out, convinced that the ERA was a lost cause.[36]

On the House floor it was anything but a lost cause. Don Edwards had effectively organized the Democrats, and Robert McClory had mobilized the Republicans. During several hours of debate, proponents, particularly the female members of the House, carefully laid out its intended results because they knew that this would be the primary legislative history to which the courts would turn when interpreting how the ERA applied to specific cases. The year of lobbying and debate paid off when the Wiggins amendment was overwhelmingly rejected by 87 to 265, and the ERA approved by 354 to 24 with only the altered clauses reflecting the compromises of the previous year. The specter of the "Hayden rider" and its progeny had finally been surmounted.[37]

In the Senate, Ervin struck back. On November 22 he persuaded the Senate Subcommittee on Constitutional Amendments, by a vote of 6 to 4, to replace the ERA with substitute language: "Neither the United States nor any State shall make any legal distinction between the rights and responsibilities of male and female persons unless such distinction is based on physical or functional differences between them." This combined all the worst aspects of the old Status Bill and the Hayden rider. Further action in the Senate was delayed in deference to Sen. Bayh whose wife was dying of cancer. When the full Judiciary Committee met in February, Bayh was back in force. Not only did the committee vote on February 29 to report the House version of the ERA with only Ervin dissenting, but it rejected five other amendment attempts, including two to exempt women from the draft. The final Committee Report was one of the strongest pro-ERA statements to come out of Congress, marshaling the arguments that had been developed for the past eighteen months to counteract the multitudinous objections.[38]

In the interim Griffiths told the pro-ERA forces that they needed to generate a million pieces of mail to counteract Sen. Ervin's opposition. They did that and more. The Ad Hoc Committee alone sent out over 40,000 letters to presidents of different organizations asking them to write their congressmen and publish items on the ERA campaign in their newsletters. All of Common Cause's 215,000 members received a letter to do the same, and a battery of volunteers made over 51,000 phone calls on Common Cause's WATTS lines. BPW sent at least 100,000 letters to state officers and local club presidents, and served as the spearhead of the pass-ERA drive in many locales where feminist organizations were anathema. As a result, some Members of

Congress received as many as 1,500 letters a month. The coordinated effort worked so well, according to congressional aide Val Fleishhacker, that "toward the end, it got so you could make twelve phone calls and get five to ten thousand letters." The lobbying effort was similarly intense. The Ad Hoc Committee assigned each senator to one of nine women and coordinated the activities of approximately forty full- and part-time volunteers who literally lived in the halls of Congress. According to one estimate, the total number of letters ran to over five million, but that was probably for the entire two-year campaign.[39] Griffiths joined in this effort by

> going to see [Senators] personally, "begging" the southern senators to vote for the bill. Within senatorial offices, secretaries helped by sharing with Griffiths the current thinking of the men for whom they worked. Griffiths gives great credit to Carol Burris of NOW, who would go from office to office in the Senate gathering this type of information. Burris also collected anything that could be gleaned about the thoughts of senators' wives, daughters, and granddaughters' opinions regarding ERA. Those who supported it were contacted and asked to talk with negative or wavering senators. Many a senator was persuaded to commit himself by a personal case of discrimination against one of the women close to him.[40]

When debate in the Senate began on March 17 proponents had combed the corridors so thoroughly that they knew they had the votes. Nonetheless both Bayh and Ervin girded themselves for a major battle, getting permission from the Senate for their aides to be on the floor to hand them material for each argument as it came up. Griffiths was also on the floor as were Reps. Margaret Heckler (R-MA) and first-termer Bella Abzug (D-NY). They sat in the back and counted each vote.[41] Unlike the House debate where each of the congresswomen, and several of the men, had had their turn on the floor, the Senate debate was primarily an exchange between Ervin and Bayh. While the issues they argued about were largely legal ones, it was clear that behind each reasoned argument lay fundamentally different conceptions of women and their proper role. This was only nominally a debate over the Equal Rights Amendment; in reality it was a debate over the desirability of women's liberation. Ervin saw women as the complement to men, and the ERA, which he denounced as the "unisex" amendment, as a threat to women's function of nurturing and maintaining the stability of the family. Bayh, and cosponsor Marlow Cook, discoursed on the evils of discrimination and the importance of the ERA in making women first-class citizens. Neither side really spoke to the concerns of the other, though they did speak to those of their separate supporters.[42]

The first test of strength came on March 21, when Ervin introduced his amendment to exempt from the ERA any laws on compulsory military service. As the clerk called the roll senators who had voted in favor of a similar amendment the year before added their "nays" to the lengthening list. When the final tally showed that only 18 senators agreed with Armed Services Committee Chairman John C. Stennis (D-MS) that the ERA posed "a very grave question from the standpoint of national security as well as the treatment of womanhood," everyone knew it was all over. The unamended ERA was supported by 73 senators, including 14 who had voted for the draft exemption two years before. Despite the overwhelming vote, Ervin persisted. That day he proposed and lost two more amendments: one exempting women from combat duty, which Ervin said was "designed to prevent the conversion of . . . the service academies into co-educational war colleges," and another protecting all laws "which extend protections or exemptions to women." They lost by 18 to 71 and 11 to 75, respectively.[43] President Nixon, who had not publicly commented on the ERA since his election, had sent a supportive letter to Sen. Hugh Scott (R-PA) on March 18, which the *New York Times* speculated might have contributed to the overwhelming vote. Neither the sponsors or the women who had worked on the campaign gave this belated gesture any credit for their victory.[44]

On March 22, 1972, the Senate galleries were so full that spectators were rotated in twenty-minute shifts. Many people who had devoted major portions of their lives to the ERA for the previous two years milled about outside. Ervin knew he had lost, but he wasn't giving up without a fight. All he needed was one change in the wording from that passed by the House, no matter how innocuous, to force a conference which Celler would chair. If he couldn't get that at least he could score debating points by forcing his colleagues to vote against "motherhood and apple pie"—otherwise known as protection of true womanhood. One by one he proposed five more amendments. The amendment to protect laws "which extend protections or exemptions to wives, mothers or widows" was rejected by 14 to 77. The amendment to protect laws "which impose upon fathers responsibility for the support of their children" lost by 17 to 72. The amendment to protect laws "which secure privacy to men or women, or boys or girls" went down by 11 to 79. The amendment to protect laws "which make punishable as crimes sexual offenses" was defeated by 17 to 71. His next maneuver was to offer as a substitute the version proposed by the Judiciary subcommittee. It lost by 12 to 78. And his final ploy was to offer to the states the alternative of accepting either the language passed by the House or an omnibus ERA incorporating all of the exemptions the Senate had just voted down. Even some of his supporters couldn't go along with this, and it lost 9 to 82. Finally Ervin sat down, and the ERA itself was passed by 84 to 8. As the final tally was read the galleries erupted into cheers and cowboy yells which could not be gaveled into silence.[45]

With the announcement of the Senate vote hundreds of women in the Capitol and thousands of women throughout the country thanked their congressional leaders, in person and by mail. On May 10, Women United held a victory celebration attended by almost seven hundred people, including 79 Members of Congress, at which Griffiths, Bayh, and Cook were honored and presented with silver trays.[46]

Of all the people who had given so much time and devotion to the ERA, one was not celebrating. Six months later Alice Paul, who had retired to her house in Connecticut, concluded the story of her lifelong struggles for *Suffrage and the ERA* by telling interviewer Amelia Fry, "So we lost it, you see."

> *Paul*: But I don't believe it's Bayh that's doing it, at all. I think that there's some master mind that's planning all these things and making use of Mr. Bayh.
>
> *Fry*: Some interest group.
>
> *Paul*: Some interest group perhaps. Somebody who wants its defeat, anyway. That's it. . . .[47]

Notes

1. As originally passed by Joint Resolution of both Houses, the ERA contained the following preliminary language:

> Resolved by the Senate and House of Representatives of the United States of America in Congress assembled (two-thirds of each House concurring therein), That the following article is proposed as an amendment to the Constitution of the United States, which shall be valid to all intents and purposes as part of the Constitution when ratified by the legislatures of three-fourths of the several States within seven years from the date of its submission by the Congress.

The original deadline of March 22, 1979, was extended to June 30, 1982, by the 2nd session of the Ninety-fifth Congress. No more states ratified during the extension.

2. *New York Times*, February 18, 1970, 20:6.

3. *New York Times*, February 27, 1970, 40:4. *National Woman's Party Bulletin* 4 (Spring 1969): 2, reports that the legal counsel of the Judiciary subcommittee told the NWP that hearings on the ERA were planned for 1970, but this may have been a standard putoff rather than a serious commitment; Reel 158, NWP papers.

4. East 1983b, 38; Freeman 1975, 212; Rawalt 1983, 63. The sixteen-page memo, "The Proposed Equal Rights Amendment to the U.S. Constitution," can be found in

Cong. Rec. 116, March 26, 1970, 9684–88; U.S. Senate, *ERA* hearings, May 1970, 369–90; and on Reel 111, NWP papers. The CACSW endorsement appears in Citizen's Advisory Council on the Status of Women 1970, 2; and the CACSW press release of February 7, 1970, on Reel 111, NWP papers. According to Rawalt there was only one disenting vote in the CACSW, Margaret Mealey of the National Council of Catholic Women: Rawalt oral history, 1980, 712.

5. Hole and Levine 1970, 105–6. The UAW was not the first union to support the ERA, though its public support cracked organized labor's wall of opposition. Teamsters president Jimmy Hoffa had supported the ERA as early as 1964, although that may have been an individual decision rather than a union resolution. See his statement on Reel 109, NWP papers.

6. Gabin 1985, 1991. At EEOC hearings held in 1967, the UAW representative described how "employers have used these laws to circumvent our collective bargaining contracts and to discriminate against the women who are members of our unions," while the representative of the AFL-CIO, Andrew J. Biemiller, testified in support of protective labor laws; Babcock et al. 1975, 263–65. Steinberg 1980, 195, points out that protective laws did not keep pace with changes in the industrial workplace. In 1910, the average workweek was fifty-seven hours; laws prohibiting women from working over fifty-four or forty-eight hours were a benefit. By 1970 the average work week ranged from thirty-five hours to forty-three. A forty-eight-hour ceiling had no effect on the average workweek; it only limited overtime work at premium pay.

7. Statement of Dorothy Haener, representing the International Union of the United Auto Workers, August 19, 1968; Reel 111, NWP papers.

8. East 1982a, 8; East 1983b, 38.

9. U.S. Senate, *ERA* hearings, May 1970.

10. Freeman 1975, 213; East 1982a, 8–9.

11. The conference program, resolutions, and petitions appear in Reel 111, NWP papers.

12. Freeman 1975, 213; Griffiths 1983, 199; *CQ Almanac* (1970): 707; *Congressional Digest* 50 (January 1971): 9; *Cong. Rec.* 116 (July 20, 1970): 24999. In a 1973 interview Griffiths told me that the suggestion of a discharge petition was made by Catherine East to commemorate the fiftieth anniversary of suffrage. In the Ingersoll interview she gives credit to Rawalt and Allan and in her biography to Rawalt and East; George 1982, 169.

13. Freeman 1975, 213–24; Griffiths 1983, 199; Rawalt 1980, 734–37; Letter of June 15, 1970, from Gladys O'Donnell and of June 16, 1970, from Geri Joseph, Reel 111, NWP papers.

14. Freeman 1975, 214; Griffiths 1983, 199–200; Rawalt 1980, 738. Two of the ten women in the House did not sign the discharge petition: Lenore Sullivan (D-MO) and Patsy Mink (D-HI).

15. Rawalt 1980, 740–41; *Cong. Rec.* 116 (August 10, 1970): 27999–28037; *CQ Almanac* 1970: 706, 54–55H; *New York Times*, August 11, 1970, 1:8. Nine of the ten congresswomen voted for the ERA, including Edith Green (D-OR), the only woman

to vote against the "sex" amendment to Title VII of the 1964 Civil Rights Act. Lenore Sullivan (D-MO), who was opposed to the ERA, did not vote.

16. Rawalt 1980, 743.

17. S.J. Res. 231.

18. U.S. Senate, Judiciary Committee, 1970: 2, 74, 163–5, 399, 402. Ervin cited the Kanowitz phrase to a law review article he had published in 1968, 182. However the version of that article that appears as chapter 7 of Kanowitz's 1969 book does not contain this phrase, though it does oppose the ERA. The telegram was solicited by a NOW member and former Harvard Law student and sent on September 28. It's reprinted in *Cong. Rec.* 116 (October 7, 1970): 35473. See also 36865 for a reprint of a *Washington Post* article on this by Elizabeth Shelton. The hearings were reported by the *New York Times*, on September 10, 1970, 47:1; September 11, 1970, 17:1; September 12, 1970, 6:4; September 13, 1970, IV:6:5; September 16, 1970, 9:1.

19. *CQ Almanac* (1970) 706, 708–9, S-60; *Cong. Digest* 50 (January 1971): 9; East 1982a, 9–10; Rawalt 1983, 64; Rawalt 1980, 751–54; *New York Times*, October 8, 1970, 28:1; October 9, 1970, 1:1; October 14, 1970, 1:1; October 15, 1970, 31:1; November 3, 1970, 19:5; November 12, 1970, 19:3.

20. Freeman 1975, 215; *Woman Activist* 1, no. 1 (January 14, 1971): 2–3, on Reel 112, NWP papers.

21. Copies of Women United letterhead stationery with officers can be found on Reels 111 and 112 of the NWP papers. Also see Rawalt 1983, 64–65; Rawalt 1980, 760–64.

22. S.J. Res. 8 and 9; Rawalt 1980, 765.

23. Marguerite Rawalt to Mitchell McConnell, office of Sen. Marlowe Cook, and P.J. Mode, office of Sen. Birch Bayh, January 18, 1971. Also see the NWP's "Memorandum on Enforcement Clause of the Proposed Equal Rights Amendment to the U.S. Constitution," January 27, 1971, Reel 112, NWP papers.

24. Statement of support by Nixon of the ERA made on September 2, 1960, Reel 106, NWP Papers. Eisenhower had endorsed it in 1957. U.S. House, *ERA hearings*, March and April 1971, 311–31. During subsequent House debate on the ERA, Rehnquist's testimony was cited by both Wiggins and Celler: *Cong. Rec.* 117 (October 21, 1971): 35301, 35759; East 1982a, 10; Freeman 1975, 218–29; Rawalt 1980, 768–69.

25. U.S. Senate Armed Services Committee, February 1971, 579–82.

26. U.S. House of Representatives 1971, 486–96.

27. Rawalt 1980, 777–78.

28. Testimony reprinted by Sen. Margaret Chase Smith in *Cong. Rec.* 118 (March 2, 1972): 6765.

29. Freeman 1975, 215–56.

30. The NWP was constantly compiling lists of supporters and several appear on Reel 112, NWP papers, which covers this period. One list was reprinted in *Cong. Rec.* 117 (September 28, 1971): 33745; and another in *Cong. Rec.* 118 (March 17, 1972): 8900. See also the telegrams of support sent to the NWP from Tom Boyle, president of the International Chemical Workers Union, on October 22, 1970, and

Cesar Chavez of the United Farm Workers on October 6, 1970, Reel 112, NWP papers. Chavez was still (inaccurately) being listed among opponents in lists printed as late as 1972, as was Dorothy Kenyon of the ACLU; *Cong. Rec.* 118, March 21, 1972, 9368, although that was just a reprint of a 1970 list printed at Cong. Rec. 116 (October 8, 1970): 35625. Also see *Woman Activist* 1, no. 7 (July 1, 1971): 2. Mary Keyserling, former director of the Women's Bureau, was also listed. She testified against the ERA in the 1971 House hearings, but reported (1982, 266–67) that she began to look into the court cases afterwards and changed her mind, though she didn't specify when. In 1981 she wrote an article on "Why I am a strong advocate of the ERA," 10–12.

31. 1971 CQ *Almanac,* 657; *Woman Activist* 1, no. 7 (July 1, 1971): 1; *New York Times,* June 24, 1971, 45:4; NFRW press release of July 24, 1971 on the RNC endorsement, Reel 112, NWP papers. It was also reprinted by McClory in *Cong. Rec.* 117 (July 31, 1971): 28594–95. Also see *Cong. Rec.* 117 (October 6, 1971): 35309; East 1982a, 10; East 1982b, 218; Rawalt 1980, 718; Griffiths 1983, 200. This was the only partisan vote on the ERA in the 1970–1972 period.

32. *CQ Almanac* 1971, 657.

33. Paul 1972, 541–42.

34. Women United Press Release No. 5 of 3 June 1971 on Reel 112, NWP papers.

35. S.J. Res. 79.

36. Paul 1972, 544–48.

37. *Cong. Rec.* 117, October 6, 12, 1971, 35289–90, 35295–326, 35782–815. CQ *Almanac* 1971, 657–68, gives a summary, as does *New York Times,* October 7, 1971, 43:3 and October 13, 1971, 1:2. Nine of the eleven women in the House voted for the ERA. Lenore Sullivan (D-MO) spoke and voted against it, and Edith Green (D-OR) was not present. See *Woman Activist* 1, no. 11 (October 15, 1971): 1.

38. *CQ Almanac* 1972, 200; U.S. Senate, Judiciary Committee, 1972.

39. *Newsweek,* April 3, 1972, 28–29. Interview with Val Fleishhacker, February 1973. She worked for Rep. Don Fraser (D-MN), whose office was the unofficial congressional headquarters of the Ad Hoc Committee. *Woman Activist* 1, no. 13 (December 15, 1971): 4–5; *Woman Activist* 2, no. 3 (March 1972): 2. Isabelle Shelton of the *Washington Star* dubbed this group "Crater's Raiders": *Sunday Star* (Washington DC), March 26, 1972, G-3. For a list see *Woman Activist* 2, no. 4 (April 1972): 4. Also see Rawalt 1980, 804.

40. Ingersoll's summary of Griffiths interview, 1983, 201.

41. Rawalt 1980, 803.

42. *Cong. Rec.* 118, March 17, 1972, 8899–911; March 20, 1972, 9080–106; CQ *Almanac* 1972, 200–201.

43. *Cong. Rec.* 118, March 21, 1972, 9314–72.

44. *New York Times,* March 22, 1972, 1:5; "Letter to the Senate Minority Leader About the Proposed Constitutional Amendment on Equal Rights for Men and Women," March 18, 1972, *Public Papers: Nixon, 1972,* 1974, 444. Nixon's public papers contain no other mention of the ERA during his first term. His State of the

Union address on January 20, 1972, had devoted three paragraphs of the written version to women without mentioning the ERA: *CQ Almanac 1972*, 199–202, 13-A.

    45. Cong. Rec. 118, March 22, 1972, 9513–40, 9544–99; *New York Times*, March 23, 1972, 1:6; *CQ Almanac 1972*, 201–2; Rawalt 1983, 65; Rawalt 1980, 812.

    46. Rawalt 1983, 66.

    47. Paul 1972, 549–50.

References

Babcock, Barbara A., Ann E. Freedman, Eleanor Holmes Norton, and Susan C. Ross. 1975. *Sex discrimination and the law: Causes and remedies*. Boston: Little, Brown.

Citizen's Advisory Council on the Status of Women. 1970. *Women in 1970*. Washington, D.C.: Government Printing Office.

East, Catherine. 1982a. The first stage: ERA in Washington, 1961–1972. *Women's Political Times*, September: 1, 7–10.

———. 1982b. Oral history interview for the Women in Federal Government Project. Schlesinger Library, Cambridge, Mass.

———. 1983a. *American women: 1963, 1983, 2003*. Washington, D.C.: National Federation of Business and Professional Women's Clubs.

———. 1983b. Newer commissions. In *Women in Washington*, ed. Irene Tinker, 35–36. Beverly Hills: Sage.

Freeman, Jo. 1975. *The politics of women's liberation: A case study of an emerging social movement and its relation to the policy process*. New York: Longman.

Gabin, Nancy. 1985. Women and the United Automobile Workers' Union in the 1950s. In *Women, work and protest: A century of women's labor history*, ed. Ruth Milkman, 259–79. Boston: Routledge and Kegan Paul.

———. 1991. *Feminism in the labor movement: Women and the United Auto Workers, 1935–1975*. Ithaca, N.Y.: Cornell University Press.

George, Emily, R.S.M. 1982. *Martha W. Griffiths*. Washington, D.C.: University Press of America.

Griffiths, Martha. 1983. Interview with Fern S. Ingersoll, summarized and excerpted in Former congresswomen look back. In *Women in Washington*, ed. Irene Tinker, 199–201. Beverly Hills: Sage.

Hole, Judith, and Ellen Levine. 1971. *Rebirth of feminism*. New York: Quadrangle Books.

Kanowitz, Leo. 1968. Constitutional aspects of sex-based discrimination in American law. *Nebraska Law Review* 48, no. 1: 131–67.

———. 1969. *Women and the law: The unfinished revolution*. Albuquerque: University of New Mexico Press.

Keyserling, Mary. 1981. Why I am a strong advocate for the ERA. *Barnard Almanac Magazine*, Winter, 10–12.

———. 1982. Oral history interview for the Women in Federal Government Project. Schlesinger Library, Cambridge, Mass., February 1–4.

National Woman's Party Papers 1913–1974. 1979. Sanford, N.C.: Microfilm Corporation of America.

Paul, Alice. 1972–1973. *Conversations with Alice Paul: Woman suffrage and the ERA.* Oral history interview by Amelia Fry. Suffragists Oral History Project, Regional Oral History Office, the Bancroft Library, University of California, Berkeley, November 1972 and May 1973.

Presidential Task Force on Women's Rights and Responsibilities. 1969. *A matter of simple justice: Report of the Presidential Task Force on Women's Rights and Responsibilities.* Washington, D.C.: GPO.

President's Commission on the Status of Women. 1963. *American women: Report of the President's Commission on the Status of Women.* Washington, D.C.: GPO.

Public Papers of the Presidents of the United States: Richard Nixon. Containing the public messages, speeches, and statements of the President. 1971–1975. Washington, D.C.: GPO.

Rawalt, Marguerite. 1980. The reminiscences of Marguerite Rawalt. Oral History Research Office, Columbia University, New York.

———. 1983. The Equal Rights Amendment. In *Women in Washington*, ed. Irene Tinker, 49–78. Beverly Hills: Sage.

Steinberg (Ratner), Ronnie. 1980. The paradox of protection: Maximum hours legislation in the United States. *International Labour Review* 119, no. 2 (March–April): 185–98.

U.S. House of Representatives, Judiciary Subcommittee No. 4. 1971. *Equal Rights for Men and Women.* Hearings on H.J. Res. 208, March 24, 25, 31 and April 1, 2, 5.

U.S. Senate, Armed Services Committee. 1971. Hearings on Selective Service and Military Compensation. February 2, 4, 8–10, 19, 22.

U.S. Senate, Judiciary Committee. *Equal Rights 1970.* Hearings on S.J. Res. 61 and S.J. Res. 231, September 6, 10, 11, 15, 1970.

———. 1972. *Equal Rights for Men and Women.* Senate Report 92-689, March 14.

U.S. Senate, Judiciary Subcommittee on Constitutional Amendments. 1970. *The Equal Rights Amendment.* Hearings on S.J. Res. 61, May 5, 6, 7.

Useful Webpages

Constitutional Amendments Not Ratified: www.house.gov/house/Amendnotrat.shtml

Biographical Directory of the U.S. Congress: bioguide.congress.gov/biosearch/biosearch.asp

Platforms of the Political Parties: www.presidency.ucsb.edu/platforms.php

The Equal Rights Amendment: www.equalrightsamendment.org

Shirley Chisholm's speech in favor of the Equal Rights Amendment on August 10, 1970: www.americanrhetoric.com/speeches/shirleychisholmequalrights.htm

CHAPTER FOURTEEN

~

Comparable Worth*

The concept of equal pay for work of equal value, also known as comparable worth, pay equity, and sex-based wage discrimination, has been called by friends and foes alike the women's rights issue of the 1980s. However, even among proponents there is little consensus on what it is, what to call it, and whether any legislative action should be taken to achieve it.

The issue came to national prominence in the fall of 1983 when U.S. district judge Jack E. Tanner of Tacoma, Washington, ruled that the state of Washington had discriminated against its employees in predominantly female job classifications by paying them significantly less than employees in predominantly male job classifications which required equivalent skill, responsibility, effort, and working conditions. Washington State had conducted a study in 1974 which revealed a 20 percent disparity between the average wages of traditionally male and female job classifications. It was sued by its employees' union, American Federation of State, County, and Municipal Employees (AFSCME) when the state legislature acted slowly and inadequately to eliminate the difference.

Since Tanner's ruling several bills or resolutions have been introduced into Congress and hearings have been held by four different congressional committees. However, his decision is being appealed and the Justice Department has said it might enter the case on the side of the state of Washington. Nonetheless, the House Committee on Government Operations recently

---

*Slightly revised from a three-part series published in *In These Times*, August and September 1984.

Figure 15. The AFSCME legal team in the Washington State case. From left to right: Ed Younglove of Olympia, WA, attorney; Lisa Newell of Washington, DC, attorney; Winn Newman of Washington, DC, lead attorney; George Masten, executive director of the Washington Federation of State Employees (AFSCME Council 28). Photograph provided by Elaine Newman. Identification of other people in photo by Paul Booth of AFSCME. Exact date of photograph is unknown, but probably taken in 1983. The photographer is most likely Mark Brown, who was on the staff of the Washington Federation of State Employees.

recommended that the Equal Employment Opportunity Commission (EEOC) file on the side of the employees.

Although some have called comparable worth a radical proposal that would completely restructure the American economy, to those most intimately involved in the legal cases or in implementation it is neither new nor radical. Winn Newman, the attorney on the Washington State and other key cases, says it is "really nothing more than plain old garden variety job rate inequity with which the labor movement has historically wrestled. Unions have regularly grieved and arbitrated the proper rate for the job—and arbitrators have regularly been called upon to resolve disputes over these rates and to establish rates that employers must pay."

Nina Rothchild, commissioner of employee relations of the state of Minnesota, asserts that "the principles of pay equity are simple and clear. Sex-based wage discrimination is against the law. Pay equity is a method to uncover and eliminate sex-based wage discrimination."

Newman declines to use the terms "comparable worth" or "pay equity" on the grounds that they are popular terms, not legal ones, and that they obfuscate what is really at stake. He has spent over fifteen years litigating cases charging employers with "sex based wage discrimination," which is prohibited by Title VII. The initial cases were filed on behalf of the IUE (International Union of Electrical, Radio and Machine Workers) of which he was general counsel. These cases sought to rectify long-existing wage inequities that had been identified as early as World War II.

Under pressure from the War Labor Board to stabilize wages and avoid strikes, employers such as General Electric and Westinghouse hired consultants to evaluate jobs in their plants and assign them points based on the skill, effort, responsibility, and working conditions involved. Relative wages were determined by each job's relative point values, except that those jobs in which women predominated had their rates lowered by one-third so that the highest-paid "women's jobs" paid less than the lowest-paid "men's jobs."

The Equal Pay Act (EPA) passed in 1963 had no effect on these wage rates because it only required equal pay when men and women were doing substantially the same work. The equal pay bill originally proposed in 1945 by Senators Claude Pepper (D-FL) and Wayne Morse (D/R-OR)—who as a member of the War Labor Board had seen many of these cases—would have made paying women less than men for *comparable* work an unfair labor practice. The scope and enforcement provisions were narrowed in 1962 to make passage possible. The EPA had no effect on the common practice of channeling women and men into different jobs based on their sex. Although Title VII prohibits segregation of jobs by sex, employers did not change their practices after it was passed in 1964. Instead they changed the names of "female" and "male" blue-collar jobs to "light" and "heavy."

Women have used court cases, grievances procedures, and complaints to the EEOC to attack this job segregation since 1965, but change has been slow. According to sociologist Barbara Reskin of the University of Michigan, overall job segregation decreased by only 10 percent between 1970 and 1980. However, even this improvement hides segregation within job categories. For example, the Bureau of Labor Statistics shows that there has been a vast increase in women bus drivers. But virtually all have part-time jobs as school bus drivers. Few have gained the higher-paying full-time permanent jobs of metropolitan or interstate bus drivers.

Sex-based wage discrimination cases would have no effect on the relative incomes of these different types of bus drivers, because they largely have different employers. However, the Washington State case, and several less publicized ones which preceded it, have opened the legal door to challenging pay practices by a single employer when the jobs are quite different if it can be shown that the difference in pay results from a difference in the sex of the job holder where the employer knows that the jobs are equivalent in skill, effort, responsibility, and working conditions.

Opponents do not view comparable worth as narrowly as proponents do, nor do they use the term sex-based wage discrimination. In 1984 hearings by congressional committees and the Civil Rights Commission, opponents claimed that adoption of comparable worth policies would be the "entering wedge" to "social engineering" by a federal agency which will eventually determine everyone's wages and make U.S. industry uncompetitive with the rest of the world.

They claim that the only proper determinant of wages is the market, and that if women are working at jobs that pay poorly it is because they choose those jobs for benefits they provide other than wages. Several have testified at the hearings that if women want to be paid like a man, they should "get a man's job." Some have even advocated "affirmative action" (but not quotas) to achieve this end! Opponents also claim that it is impossible to evaluate jobs impartially because too many value judgments are involved, that different jobs are valued differently by different employers, and that individual skill and ability should be rewarded differently.

Proponents' views are no more uniform than opponents', but some generalizations can be made. They deny that the market works very well for most jobs and argue that women are discouraged from entering the better-paying "male" jobs. They would agree with the latter claims, but the comparable worth policies most proponents have in mind would not require any new agency, the creation of an impartial job evaluation system, or comparisons between employers or individuals.

Rather employers, particularly in the public sector, would be encouraged to do internal studies using job evaluation systems developed over thirty years, refined to account for sex bias. These systems all evaluate jobs, not the people doing them, and thus do not affect rewards based on performance. In order to work they require that a consensus be achieved by representatives of different interests within a firm on the relevant job factors and the number of points to be given to each one.

Opponents argue that the cost of such studies would be prohibitive, and might only create more litigation on their validity. Proponents claim that full-dress evaluations are not necessary, that inquiries can be restricted to ascertaining the amount of sex-based wage discrimination, and that the informal job evaluation systems most employers already have would be sufficient in most cases. Since sex discrimination is illegal, a court might order a wage disparity analysis if employers failed to do them on their own, thus they would not necessarily avoid litigation by inaction.

The remedies most frequently mentioned by proponents of pay equity are legislation, litigation, and collective bargaining. Most unions would prefer to achieve wage gains by collective bargaining, backed up by the threat of litigation. AFSCME only sued the state of Washington because state law prohibited public employees from bargaining over wages. Legislation by states to compel pay equity studies of their own employment practices is also encouraged. However, since the courts have said that Title VII encompasses sex-based wage discrimination claims (and by inference race, religion, and national origin as well), Joy Ann Grune, former director of the National Committee on Pay Equity (NCPE), feels that "substantive legislation is not necessary. What we need is enforcement of Title VII." The NCPE is an umbrella group of over seventy-five organizations, including a dozen trade unions.

Several members of Congress who support comparable worth and would like to attach their names to the cause have submitted bills or resolutions, as well as calling numerous hearings. Sen. Dan Evans (R-WA), who ordered the original Washington State study while governor but left office before it could be implemented, and Rep. Olympia Snowe (R-ME) have called for pay equity studies of the legislative branch and implementation of their findings. Rep. Mary Rose Oakar's (D-OH) bill would order the Office of Personnel Management to do a similar study of the civil service. Sen. Alan Cranston (D-CA) and Rep. Pat Schroeder (D-CO) are exhorting the EEOC and other relevant agencies to pursue sex-based wage discrimination claims, a demand that would not have been necessary under previous administrations.

Schroeder had originally drafted bills to amend Title VII and the Equal Pay Act to incorporate sex-based wage discrimination claims but was asked to drop them by pay equity advocates. Such bills would have implied that sex-based wage discrimination was not already illegal, and that was not a good message to send the courts. If AFSCME v. Washington is overturned by a higher court, interest in such a bill may revive.

Politicization

Comparable worth officially became a partisan issue when the 1984 Republican Party convention adopted a platform provision opposing it one month after the Democratic Party adopted a platform that declared support. To those who have followed the Reagan Administration's consistent attempts to undermine all pay equity efforts this is not surprising. This pattern of opposition by all federal agencies concerned with discrimination led Lane Kirkland, president of the AFL-CIO, to tell a congressional committee last April that "the message the Reagan Administration . . . is sending to the employers of America is that sex discrimination in wages and salaries is not really very important or very wrong."

Even before the final draft of the platform, written by White House staff, was made public, the administration's attitude was apparent in hearings (called "consultations") on June 6–7 by the supposedly independent Civil Rights Commission. Although witnesses were invited to give academic papers, they were cross-examined by commissioners who acted as though they represented the prosecution or defense rather than the disinterested fact finding agency it is supposed to be. Leading the pay equity defense team was Howard Law Professor Mary Berry (joined solely by Blandina Ramirez). She was dismissed from the commission by President Reagan when he took office, but reappointed by House Speaker Tip O'Neill (D-MA) after Congress reconstituted the commission under a different format.

Berry told this reporter that the commission had actually come out against comparable worth several months ago and agreed to hold hearings only after she challenged their legal right to take a position without investigation. She has accused the commission of "being a public relations arm of the White House."

The White House was in need of a public relations arm after a memo to Office of Personnel Management (OPM) director Donald Devine was leaked in May, resulting in hurriedly called hearings by Congresswoman Mary Rose Oakar (D-OH). Oakar has two pay equity bills before Congress, one of which would require that OPM do a study of pay practices in the civil service much like the one that eventually led to the Washington State suit. The memo to Devine said that if Congress does require a pay equity study, it could be used to "show a clear picture to the private sector about how ridiculous the concept of comparable worth is."

It went on to say that "the political possibilities of this situation should not be underestimated. By doing job evaluations across clerical and blue collar occupations, a comparable worth study would immediately divide the white collar and blue collar unions. . . . since [the latter] would be the inevitable losers in such a comparable worth adjustment process." The memo advocated using the Oakar bill to "further divide this constituency of the left

. . . [and] create disorder within the Democratic House pitting union against union and both against radical feminist groups."

Devine followed up on this suggestion a few days later by inviting representatives of several unions representing government employees to a briefing in his office on May 22 where they were lectured on how blue-collar pay scales would suffer if a pay equity bill was passed. At the May 30 hearings the union representatives all said that the purpose of the meeting was to mislead them into opposing Oakar's bill. They endorsed the goal of pay equity and denounced the clumsy political manipulation of the OPM. Saul Stein, research and education director of the Metal Trades Department of the AFL-CIO, demanded that Devine and the deputy who wrote the memo resign on the grounds that it was "a clear violation of the Hatch Act" which prohibits political activity by federal employees.

After the hearings Oakar amended her bill to require that the study be done by an outside consultant "in cooperation with OPM and federal labor and women's organizations" so that "the final product will not be subject to manipulation or partisan politics." She also attached it to another bill on civil service pay which was supported by the administration in order to prevent a veto. This bill was passed by the House 413 to 6 in late June.

According to Winn Newman, the attorney who has handled the leading pay equity cases for fifteen years, all the federal agencies obligated to enforce equal employment opportunity laws have been remiss since Reagan became president. In testimony before the House Committee on Government Operations last February he said the Equal Employment Opportunity Commission had interpreted Title VII broadly prior to 1981, but that "President Reagan's appointees to the EEOC lost no time in expressing their opposition to correcting sex-based wage discrimination." He said the EEOC has taken no action on over 250 charges currently filed with the agency alleging some form of wage discrimination and listed several potential cases the EEOC could have brought to court or referred to the Justice Department for action which the agency has ignored.

EEOC chair Clarence Thomas claimed that there are no sex-based wage-discrimination complaints before the EEOC, only comparable worth cases, which "are not cognizable under Title VII." He told the Government Operations Committee that the EEOC considers sex-based wage discrimination to be a "priority" issue, but has not been able to act on "comparable worth" cases because it does not yet have a policy on how to handle them. The committee concluded that the "EEOC has placed itself in a 'Catch-22' situation by refusing to act without a policy while at the same time refusing to squarely address the issue and adopt a policy." It found that "the Commission did not initiate any action until the Committee began its investigation" and that it "has failed in its responsibility as the lead Federal agency for enforcement of employment discrimination law."

The courts have not expressly permitted the bringing of "comparable worth" claims, but have said that sex-based wage discrimination is a violation of Title VII. The EEOC's semantic distinction between a popular term and the legal one permitted it to claim that it was fulfilling its legal mandate without having to violate the then unstated policy of the Reagan administration to oppose pay equity efforts.

An earlier internal EEOC memo recommended dismissal of all comparable worth complaints, in part because most of them were against state or municipal governments. While the EEOC can investigate and attempt to conciliate complaints against governmental bodies, Title VII only permits the Justice Department at its discretion, not the EEOC, to sue them. It is the responsibility of the EEOC to decide which governmental cases to refer to the Justice Department for possible legal action. The EEOC memo said the Justice Department was "not likely to file suit." The Justice Department declined to testify before the Government Operations Committee on the grounds that it had "had no occasion" in the last three years to file a wage discrimination case. EEOC chair Thomas had originally decided not to testify until threatened with a subpoena by the committee.

The Labor Department has also declined to take action on comparable worth issues, and has tried to undo the achievements of the Carter administration. In 1978, when Ray Marshall was secretary of labor, suit was filed against the Kerr Glass Manufacturing Corporation charging that Kerr channeled its unskilled men and women into different but comparable entry-level jobs whose evaluation was skewed to achieve sex-discriminatory wage rates. Reagan's Department of Labor settled the case four years later by agreeing to drop wage discrimination and related back pay claims.

In 1979 the Labor Department's Office of Federal Contract Compliance Programs proposed revisions to its Sex Discrimination Guidelines that included a section on comparable worth. The new rules were frozen by Reagan shortly after he took office and when finally issued on August 26 (the anniversary of the Nineteenth Amendment) the comparable worth language had been deleted.

Opposition to pay equity has been so consistent and appeared so early that it is unlikely to have been arrived at independently by each of the federal agencies involved. Comparable worth was not officially a partisan issue until the 1984 party platforms were adopted and prominent supporters and opponents are still to be found in both parties. However, the person who has been most influential in shaping the Reagan administration's policies on women has been Phyllis Schlafly. Members of her Eagle Forum inundated the 1980 Reagan/Bush campaign with angry phone calls after it appointed many supporters of the ERA and pro-choice to a Women's Policy Advisory Board. This convinced administration policy makers, particularly Attorney General Ed Meese, that Schlafly, not feminist Republicans (most of whom had supported Ford or Bush), was the one to listen to on issues affecting women.

Schlafly and her Eagle Forum have consistently opposed comparable worth and have alarmed many conservative Republicans with their claims that it would lead to government wage controls. She has also opposed any studies being done by government agencies on wage-based sex discrimination on the grounds that they are a preliminary step to expensive lawsuits. When Congressman Jack Kemp (R-NY), a 1988 presidential aspirant, spoke at Jerry Falwell's Family Forum III on August 18 he was criticized from the audience by an Eagle Forum member for voting for the Oakar bill. She claimed comparable worth was "an attempt to bring in the ERA through the back door."

State and Local Activities

While academics and politicians are arguing the merits of comparable worth in Washington, it is being legislated, litigated, and bargained for in the states. The first lawsuit was filed by the International Union of Electrical, Radio and Machine Workers (IUE) in 1970. The first job evaluation study specifically designed to test for wage disparities between predominantly male and female jobs was conducted by the state of Washington in 1974. It became the model for numerous other studies by state and local governmental units at the urging of their employees' unions and women's organizations. It has not been the model for implementation.

The tipping point for activity on comparable worth was in 1981. Prior to that time there was some question as to whether sex-based wage discrimination claims under Title VII, which prohibits discrimination in employment on the basis of sex, race, religion, and national origin, were limited by the requirement of the 1963 Equal Pay Act that the work be substantially equal. As originally proposed in 1945 the EPA required that work be comparable, but it was narrowed in 1962 to make passage possible. When sex was added to Title VII during floor debates in 1964 a special exemption permitted employers to differentiate wages by sex where authorized by the EPA.

Consequently most cases claiming that predominantly female jobs were paid less than predominantly male ones which were not substantially equal but were equivalent in skill, effort, responsibility, and working conditions were dismissed by the courts unless women could show that the wage disparities were intentional. Title VII generally does not require that discriminatory intent be proved. Many of the sex-based wage discrimination cases filed prior to 1981 were settled out of court because there was a long history of intentional wage discrimination.

On June 8, 1981, in *County of Washington v. Gunther*, the Supreme Court declared that Title VII was broader than the Equal Pay Act. However, it made a point of stating it was only ruling on the question of scope and not "on the controversial concept of 'comparable worth.'" Thus it is not surprising that the decision by U.S. district judge Jack E. Tanner last fall that the state of Washington violated Title VII when it failed to remove wage disparities between predominantly female and male jobs uncovered by its own studies has been appealed.

1981 also saw the first strikes over comparable worth. In July of that year city employees in San Jose, California, went on strike for nine days after a four-year effort to obtain pay equity had failed. A job evaluation study showed that the workforce was heavily sex segregated and that there was an 18 percent difference in wages for equivalent jobs where 70 percent of the occupants were either men or women. The employees' union (AFSCME) was unable to reach a settlement with the city even though San Jose had a woman mayor and a female majority on the city council. The strike ended when the city agreed to provide 1.5 million dollars for wage adjustments of 5 to 15 percent over a two-year period in addition to a 15.5 percent across-the-board pay raise.

Going on strike was forbidden by law in the state of Washington, so AFSCME sued. The 1974 study had been initiated by Governor Dan Evans at the request of the Washington Federation of State Employees. It was updated three times, with each investigation revealing still more sex segregation and wage discrimination. Evans's last budget request before leaving office included seven million dollars to begin implementing the results of the studies, but it was deleted by his successor, Dixie Lee Ray, even though there was a budget surplus that year. The legislature took no further action until the AFSCME suit was filed, when it set up a ten-year implementation plan. The judge found this to be too little, too late and not only ordered the state to implement pay equity immediately, but to pay the employees it had shortchanged (10 percent of whom are men) several hundred million dollars in back pay.

The size of the award has frightened many state legislators. At an annual meeting of the National Conference of State Legislatures last December several participants said that their states would be reluctant to conduct studies out of fear that they would be obligated to immediately budget millions of dollars they might not have to remove any sex-based wage disparities. AFSCME and other proponents counter that the size of the award was largely for back pay, not implementation per se. AFSCME contends that there would be no lawsuits, and hence no back pay awards, if states would act "reasonably and responsibly" to bring the wages of women's jobs in line with men's.

In contrast to the state of Washington, the state of Minnesota is held out as the right way to respond to pay equity demands. In 1981 the Minnesota Commission on the Economic Status of Women created a pay equity task force of legislators, labor, management, and the general public which put out a report estimating the undervaluation of predominantly female jobs based upon a job evaluation previously done by an outside consultant. The following year the legislature appropriated twenty-two million dollars for initial pay equity adjustments. Over eight thousand employees received adjustments— some as high as $1,600—in addition to the 8½ percent general increase. The legislature also changed the state personnel law to make pay equity a primary policy and to compel local governments to implement it.

Since 1974 over a dozen states and dozens of local jurisdictions have mandated comparable worth studies and several have passed laws to add it to their equal pay acts or incorporate it into their public employee wage policies. Some of these studies, such as that in New York, are extremely elaborate. However, only Minnesota, Washington, New Mexico, and Connecticut, and several cities, have actually allocated money to eliminate wage disparities. Washington did so under threat of a lawsuit and Connecticut has been sued by AFSCME because the amount it allocated was so inadequate.

In those jurisdictions which permit public employee unions to participate in wage setting, authorization of the studies and implementation of their findings are usually done through a combination of collective bargaining and legislation. In other jurisdictions, political pressure has been the key ingredient. This political pressure has largely been a consequence of the increasing numbers of women state legislators and the increasing sophistication of women's organizations, some of it gained through ERA struggles.

At the Forum for Women State Legislators in San Diego last December (1983) workshops on pay equity had twice the attendance of any other. Women legislators from ten states asked for model bills to take home with them. The women's network of the National Conference of State Legislatures engineered passage of a resolution supporting pay equity by the NCSL a couple of years ago. There has been some sort of pay equity activity in at least forty states and fifty-two municipalities. Nonetheless, one member of this network told a NCSL workshop last December that "this is only the beginning. Comparable worth is about to explode in the states."

Postscript

On September 4, 1985, the Ninth Circuit Court unanimously reversed the district court in *AFSCME v. State of Washington*, 770 F.2d 1401, holding that reliance on a free-market system to set wages did not violate Title VII, even when it resulted in lower wages for women. Since the Ninth Circuit is one of the most liberal courts, this decision eliminated litigation as a means to remove sex-based wage disparities. Some state and local governments, including that of Washington State, chose to implement it anyway. Although it was still possible for unions to bargain for comparable worth, by any name, its pursuit faded as a legal and political issue. The judge who wrote the Ninth Circuit decision, Anthony Kennedy, was appointed associate justice of the U.S. Supreme Court in 1988. EEOC Chairman Clarence Thomas, who did not believe Title VII encompassed comparable worth, was appointed to the U.S. Supreme Court in 1991.

Suggested Readings

Aaron, Henry J., and Cameron M. Lougy. 1986. *The comparable worth controversy.* Washington, D.C.: Brookings Institution.

Acker, Joan. 1989/1991. *Doing comparable worth: Gender, class, and pay equity.* Philadelphia: Temple University Press.

Blum, Linda M. 1991. *Between feminism and labor: The significance of the comparable worth movement.* Berkeley: University of California Press.

Cook, Alice H. 1986. *Comparable worth: A case book 1986 supplement.* Industrial Relations Center, University of Hawaii at Manoa.

Evans, Sara M., and Barbara N. Nelson. 1989/1991. *Wage justice: Comparable worth and the paradox of technocratic reform.* Chicago: University of Chicago Press.

Mezey, Susan Gluck. 1992. *In pursuit of equality: Women, public policy, and the federal courts.* New York: St. Martin's Press.

Nelson, Robert, and William P. Bridges. 1999. *Legalizing gender inequality: Courts, markets, and unequal pay for women in America.* New York: Cambridge University Press.

Paul, Ellen. 1989. *Equity and gender.* New Brunswick, N.J.: Transaction.

Remick, Helen, ed. 1984, 1985. *Comparable worth and wage discrimination: Technical possibilities and political realities.* Philadelphia: Temple University Press.

Treiman, Donald, and Heidi Hartmann, eds. 1981. *Women, work and wages: Equal pay for jobs of equal value.* Washington, D.C.: National Academy Press.

U.S. Commission on Civil Rights. 1985. *Comparable worth: Issue for the 80s*, vol. 1. Washington, D.C.: GPO, June.

———. 1985. *Comparable worth: An analysis and recommendations*. Washington, D.C.: GPO.

U.S. Equal Employment Opportunity Commission. 1981. *Comparable worth: A symposium on the issues and alternatives: Proceedings of November 21, 1980*. Washington, D.C.: GPO.

Court Cases

AFSCME v. Washington, 578 F. Supp. 846 (W.D. Wash. 1983)

AFSCME v. State of Washington, 770 F.2d 1401 (9th Cir., 1985).

County of Washington v. Gunther, 452 U.S. 161, 173–76, 101 S. Ct. 2242, 68 L. Ed. 2d 751 (1981).

Figure 16.   Top: Nancy Pelosi celebrates her election as Speaker of the U.S. House of Representatives at a reception for her supporters in the Cannon House Office Building on January 5, 2007. To her right is Rep. Jerry Nadler (D-NY) and to her left is Rep. Steny Hoyer (D-MD). Photograph by Jo Freeman. Bottom: Pelosi pins from the personal collections of Jo Freeman (by gift of Lara Levison) and Catherine Dodd.

EPILOGUE

∼

The Long Road to Madam Speaker*

If women want to succeed in politics, Eleanor Roosevelt wrote in 1928, they "must learn to play the game as men do." When Nancy Pelosi, Member of Congress from California's Eighth Congressional District, was sworn in as Speaker of the House of Representatives on January 4, 2007, to the highest elected post ever held by a woman in the United States, it was because she had learned to do just that. During her lifetime both the political world and opportunities for women to operate effectively in that world changed a great deal. She grew up in one world but rose to power in another. It was her ability to apply the lessons learned from both, in the context of major social changes in the status of and opportunities for women, that made her achievement possible.

The World That Was

When Nancy D'Alesandro was born on March 26, 1940, in Baltimore, Maryland, four of the seven women then serving in Congress were political widows—three had followed their husbands into the House and one into the Senate. Later in the year two more political widows would succeed their deceased husbands in the House after winning special elections (Chamberlin 1973, 367–75). While being a political widow was an asset for

---

*This chapter was written in the winter of 2007 while I was a Senior Scholar at the Woodrow Wilson International Center for Scholars in Washington, DC.

a woman candidate, being a wife was a handicap. The other three women MCs were not married (two were widows, one never married). The Maryland House of Delegates had five women among its 120 members (Cox 1996, 144) but Maryland still hadn't ratified the Nineteenth Amendment. It would do so on March 29, 1941, and two months later elect its first congresswoman—another political widow who would serve only one term. Women had had equal suffrage with men for almost twenty years but voted at much lower rates because many in the older generation thought that anything to do with politics was "men's business." While women had been working in politics for at least sixty years, they had gained entry as party loyalists and supporters of "good men." They were not expected to have ambitions for themselves, and any effort to organize as women to support women was denounced as unpatriotic (Freeman 2000, 124–27).

Politics runs in families. The political gene is often passed on from parent to child, though how progeny express that gene can vary widely. Nancy D'Alesandro learned how to play the political game at her father's knee. In 1940, Thomas D'Alesandro, Jr.—better known as "Tommy the Elder"—was a freshman Member of Congress—just the latest office since he was first elected to the state legislature at the age of twenty-three. He would become mayor of Baltimore in 1947 and serve for twelve years. The oldest of her five brothers, "Tommy the Younger," served one term as mayor after many years on the city council. For her entire childhood and adolescence Nancy was immersed in the family business. She learned the basic premise of machine politics: Take care of the people who take care of you. Politics was not about issues. It was about who got what (Feuerherd 2003; Duke 2006; Mayhew 1986).

The political world that ER knew in 1928 had not changed much for women by 1940. "Politically," she wrote, "women are generally 'frozen out' from any intrinsic share of influence in their parties. . . . They are called upon to produce votes, but they are kept in ignorance of noteworthy plans and affairs" (Roosevelt 1928, 78–79). Women's biggest political assets were family connections, name recognition, and money—and even these brought them little more than superficial recognition when they answered the call to serve. Of the twenty-six women who served in Congress in 1940 or earlier twenty-one were born or married into political families and seven were quite wealthy. First-term women were also older than their male peers and unlikely to have had a professional career (Gertzog 1984, 38, 42). Major changes initiated by World War II rippled through succeeding decades. Women were employed outside the home in greater numbers than ever before. While they were forced out of many paid jobs when the war ended, they didn't forget the experience. As men were drafted into the war women replaced them in the low-level jobs of the political world. Party leaders discovered that women were better at the mundane tasks of politics—the lickin', stickin', and doorbell ringing—and that they demanded little in return. After the war, women lost their paid jobs in the labor force but kept their unpaid ones in politics. The war changed the political labor force from one of patronage workers to one primarily of volunteers; 90 percent were women (Freeman 2000, 176–77). The volunteer era of politics would last thirty to forty years.

Nancy would become one of those volunteers, but not until she had married and borne five children in six years. While attending Trinity College, a small Catholic women's college in Washington, DC, she met Georgetown University student Paul Pelosi of San Francisco. Whatever ambitions Trinity fostered, they lay dormant while she did what was expected of a good Catholic girl. Paul and Nancy married in 1963 and moved to New York City where he pursued his career as an investment banker. While other women her age in New York were protesting in the streets and forming feminist consciousness-raising groups, she was pregnant most of the time and always looking after small children. In 1969 the family moved to San Francisco, where there was a vibrant feminist movement. This movement burst into the public eye in 1970 and began to alter conceptions of women's place permanently (Freeman 1975).

A Woman's Place

During the 1970s the traditional view that "a woman's place is in the home" was challenged by the declaration that "a woman's place is in the House—of Representatives." The number of women in the House had increased slowly after World War II and gone down during the sixties. Once the feminist movement raised consciousness about women it rose again, but slowly; in 1972 Maryland elected its second female Member of Congress and California elected its fourth. The characteristics of the new women and their route to Congress were becoming more like men's. Political widows gave way to career women. Women elected to Congress were more likely to have held a previous public office, to be currently married, and to have had a professional career (Thompson 1985).

But they were still marginal Members. Much of the business of Congress is conducted through informal groups and friendship networks, which are crucial to shaping legislation. Women were either excluded or at best peripheral. Men felt uncomfortable with women present while "women [seemed] to deliberately avoid being considered a bloc" (Gehlen 1969, 38–40). The women first elected in 1972 were a new breed. They met together informally to exchange information until they finally formed a formal caucus in 1977—after the senior women who were not sympathetic to feminism had retired. Bipartisan and closed to men, the Congresswomen's Caucus provided the benefits of an informal social support group and an institutionalized place to identify and work on policies affecting women. However, the requirement for unanimity in order to publicly support any policy at a time when the parties were polarizing on issues affecting women created barriers to action, and the small number of congresswomen made it difficult to support a staff from Members' dues and contributions. The Congresswomen's Caucus's greatest success was in persuading Congress to extend the deadline for ratifying the Equal Rights Amendment from March 22, 1979, to June 30, 1981. Faced with a declining membership and a hostile administration after Ronald Reagan became president in 1981, the caucus transformed itself into the Congressional Caucus for Women's Issues (CCWI) on October 21, 1981. The addition of men with feminist attitudes from liberal districts and the loss of Republican women significantly altered the nature of the caucus, but also made it more effective (Gertzog 1984, 195–227).

Dedicated Democrat

As raising her five children consumed less of her time, Nancy Pelosi spent more of it serving the Democratic Party—a choice predestined by her family background. Party service was her route into politics. Party service was also a common route for men, but was more common for women, perhaps because so much of it is unpaid. Men are more likely to have served their apprenticeship to an elected office as paid staff of another elected official, or to have held a lower elected office (Thompson 1985, 80–81).

Pelosi moved up fast in the California Democratic Party. In addition to volunteering her time (and sometimes that of her children) to work on campaigns, she made her spacious home available for fundraising parties and developed a skill at persuading others to donate money. Her husband's investment business allowed them to travel in wealthy circles, but usually ones that shared their liberal values. In 1976 she used her connections in her home state of Maryland to help California governor Jerry Brown, then an aspiring presidential candidate, win that state's Democratic primary race. One consequence of the new national party charter was that the Democratic National Committee expanded to reflect each state's population. As a reward for her service to the party she was appointed as one of the new committeewomen from California. In 1977 she became chair of the northern section of the California Democratic Party and in 1981 state party chair. Only the second woman to hold this position, she was treated far more civilly than Elizabeth Snyder had been when she was Democratic state party chair from 1954 to 1956 (Freeman 2000, 118). In 1984 Pelosi chaired the host committee when the Democratic National Convention met in San Francisco, where Geraldine Ferrero (D-NY) became the first woman to be nominated for vice president by a major party. Pelosi was one of six people to run for chair of the national party after that convention, but dropped out when it became clear that she could not win. Instead, she became finance chair of the Democratic Senatorial Campaign Committee—where she could put her fundraising skills to good use and make friends among Democrats all over the country. Her efforts helped turn a 47–53 Democratic minority into a 55–45 Democratic majority after the 1986 elections.

Pelosi's rapid rise was aided by the convergence of two social movements: one of women nationally, and one of idealistic liberals in the California Democratic Party. California was fertile ground for the new feminist movement. During the 1970s the movement was expanding into all facets of American life and was much in the news (Rosen 2000). Within the Democratic Party women pushed for equal representation in all party bodies, and were largely successful (Shafer 1983). As party leaders looked for women to appoint or support for elective office, Pelosi was available and visible. She was a women whom men felt comfortable with and she was first and foremost a loyal Democrat. As had been true in the 1920s, when male party leaders also worked to bring women into the party, loyalty was a prime concern (Freeman 2000).

The movement inside the Democratic Party began during Adlai Stevenson's 1952 presidential campaign when thousands of Democratic clubs were formed throughout the country. Unlike the traditional party clubs these brought into politics Democrats who were educated, professionally employed, and motivated by ideals rather than the desire for patronage. Many of the California clubs coalesced in January of 1953 to found the California Democratic Council (CDC) in order to endorse candidates in the Democratic primaries—something the official party was legally forbidden to do—and mobilize support on their behalf. CDC built a network of Democratic clubs dedicated to electing liberal Democrats (Wilson 1962, 1966).

The Burton Machine

One product of this movement was San Francisco attorney Phil Burton, who defeated an incumbent Republican to be elected to the state assembly on his second try in 1956 (Bell 2006, 509; Jacobs 1995, 57). Phil's two brothers,

John and Bob, worked with him, as did his wife, Sala. They brought into their group other up-and-coming liberals in the Bay Area, such as Willie Brown and John's best friend, George Moscone. Their success lay in persuading middle-class liberals, especially those in the Young Democrats, to spend hours doing mailings and going door to door in poor and minority neighborhoods to elect the Burton brothers and the candidates that they supported. Collectively they were known as the Burton machine. In the fall of 1963 the Burton machine elected Congressman Jack Shelley as mayor of San Francisco in order to free up his seat for Phil Burton. John Burton took Phil's place in the California Assembly. Willie Brown was also elected to the assembly in 1964. After he became Speaker of the assembly in 1981 he became the "go to" man in California. In 1973 John became chair of the state Democratic Party, and in 1974 he too was elected to Congress in a special election to fill a vacant seat next to Phil's district. Moscone was elected mayor of San Francisco in 1975 (Jacobs 1995, 94, 280, 287).

The Burton machine was unlike the one that Nancy Pelosi grew up with. It was based on ideological cohesion, not distribution of jobs and state contracts. Once in office, the Burton brothers, Willie Brown, and the other liberal Democrats pushed for legislation which helped unions, the poor, and minorities. Initially the laws they pursued represented an extension of New Deal welfare legislation (Bell 2006, 517–20). As the sixties social movements raised new issues, especially ones about the treatment of minorities, women, and gays, the Burtons incorporated laws and policies benefiting these groups into their program. The fact that the Burtons embraced their causes did not mean that these groups always embraced them. The more power they got the more they were seen as the establishment.

Phil Burton was an ambitious man. Wanting to lead not only in San Francisco but in Congress, Burton "ascended by winning chairmanship of the Democratic Study Group and later the House Democratic Caucus." He made his move for a major leadership position in 1976 by running for majority leader. Although he campaigned for two years, he lost by one vote to Jim Wright—whom Speaker Tip O'Neill preferred as his second-in-command (Jacobs 1995, 219, 321). To elect like-minded people and put them into his debt, Phil Burton became an expert on redistricting. In the 1960s he influenced the drawing of assembly district lines to create a seat for Willie Brown. The district lines he shaped in the 1970s were thrown out by the court (Jacobs 1995, 121, 286). After the 1980 Census, he took control of the process once again and drew lines to maximize the number of Democrats as well as to help those who voted his way. However, Phil Burton did not live long enough to see all the fruits of his labor. He died on April 10, 1983.

When John Burton retired from Congress at the end of 1982 Phil offered the seat to several of his friends, including Nancy Pelosi. She turned it down because she thought her children were still too young. It finally went to Barbara Boxer, who ran one of John Burton's district offices. Nor was Pelosi interested (or offered) Phil's seat when he died the following April. His widow, Sala Burton, easily took his place. Sala wasn't the last of the political widows in Congress, but they were becoming rare. When Sala died of cancer on February 1, 1987, Nancy Pelosi was ready. On her deathbed, Sala asked her to run. Nancy said yes (Jacobs 1995, 445, 488, 489).

Congresswoman Pelosi

The special election to fill the vacancy in the Fifth Congressional District was held on April 7, 1987. With fourteen candidates running, Pelosi got barely 36 percent of the vote but Supervisor Harry Britt, her only serious challenger, got almost 4 percent less. Pelosi had the full support of the Burton machine as well as a plethora of Democratic officeholders. Sponsorship by established politicians is very valuable to any candidate but is particularly valuable to anyone who has not previously run for office and is without a personal political base; at the very least it signals to voters the belief that a candidate can do the job. However, in San Francisco, long a petri dish for social change movements, being the establishment candidate can also be a liability. Britt, who was openly gay, was the "outsider" candidate, supported by gays and left-wing Democrats. Feminists, who are often antiestablishment even when the candidates are women, rallied behind Pelosi. The San Francisco chapter of the National Organization for Women (NOW) endorsed her. Pelosi never came that close to losing again. Almost 80 percent of those voting reelected her in 1988 and 1990; after redistricting over 80 percent of those voting in her new Eighth Congressional District gave her their blessing. For her first two campaigns (1987 and 1988) she spent over a million dollars. After that she spent less than half a million.

In her first few years as a congresswoman, Pelosi championed issues of concern to her San Francisco constituents. At the top of her list was AIDS, in particular funding for research into treatment and programs to support the afflicted. China policy was also high on her agenda. As a member of the House Banking Committee she tried to restrict World Bank loans to China and opposed efforts to grant it "most-favored-nation" trading status (i.e., "normal" trade relations) because of its numerous human rights violations. She joined the CCWI and quickly became a committed and active member, always voting on the feminist side of issues concerning women—such as the

Family and Medical Leave Act (vetoed by Reagan; signed by Clinton), and easier availability of abortions for poor women and military women. Pelosi also reflected the values of one of the most strongly Democratic and racially diverse districts in the country by voting against the invasion of Iraq both in 1991 and in 2002, against aid to the Nicaraguan contras, for the Civil Rights Restoration Act in 1988, and for shifting funds from defense to domestic programs in 1992. Through her work on bills she gained a reputation for picking issues carefully and pursuing those chosen tenaciously (*Politics in America*, various years, "Pelosi").

When Nancy Pelosi became a Member of Congress in 1987 it was still very much a men's club. The number of women in the House had crept up to a little over 5 percent of the 435 Representatives but was far short of the critical mass necessary to change the culture. A study of congresswomen in the mid-1980s found that men's attitudes toward the women serving with them were more collegial and less patronizing than previously, but still had a ways to go. One interviewee "estimated that there were about 100 'macho sons-of-bitches' in the House, about 100 'decent, sensitive guys,' and about 200 'in between'" (Gertzog 1984, 66). However, the older members were more likely to be in the first category, and thus in the leadership of both parties. Men in Congress, like men elsewhere in the United States, were changing their attitudes and behavior toward women, but slowly and unevenly. As was true of many institutions, the older generation simply had to die off or retire to allow room for the more egalitarian attitudes to grow.

Changing attitudes did not by themselves create more opportunities for women MCs. There was still a glass ceiling on leadership positions. By the late 1980s women had obtained only a handful of positions at the middle levels of the leadership hierarchy and these came largely because the number of midlevel positions had increased, creating "open" seats. Pelosi was one of five Democratic (and two Republican) women appointed to one of the new whip positions in 1989 (her title was Assistant Whip). Overall, Republican women did a bit better than Democrats in getting the secondary positions, but none could break the barrier into the top posts where the real decisions were made. One who tried was Lynn Martin (R-IL), who ran for chair of the House Republican Conference in 1988 after serving four years as vice chair. She lost narrowly. A couple others ran and lost. Most women did not run (Gertzog 1995, 97, 100, 107–8, 281–83).

Changing Times, Changing Women

In the 1990s major changes took place for women in Congress. Their numbers leaped upwards after the 1992 elections—from twenty-nine to forty-seven representatives and from two to six senators—to become 10 percent of the total Members in the 103rd Congress. Of the twenty-four new women in the House, five were African Americans; two were Hispanic; five were from California; only three were Republicans. All of the new Democratic women but only one of the new Republican women joined the CCWI. The four new women senators were all Democrats; two were from California and one was black. A seventh senator would join them after a June 1993 special election, doubling the number of female Republican senators. Together, the women sworn in for the first time in 1993 shifted the congressional women's caucus in a decidedly liberal, Democratic direction.

The women who won these elections were not novices; they had been working their way through the political pipeline for years. Twenty years earlier, the number of women in the state legislatures escalated after the 1972 elections. In the 1980s many women ran for Congress, usually losing to incumbents. Redistricting, retirement, and scandals created ninety-one open seats in 1992, as well as some seats whose incumbents were vulnerable (Gertzog 1995, 4). Events that year prompted 211 women to seek their party's nomination for Congress; 104 received it (Palmer and Simon 2001, 67). The women who had been working in the wings moved into the spotlight. The new women MCs joined those who had been building seniority and acquiring knowledge of how things were done to create a significant pool of female political talent in the 103rd Congress. Sheer numbers meant there would be at least one woman on every House committee.

Emboldened by all the new Democratic women, the CCWI flexed its muscles for two years. It pressured the new Democratic administration to appoint women to top positions. It prodded the 103rd Congress to pass "more legislation addressing the needs of women and their children than any Congress in history" (Gertzog 2004, 43). Among the sixty-six measures it endorsed were ones dealing with women's and children's health, education, and a variety of economic needs. These included the Family and Medical Leave Act, the Violence Against Women Act, the Economic Equity Act, and numerous provisions in other bills (Gertzog 2004, 45–53). Working with two other congresswomen on the Labor, Health and Human Services Subcommittee of the Appropriations Committee—Nita Lowey (D-NY) and Rosa DeLauro (D-CT)—Pelosi was able to increase the funding for breast and cervical cancer research significantly (Dodson 2006, 163). The CCWI stepped into a minefield when it voted to support a woman's right to choose abortion. Previously, the CCWI had stayed away from abortion as too divisive. Early in 1993 it voted to support reproductive rights measures and succeeded in adding clauses to some laws which made some abortions more accessible for some women.

However, when the Republicans became the majority party (in both houses) after the 1994 elections, the CCWI was gutted. The new Speaker, Newt Gingrich, removed the funding for the formal caucuses and study groups because he thought they mostly helped Democrats. The CCWI was high on his target list. It moved out of the Rayburn House Office Building to private office space two miles away and changed its name to Women's Policy, Inc (WPI). The congresswomen reorganized themselves into a Members' organization, but kept the name. As a result, male Members no longer belong to the CCWI. It became much smaller, and not just because of the absence of men.

Seven of the eleven new women elected in 1994 were Republicans and only one of them joined the caucus (Sue Kelly, NY). Most of the other six were militantly opposed to everything the caucus stood for. Speaker Gingrich met separately with Republican women in order to make a bipartisan congresswoman's caucus irrelevant, and almost succeeded because the Republican agenda was so contrary to that of the CCWI. The fact that there were a critical number of women willing to block CCWI proposals encouraged congressmen to do so as well. Programs benefiting women that had been passed by the 103rd Congress were denied funding by the 104th. Antiwelfare legislation as well as anti-abortion bills enlarged the partisan divide. In the 104th Congress "more than fifty roll call votes were taken on reproductive rights issues" and the pro-choice position lost on all but four minor ones (Gertzog 2004, 59, 87–88, 96, 104, 110).

The CCWI partially recovered in the 105th Congress (1997–1998) largely because of the personal efforts of moderate Republican Nancy Johnson (CT) and her promise to take reproductive rights off of the agenda. With the Republicans firmly in control of both branches through 2006, the CCWI struggled to find issues on which it could succeed. One of these was support for women business owners. Others had to do with women's health (but not reproduction). Since most members were Democrats, the CCWI had cordial relations with the Clinton White House, but distant ones with the Bush White House. Understaffed and underfunded, the WPI could not provide the research services of the old CCWI. However, it has managed to survive, as has the skeletal Congresswoman's Caucus, by looking for common ground. Virtually all Democratic women join, as do most Republican women, though most of the moderate Republican women are gone. Issues on which there is a sharp partisan divide are avoided (Gertzog 2004, 119–20, 123, 131, 164, 172). Even on issues on which there is consensus, what the caucus and the WPI can do depends a great deal on factors beyond their control, such as which party controls the House—and the White House.

Money

The political environment also changed, largely because of the need for and availability of large sums of money to campaign for public office. While money has always been "the mother's milk of politics," the ability to mobilize and channel large amounts of volunteer time was also very important for three to four decades after World War II. During the 1970s this resource declined as more women moved into the paid labor force. At the same time, the passage of campaign finance acts and the growth of media markets enhanced the importance of paid professionals using modern technology. Raising money to buy these resources—plus pay for traditional tasks like petitioning and phonebanking that were once done by volunteers—became the most important campaign job.

Need was fueled by availability. Federal financing of presidential campaigns from 1976 onward freed private money to go elsewhere. Initially it flowed into state campaigns, which were not regulated by federal law. California in particular was a state where money mattered. In the 1960s Assembly Speaker Jesse Unruh funneled lobbyist money to incumbents and challengers he wanted to help, and to put into his debt. Assembly Speakers Leo McCarthy (1974–1980) and Willie Brown (1981–1995) turned the acquisition and distribution of campaign cash into a fine art and a major enterprise (Masket 2002, 31–32). McCarthy, though from San Francisco, was not part of the Burton machine. He became one of Pelosi's mentors, especially in the expeditious use of money.

In the 1990s campaign costs skyrocketed. Although there were fewer competitive congressional districts, the balance between the two major parties in the House was so close that both national parties funneled large amounts of money into races that were once won or lost on a local level. Not only did the House and Senate Democratic and Republican campaign committees raise and distribute large amounts of money, but individual Members did as well through the creation of "Leadership PACs." The ability to raise and distribute money to party candidates was "routinely and systematically used [by Members] to improve their chances of being elected [and appointed] to party leadership." The ability to raise money for other candidates' campaigns was particularly helpful to Republicans' leadership ambitions, but was also valuable to Democrats (Heberlig, Hetherington, and Larson 2006, 993–94).

Leadership

Throughout the 1990s and into the twenty-first century, women moved a bit higher into the leadership of each party in both the House and the Senate.

More and more women ran against men for leadership posts within each party in each house. Sometimes they won. Sometimes the fact that they did well led to their appointment to a different position within the overall party leadership (Gertzog 1995, 108; Rosenthal 2006, 6–7; Baer 2006, 20). This constant pounding on the glass ceiling created cracks—repetition made men more comfortable with women's aspirations for leadership.

"Leadership" is just one of several career paths ambitious Members of Congress can attempt. Another is to become a committee chair. While committee chairs have a lot of power over their subject areas, they are only rarely elected to the party leadership. The time one spends becoming a policy expert and promoting legislation competes with the time necessary to cultivate the broader relationships necessary to be elected a leader. A third course is to make a name for oneself in order to run for the Senate or a statewide office. Such members are often criticized by other MCs for being "showhorses" rather than "workhorses," but the publicity helps in their home states. Which route a Member follows is a matter of luck and opportunity as well as personal choice and political skill. For women there were barriers on all of these routes. While obstacles on all of them crumbled during the 1990s, those to the higher levels of leadership were probably the last to go.

There are several types of leadership positions. The majority and minority leaders and their whips organize the floor action of each house. The majority leader sets the daily calendar. Whips keep track of each party's members, where they are, and how they intend to vote. Each party has its own organization which elects the floor leaders, assigns members to committees, and chooses its legislative priorities. The Republican's is called the Conference and the Democrat's is called a Caucus. Delegates as well as representatives can vote in these bodies (since each determines its own membership and has chosen to include delegates). Each party also has a policy committee and a campaign committee. These party organizations usually have officers who are different from the party floor leaders. Within each of these committees there is a variety of positions and titles, which sometimes change. Whether members are elected, "selected," or appointed can also change. Even when they don't change, the political world is one in which informal relationships are often more important than formal ones (Baer 2006). Thus titles don't always tell much about real influence, which is harder to measure.

In 1995 the Republican House Conference adopted the practice of having a vice chair of the opposite sex of the chair—a pattern already in place at the RNC (called co-chair rather than vice chair) and many other Republican Party committees. Three women were vice chairs of the conference between 1995 and 2003. In 2003 Deborah Pryce (OH) became the first woman to move up to chair of the House Republican Conference, making her the fourth-ranking Republican in the House. She served the standard term of four years, with a male vice chair. There had already been one, and only one, female chair of the Republican Conference in the Senate: Margaret Chase Smith of Maine held the job from 1967 to 1972. Kay Bailey Hutchison of Texas served as vice chair for six years before becoming chair of the Republican Policy Committee in 2007. The chairs of the Republican Conference and the Policy Committee are the third- and fourth-ranking members of the Republican Party in the Senate. The National Republican Senatorial Committee (NRSC), which raises money for Republican Senate candidates, was headed by Elizabeth Dole (NC) in 2005–2006.

The House Democratic Caucus created the position of Caucus Secretary for women in the 1940s. After the title was changed to vice chair in 1987 only one other woman ever held the job (Barbara Kennelly, CT, 1995–1999). No woman has chaired the caucus, though some have run and lost. Eva Clayton (NC) was co-chair of the House Democratic Policy Committee from 1995 to 1999. In 2001–2002, Nita Lowey (NY) was the first (and only) female chair of the Democratic Congressional Campaign Committee. In 2003 Rose DeLauro (CT) became chair (or co-chair) of the House Democratic Steering Committee. In the Senate, the post of Caucus Secretary was created in 1903 as the third-ranking position. It became a woman's job in 1995; Barbara Mikulski (MD) held it for ten years. She was followed by Debbie Stabenow (MI) and Patty Murray (WA), but the ranking was bumped with the creation of the position of vice chair, a position which has so far only been held by men. Murray is still caucus secretary, but Stabenow moved on to become chair of the Steering Committee. Murray had been chair of the Democratic Senatorial Campaign Committee in 2001–2003.

Nancy Pelosi has been on the "leadership" track since she joined the House. She lobbied to join the Appropriations Committee—one of the power committees in the House—and succeeded when the 102nd Congress began in 1991. Because its members determine how much funding different federal projects get, they make many friends, and sometimes enemies, among the other Members. An apprenticeship on this or another power committee is almost a prerequisite to joining the party leadership. Pelosi was one of the few women whom congressmen interviewed in 1993 said that they could envision as a future leader (Gertzog 1995, 117). Pelosi sought assignment to the Select Intelligence Committee and won that in 1993; eight years later she was its ranking member—one of a handful of MCs who are supposed to be consulted by the Administration on important national security matters. In 1995 she became vice chair of the Democratic Congressional Campaign

Committee, which raises and distributes money to Democratic candidates for the House, and in 1997 she joined the Democratic Steering Committee, which assigns Democrats to committees.

The threshold moment in Pelosi's rise was not her election to be Speaker, which was foreordained once the Democrats retook the House after the 2006 elections, but her election to be the Democratic Party whip in 2001. The whip's job is to count votes and round up supporters for a party's bills. That was a hotly contested race between Pelosi and Steny Hoyer of Maryland for the votes of 215 Democrats in the House. The two had been running against each other for three years, waiting for an opening in the top Democratic leadership. In the homestretch before the October 10, 2001, vote, Pelosi was able to call upon both her old friends from the Burton machine and prominent Democratic women around the country for help. Willie Brown, who had become the first African American Mayor of San Francisco after being term-limited out of the California Assembly, phoned members of the Congressional Black Caucus. Former Texas governor Ann Richards also made phone calls. Pelosi's skill in raising money for other Members had put many into her debt.

This win put her in line to become the leader of House Democrats only a year later—minority leader if they were still in the minority after the 2002 elections; majority leader if they were not. When Rep. Richard Gephardt (D-MO) decided to give up the leadership after the disappointing elections, Pelosi and Martin Frost of Texas announced for the office. After twenty-four hours Frost dropped out of the race, convinced that Pelosi would win, and Harold Ford (D-TN) dropped in. A moderate African American, he thought he could pull the votes of the Black Caucus and the more moderate Democrats away from Pelosi. However, she stayed on the phone soliciting support and when the counting was done she had 177 votes to Ford's 29. An aide told a reporter that "it took us three years to win the whip's race, and 36 hours to win this" (Sandalow 2002, A3).

In reality, Pelosi started even earlier. Her campaign committee, "Nancy Pelosi for Congress," contributed money to other candidates throughout the 1990s, but racheted up in 1997. Her donation level doubled for the 1998 election. She went into hyperdrive on March 22, 1999, when her Leadership PAC registered with the Federal Election Commission. Former California lieutenant governor and assembly speaker Leo McCarthy, her mentor in money, was its treasurer until his death a month after Pelosi was sworn in as Speaker. The purpose of "PAC to the Future" was (and is) to raise money for Democrats running for House seats. Between PAC donations and money raised through fundraising dinners, Pelosi estimated that she provided $4.5

million to Democratic candidates in the 2000 election cycle (Foerstal 2001a, 2061). Donations from her PAC alone were $753,300 (plus $39,500 to Democratic Senate candidates). After winning the Whip race she expanded her fundraising with the goal of restoring the Democrats to be the majority party in the House. In the next six years (through the end of 2006), her PAC donated $2,167,000 to House Democratic candidates (plus $131,000 to Senate candidates). This made her the top Democratic fundraiser in the House. Only former Republican majority leader Tom DeLay (TX) raised more money for his party's candidates, and he didn't raise much more (McCormick and Sandalow 2006).

As Speaker, Nancy Pelosi will have a lot more to do than raise money for Democrats. But if she wants to stay Speaker, raising money will continue to be a major priority.

Is the Glass Ceiling Gone?

As Republican John Boehner, now minority rather than majority leader in the House of Representatives, handed the gavel to Nancy Pelosi on January 4, 2007, he graciously accepted defeat by saying: "Whether you're a Republican, a Democrat or an independent, this is a cause for celebration." Pelosi herself, on accepting it, proclaimed that "this is an historic moment, for Congress, and for the women of this country. It is a moment for which we have waited more than 200 years." Members of both parties gave her a standing ovation.

When Geraldine Ferraro was nominated by the Democrats to be vice president in 1984, it was also an historic moment, but one that has yet to be repeated, let alone become routine. It was the result of a unique set of circumstances, not the end of a long road to equal opportunity for women politicians. While one will not know with certainty until more time passes, I believe that Pelosi was right when she said, "For our daughters and granddaughters, today we have broken the marble ceiling." Pelosi was elected Speaker not because the times were novel, but because the institution was ready. When Rep. Barbara Jordan (D-TX) chose not to run for reelection in 1978 after becoming a nationally appreciated figure in only three terms, one of the reasons she gave was that she saw no future for herself in Congress. The glass (or marble) ceiling looked unbreakable. Since then the slow but steady push of women into the U.S. Congress and onto the leadership track has left that ceiling in shards.

However, these shards are not "equal opportunity" impediments. Republican women will have greater trouble moving into the leadership of their party in both the House and the Senate than will Democrats. The reasons for this do *not* include greater receptivity to women by the current (and future) Democratic Members of Congress compared to Republican Members. It's the Republican voters who have to be convinced to elect more women.

Start with the numbers. Women were 16 percent of the 110th Congress that convened in 2007. While their proportion was the same in each house, it was very different between the two parties. More than 20 percent of the Democratic Members of Congress were female, but only 10 percent of the Republican Members. Or, to put it differently, although the Congress was almost evenly divided—53.7 percent of the House and 51 percent of the Senate were Democrats (including two independents)—fully 70 percent of the women were Democrats. In earlier years, the proportion of women in the two parties was very close. In the 101st Congress (1989–1990) women were 6.4 percent of Republicans and 5.6 percent of Democrats. Party distribution shifted with the 1990 elections; in the 102nd Congress women were 4.7 percent of Republicans and 6.8 percent of Democrats. The 1992 elections brought a big increase in the number of Democratic women in the 103rd Congress, but only a small one for Republicans.

The party gap emerged a decade earlier in election to the state legislatures—one of the major pipelines to Congress. In 1981, women were about 12 percent of both the Republican and Democratic state legislators. Their proportion among the Democrats rose slowly but steadily to about 30 percent by 2007. Among Republican state legislators the proportion of women rose more slowly, flattened out in the mid-1990s, and fell as the new century began—to 16 percent in 2007.

In 2007 women were 23.5 percent of *all* state legislators, but 69 percent of *women* were Democrats (Johnson 2007). For the last twenty-five years there have been more Democratic women in this important pipeline to Congress. Not unexpectedly, since 1988 more women have sought the Democratic nomination for Congress and more have received it (Palmer and Simon 2001, 70–71). While the party gap among women elected to Congress has not widened as consistently as that for women state legislators, it has grown larger.

The party gap in Members of Congress has already led to a party gap in Congressional leadership. The greater number of Democratic women in both houses (and proportionately fewer men) competing for roughly the same number of leadership positions by itself means that, all else being equal, there will be more Democratic women in their party's leadership than Republican women.

But that's not all. While seniority is no longer a prerequisite for moving up in the leadership hierarchy or becoming a committee chair, it does help. The longer one is in Congress, the more one is able to develop the relationships and acquire the credentials for a higher position. Both seniority and the time to do these things, as well as to perform leadership tasks, are more easily attained by Members in safe districts. Thus the actual pool from which leaders are chosen is much smaller than the total number of party members in Congress. The fact that Pelosi had one of the safest Democratic districts in the country freed her to look out for other Democrats. She used her fundraising prowess to help the Democrats take back the House. When the 2006 elections brought that about after twelve years in the minority, there was no Democratic opposition to her becoming the first woman to be elected Speaker.

Democratic women are more likely to be elected from safe districts than Republican women. We know that districts which are safe for Democrats have different demographics than districts which are safe for Republicans. While these characteristics change somewhat over time, today's Democratic districts come in two or three varieties. Excluding the South (which switched partisan preferences in the 1980s), the traditional Democratic district is urban, multiethnic, and blue-collar, with a disproportionate number of non-Protestants. Districts that elect African Americans are all of these things, except that black Democratic voters are Protestant. A newer type of Democratic district is urban, multiethnic, and populated by well-educated professionals. Those that aren't in big cities include university towns (Judis and Teixeira 2002). Republican districts, outside the South, are rural, white, Protestant, and generally populated by people in the middle of the socioeconomic spectrum. Swing districts, those that sometimes switch parties, combine these demographic characteristics. Many are suburban.

If one looks at the districts that have elected women to the House of Representatives since 1972, one sees that those that elect white women have distinct demographic characteristics (Palmer and Simon 2005). Districts which elect minority women do not differ from those that elect minority men, which is probably why 42 percent of the fifty female Democrats in the 110th House are from racial minorities (twelve are African American, two are Asian-Pacific, six are Latina). Of the twenty-one Republican women representatives, one is Latina. (All of the women in the Senate are white and Anglo.) The nonminority Congressional districts which are "female friendly" look very much like the newer type of Democratic district—they are urban and upscale. This is precisely the type of district that reelects Nancy Pelosi every two years. It is also similar to the type of district that elects Republican women—except that these are swing districts, not safe Republican districts. The women elected from these districts are moderate Republicans. Even when they can avoid being defeated by liberal Democratic men (as many have been), and can allot enough time from constantly running for reelection in an unsafe district to work for a leadership position, their personal politics are too liberal to fit in with the current conservative Republican leadership. Deborah Pryce of Ohio, the highest ranking woman in the House Republican leadership, won her 2004 race by only one thousand votes and announced on August 16, 2007, that she would not run again.

If the Republican Party wants more women in Congress, it will have to make a special effort to recruit them (as it did in 1984), support them, and persuade conservative Republican voters to elect them. Right now, women mostly get the Republican nomination in districts that are too Democratic for them to win. The Republican Party will also have to be more tolerant of those moderate Republican women who can win in swing districts—where moderate positions on social issues are an asset. And, if the Republican congressional leadership wants to have more than a token presence of women, it too will have to recruit women and be more tolerant of their political positions. In short, if the Republican Party wants more women in its congressional leadership, it will have to practice affirmative action.

This is not necessary for Democrats. If the glass, or marble, ceiling is truly broken, all that is necessary for the Democratic Party to do is to be gender neutral. In the natural order of things, the women will take care of themselves.

Does It Matter?

While it's nice to see women in positions of power and influence, and even nicer for Congress to be more representative of the U.S. population, in the long run, does it matter? The job of Congress is to pass laws; what difference does it make if more Members are women? If the top leadership positions are occupied by women?

There is no way to answer that question for overall legislation because one cannot separate the presence of women from the demands of the times and the context in which women work. But, because of the long history of the CCWI, one can observe that the presence of women does matter for legislation of particular interest to women. There have been two periods since the rise of the new feminist movement in which Congress has passed a bumper crop of laws of particular interest to women. The first of these was the 92nd Congress, which began in 1971, right after the highly public emergence of the feminist movement (Freeman 1975). While there were only two women Senators and thirteen women in the House, there was an enormous amount of publicity about laws and practices that discriminated against women. This followed over a decade of agitation about the evils of race discrimination and happened at a time in which the parties had not yet polarized on issues of concern to women. For a few years (the 92nd and 93rd Congresses) policies that affected women could be discussed in a context in which partisanship was not the dominant factor. Once the Equal Rights Amendment and the legalization of most abortions became highly divisive public issues, and the parties took contrary stands, congressional movement on all women's issues, including those irrelevant to the ERA or abortion, was politicized and paralyzed.

The CCWI was born about the time that paralysis set in, and at a time that women were few in numbers and without much institutional clout in Congress. Although the CCWI was bipartisan, the Republican administrations of the 1980s and the Republican Senate of 1981–1987 were not sympathetic to its positions. The moderate Republican women among its members had trouble getting their own leadership to listen. It was only during the 103rd Congress, when an overwhelmingly Democratic CCWI had a Democratic leadership in both houses and a Democratic White House to work with, that Congress passed the second bumper crop of legislation of benefit to women. This environment changed when the elections of 1994 brought in a Republican Congress that "reversed past achievements, shredded its agenda, and threatened its survival" (Gertzog 2004, 117).

What these two periods had in common was 1) organized pressure (from the outside the first time and from the inside during the second) and 2) a sympathetic (Ford and Clinton) or at least benign (Nixon) administration. Both also had a Democratic Congress, though that was important the second time, but probably not the first. Democrats now control both houses of Congress, with women in positions of influence in both of them. Furthermore, the percent of women in the Democratic Caucus is approaching critical mass. Critical mass for minority groups occurs when they are roughly between 20 and 30 percent of the total. Smaller numbers create cohesion but lack clout. As the percentage creeps into the thirties, cohesion is lost as individuals pay more attention to other identities and concerns. In between there is enough cohesion for minority group members to work together, and high enough numbers to get things done. If an administration sympathetic or at least benign to women's issues is elected which will not veto laws passed by a Democratic Congress, the presence of a critical mass of women Members should make a difference. It is also important that there be a critical mass of women (and/or feminist men) in the leadership. Pelosi is a feminist, but if she were the only one, her value would be purely symbolic. She needs a critical mass of feminist men and women around her to get past the obstacles of an organized opposition.

Sources

I'd like to thank the following people for steering me to sources of information or supplying it directly: Sarah Chilton, Elizabeth Cox, Janet Spikes, Geneva C. Jones, Lucy Sells, Janet Flammang, Pat Reuss, Helen Grieco, Judy Lemons, Jodie Evans, Mike Miller, Amy Hackett, George Smaragdis, John Grunwell, David Bair, Laura Mooney, Dagne Gizaw, Michelle Kamalich, Massie Ritsch, and Michael Rossman.
    Although I've never met Nancy Pelosi, I was one of the Young Democrats who walked precincts for Phil and Johnny Burton in 1963–1964.

Baer, Denise. 2006. Party-based leadership and gender: Beyond the chinese box puzzle of women's recruitment to political office. Paper presented at the Conference on Women and Political Leadership, American University, Washington, D.C., April 8.

Bell, Jonathan. 2006. Social democracy and the rise of the Democratic Party in California: 1950–1964. *Historical Journal* 49, no. 2: 497–524.

Bunting, Glenn F. 1992. '92 Democratic Convention: Pelosi's prominence in party on the rise: lawmaker: The San Francisco Congresswoman will deliver a speech and preside over proceedings to adopt the platform. *Los Angeles Times*, July 14, A:6:4.

Center for Responsive Politics. 2007. Contributions to federal candidates and parties from the Nancy Pelosi for Congress Committee, unpublished data for the 1990–2006 election cycles. Washington, D.C.: Center for Responsive Politics.

Chamberlin, Hope. 1973. *A minority of members: Women in the U.S. Congress.* New York: Praeger.

Cox, Elizabeth M. 1996. *Women state and territorial legislators, 1895–1995.* Jefferson, N.C.: McFarland and Co.

Dodson, Debra L. 2006. *The impact of women in Congress.* Oxford; New York: Oxford University Press.

Duke, Lynne. 2006. Pride of Baltimore; Nancy Pelosi learned her politics at the elbow of her father the mayor. *Washington Post*, November 10, C-1.

Feuerherd, Joe. 2003. Roots in faith, family and party guide Pelosi's move to power. *National Catholic Reporter*, January 24, 1.

Foerstal, Karen. 2001a. Democrats Pelosi and Hoyer stress party-building ability in House whip contest. *CQ Weekly Online* (September 7): 2061.

———. 2001b. Hoyer's and Pelosi's 3-year race for whip: It's all over but the voting. *CQ Weekly Online* (October 5): 2321–25.

———. 2002a. Emerging players: Rep. Nancy Pelosi, D. Calif. *CQ Weekly Online* (January 5).

———. 2002b. Pelosi's vote-counting prowess earns her the House Democrats' No. 2 spot. *CQ Weekly Online* (October 12): 2397–98.

Freeman, Jo. 1975. *The politics of women's liberation: A case study of an emerging social movement and its relation to the policy process.* New York: Longman.

———. 2000. *A room at a time: How women entered party politics.* Lanham, Md.: Rowman & Littlefield.

Gehlen, Frieda. 1969. Women in Congress: Their power and influence in a man's world. *Transaction* 6, no. 11 (October): 35–45.

Gertzog, Irwin N. [1984] 1995. *Congressional women: Their recruitment, treatment and behavior,* 2nd ed. New York: Praeger.

———. 2004. *Women and power on Capitol Hill: Reconstructing the Congressional Women's Caucus.* Boulder, Colo.: Rienner.

Heberlig, Eric, Marc Hetherington, and Bruce Larson. 2006. The price of leadership: Campaign money and the polarization of congressional parties. *Journal of Politics* 68, no. 4 (November): 992–1005.

Hunter, Marjorie. 1981. Congresswomen admit 46 men to their caucus. *New York Times,* December 14, 10.

Jacobs, John. 1995. *A rage for justice: The passion and politics of Phillip Burton.* Berkeley: University of California Press.

Johnson, Kirk. 2007. In state legislatures, Democrats are pushing toward parity between the sexes. *New York Times,* February 15, A26.

Judis, John, and Ruy Teixeira. 2002. *The emerging Democratic majority.* New York: Scribner.

Love, Keith, and Dan Morain. 1987. Pelosi wins Democratic contest for Burton seat. *Los Angeles Times,* April 8, I:3:2.

Masket, Seth. 2002. The power of outsiders: How activists brought party government to the California Legislature. Paper delivered at the Second Annual Conference on State Politics and Policy: Legislatures and Representation in the U.S. States. Milwaukee, Wisc., May 24.

Mayhew, David R. 1986. *Placing parties in American politics.* Princeton, N.J.: Princeton University Press.

McCormick, Erin, and Marc Sandalow. 2006. Pelosi mines "California gold" for Dems nationwide. Personal skills, wide network of wealthy donors help party's house leader gather millions. *San Francisco Chronicle,* April 3, A1.

National Conference of State Legislatures. 2007a. Women in state legislatures 2007. www.ncsl.org/programs/wln/WomenInOffice2007.htm.

———. 2007b. 2007 partisan composition of state legislatures. www.ncsl.org/statevote/partycomptable2007.htm.

Palmer, Barbara, and Dennis Simon. 2001. The political glass ceiling: Gender, in-cumbency in the U.S. House Elections, 1978–1998. *Women & Politics* 23, no. 1/2: 59–78.

———. 2005. The political geography of women friendly congressional districts. Pa-per presented at the annual meeting of the Southern Political Science Associa-tion, New Orleans, LA, January 8.

———. 2006. *Breaking the political glass ceiling: Women and congressional elections.* New York: Routledge.

Politics in America. Washington, D.C.: Congressional Quarterly, published biannu-ally.

Roosevelt, Eleanor. 1928. Women must learn to play the game as men do. *Redbook* 1, no. 6 (April): 78–79, 141–42.

Rosen, Ruth. 2000. *The world split open: How the modern women's movement changed America.* New York: Viking.

Rosenthal, Cindy Simon. 2006. En-gendering choice in congressional leadership elections. Paper presented at the National Symposium on Women and Politics, University of California, Berkeley, June 9–10.

Sandalow, Marc. 2002. Savvy, cash clinched job for Pelosi: Tightly orchestrated cam-paign followed lucrative fund raising. *San Francisco Chronicle,* November 17, A3.

Sandalow, Marc, and Erin McCormick. 2006. Pelosi's goal: Democrats back on top. Minority leader practices hardball politics to position her party for midterm elec-tion. *San Francisco Chronicle,* April 2, A1.

Shafer, Byron E. 1983. *The quiet revolution: The struggle for the Democratic party and the shaping of post-reform politics.* New York: Russell Sage Foundation.

Thompson, Joan Hulse. 1985. Career convergence: election of women and men to the House of Representatives, 1916–1975. *Women and Politics* 5, no. 1 (Spring): 69–90.

Wasniewski, Matthew A., ed. 2006. *Women in Congress.* Office of History and Preservation, Office of the Clerk, U.S. House of Representatives; Prepared un-der the direction of the Committee on House Administration of the U.S. House of Representatives; House Document 108-223, Government Printing Office, Washington, D.C.

Wilson, James Q. [1962] 1966. *The amateur Democrat: Club politics in three cities.* Chicago: University of Chicago Press.

Useful Webpages

A list of all the women who have ever served in the U.S. House of Representatives is at bioguide.congress.gov/congreswomen/index.asp

A list of all women U.S. Senators is at www.senate.gov/artandhistory/history/common/briefing/women_senators.htm

Campaign finance data for Nancy Pelosi is at
  Nancy Pelosi: www.opensecrets.org/politicians/allsummary.asp?cid=N00007360
  PAC to the Future: www.opensecrets.org/pacs/lookup2.asp?strID=C00344234
  Nancy Pelosi for Congress: query.nictusa.com/cgi-bin/com_supopp/C00213512
Several fact sheets on women in Congress and other elected offices can be found at
  www.cawp.rutgers.edu/Facts.html
The Women's Caucus webpage is at www.womenspolicy.org/caucus

Index

Note: Page numbers in italics indicate photographs or tables.

~

About the Author

Jo Freeman is the author of two prize-winning books, *The Politics of Women's Liberation* (1975, 2000) and *A Room at a Time: How Women Entered Party Politics* (2000). She is also the author of *At Berkeley in the Sixties* (2004); editor of *Social Movements of the Sixties and Seventies* (1983); coeditor, with Victoria Johnson, of *Waves of Protest: Social Movements Since the Sixties* (1999); and editor of five editions of *Women: A Feminist Perspective* (1975, 1979, 1984, 1989, 1995).

For more information, go to www.jofreeman.com.